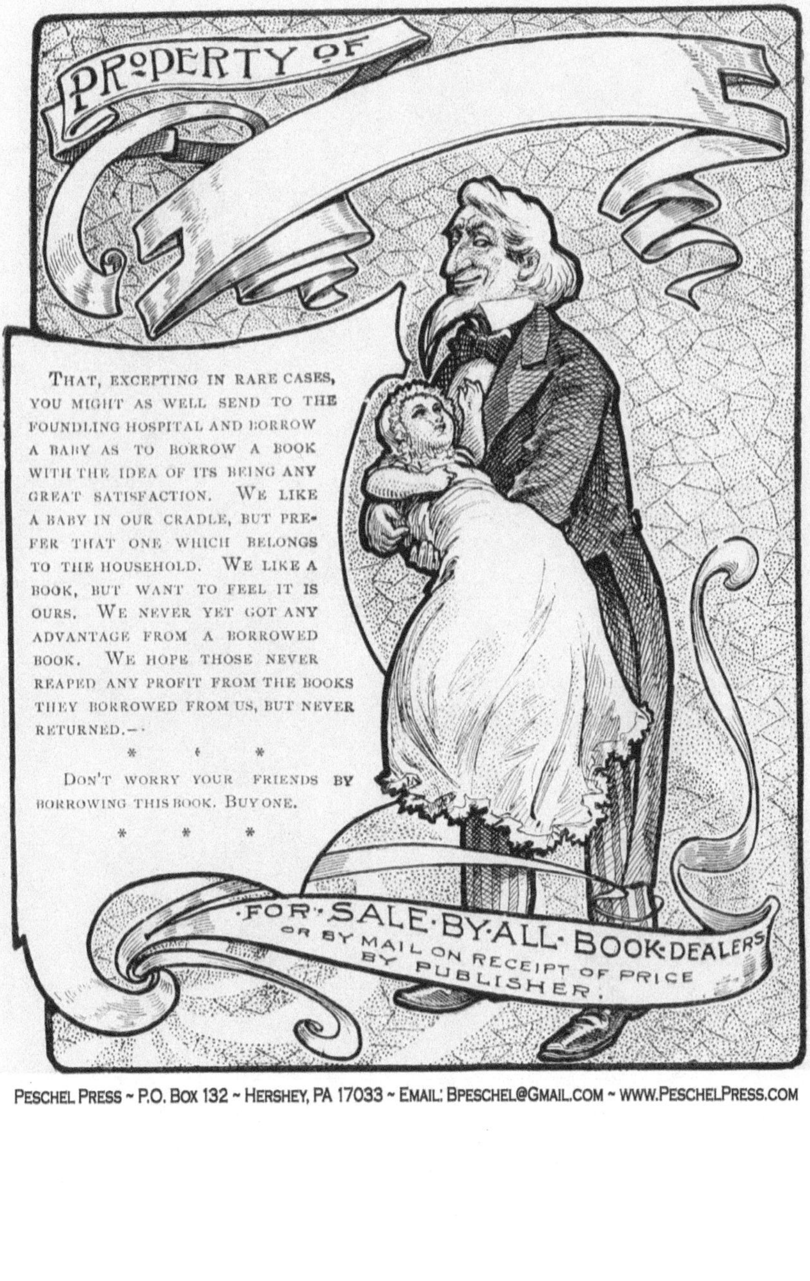

PROPERTY OF

That, excepting in rare cases, you might as well send to the Foundling Hospital and borrow a baby as to borrow a book with the idea of its being any great satisfaction. We like a baby in our cradle, but prefer that one which belongs to the household. We like a book, but want to feel it is ours. We never yet got any advantage from a borrowed book. We hope those never reaped any profit from the books they borrowed from us, but never returned.—

* * *

Don't worry your friends by borrowing this book. Buy one.

* * *

For sale by all book dealers or by mail on receipt of price by publisher.

Peschel Press ~ P.O. Box 132 ~ Hershey, PA 17033 ~ Email: Bpeschel@gmail.com ~ www.PeschelPress.com

Sherlock Holmes
Jazz Age Parodies and Pastiches II: 1925-1930

Also From the Peschel Press

The 223B Casebook Series
The Early Punch Parodies of Sherlock Holmes
Sherlock Holmes Victorian Parodies & Pastiches: 1888-1899
Sherlock Holmes Edwardian Parodies & Pastiches I: 1900-1904
Sherlock Holmes Edwardian Parodies & Pastiches II: 1905-1909
Sherlock Holmes Great War Parodies & Pastiches I: 1910-1914
Sherlock Holmes Great War Parodies & Pastiches II: 1915-1919
Sherlock Holmes Jazz Age Parodies & Pastiches I: 1920-1924
Sherlock Holmes Jazz Age Parodies & Pastiches II: 1925-1930
The Best Sherlock Holmes Parodies & Pastiches: 1888-1930

The Rugeley Poisoner Series
The Illustrated Life and Career of William Palmer
The Times Report of the Trial of William Palmer
The Life and Career of Dr. William Palmer of Rugeley

Annotated Editions
The Complete, Annotated Murder on the Links
By Agatha Christie
The Complete, Annotated Secret Adversary
By Agatha Christie
The Complete, Annotated Mysterious Affair at Styles
By Agatha Christie
The Complete, Annotated Whose Body?
By Dorothy L. Sayers

Other Books
Sew Your Own Cloth Grocery Bags
The Dictionary of Flowers and Gems
Suburban Stockade
The Bride from Dairapaska

Also by Bill Peschel
Hell's Casino
Writers Gone Wild (Penguin)

Sherlock Holmes
Jazz Age Parodies and Pastiches II: 1925-1930

Edited by Bill Peschel
PESCHEL PRESS ~ HERSHEY, PA.

SHERLOCK HOLMES JAZZ AGE PARODIES AND PASTICHES II: 1925-1930. Notes and essays copyright 2019 Bill Peschel. All rights reserved. Printed in the United States of America. No part of the notes or essays may be used or reproduced in any manner without written permission except in cases of brief quotations embodied in critical articles or reviews. For information, email peschel@peschelpress.com or write to Peschel Press, P.O. Box 132, Hershey, PA 17033.

"The Adventure of the Missing Tenants" reprinted by permission of Arkham House Publishers, Inc., and Arkham's agents, JABberwocky Literary Agency, Inc., 49 West 45th Street, #12N, New York, NY 10036-4603.

"The Adventure of the Fight Club," copyright © 2018 by Bill Peschel, first appeared in "The Casebook of Twain and Holmes," reprinted by permission of the publisher.

Cover design by Bill Peschel. Art by Eric Fraser from "The Velvet Blotting Clue."

www.peschelpress.com

ISBN-13: 978-1-950347-03-2

First edition (New ISBN edition): March 2021

Table of Contents

Introduction i

1925

ACD's Life to Date 5
The Little Dragon of Jade 8
    Edgar Wallace
Sherlock Holmes Splits Hairs 27
    George C. Henderson
Sherlock Among the Spirits 30
    Anonymous
Intelligence Service 34
    "Z. 4.999"
The Rollo Boys with Sherlock in Mayfair 40
    Corey Ford

1926

ACD's Life to Date 51
A Disciple of Sherlock Holmes 53
    Maurice Morelo
A Strange Suicide 57
    Pierre Henri Cami
Lord Camembert Smudged 60
    Earle Ennis
The Adventure of the Missing Hatrack 66
    Frederic Dorr Steele
The Ape of Agate 76
    Anonymous
The Scarlet Pimple 79
    Anthony Armstrong
The Reigate Road Murder 84
    Anthony Armstrong
The Marriage of Sherlock Holmes 89
    Gregory Breitman
Tha Grate Fur Koat Mistery 104
    Albert J. Bromley

1927

ACD's Life to Date 106
The Return of Donan Coyle 108
    "Sugatel"
The Velvet Blotting Clue 111
    Anonymous
The Commencement Mystery 118
    Anonymous
The End of Sherlock Holmes 121
    "A.E.P."
The Strange Case of the Three Revolvers 126
    Anthony Grey
Mary of the Prairie or, Should She Have Let Him? 130
    Anonymous

1928

ACD's Life to Date 136
An Adventure of Shylock Bones 139
    "Goanna Jack"
Help! Help! Sherlock! 142
    Edmund L. Pearson
The Seven Corpse Case 148
    F.M.J. Wood

1929

ACD's Life to Date 156
Expert Assistance 158
    James J. Montagne
The Adventure of the Missing Tenants 160
    August Derleth
Connie 181
    Frank Godwin
The Omnibus Murder 194
    R.E. Swartwout
The Return of the Native 201
    "Cohan and Doyle" (Lester A. Blumner)
The Modern Radio Sleuth 204

Jay Coote
The Mystery Than Which 216
　　　Rupert Hughes
Shylock Bones 220
　　　Joe Archibald
The Mary Queen of Scots Jewel 223
　　　William O. Fuller
The Indignant Lecturer and The Amateur Detective 244
　　　H.H. Ballard

1930

ACD's Life to Date 249
The Return of Herlock Sholmes 251
　　　"Kittywyn"
Baffling, Mystery Puzzle of *Sunday News'* Death 253
　　　Anonymous
Purple Peanut, A Tale of the Greyhound Track 261
　　　Anonymous
The Great Flatbush Mystery 266
　　　Ed Hughes
The Bound of the Haskervilles 271
　　　T.P.J. Mirage
The Clue of the Six Pips 276
　　　"Sir A. Roastan Boil"
The Great Detective 284
　　　Stephen Leacock
The Six O'clock Mystery 302
　　　Anonymous
The Case of the Missing Patriarchs 304
　　　Logan Clendening

Appendix

The Adventure of the Fight Club 307
　　　Bill Peschel
Bibliography 340
About the Editor 342

Introduction: Forever Sherlock

When Sherlock Holmes stepped onto the world stage in 1887, Victoria was queen, horse-drawn hansoms rolled on London's streets, God was in his heaven, and the sun always shone on the British Empire.

When he retired for good in 1914 (as recounted in "His Last Bow") Holmes was the same man and so was his creator, but the world was changing. The old order began its slow decline, hastened by the coming war, and in Britain by heavy taxation that would force the aristocracy to adapt or perish. We see this process accelerated in the last volume.

As for Holmes creator, Conan Doyle continued his crusade on behalf of spiritualism, but public interest was waning. Many who lost sons and husband found comfort in it were moving on.

Soon, Conan Doyle would be gone, but Sherlock will live on. Infinitely adaptable, he can mutate into whatever role demanded of him: humorist, marketer, communicator, or hero. In short, the same roles we've seen him perform in these seven volumes. Ever renewable, Holmes was built to live forever.

Bill Peschel
May 2019

P.S.: If you like this series, will you consider spreading the word about it? A review, a comment online, or a mention to another Sherlock Holmes fan would be very much appreciated.

How the Book Was Organized

The 223B Casebook Series has two goals: To reprint the majority of the parodies and pastiches published in Conan Doyle's lifetime, especially rare items not readily available, and stories collected about a single subject, such as *The Early Punch Parodies of Sherlock Holmes*.

The stories in the chronological books appear in the order in which readers of the time would have seen them. This way, we can see how writers changed their perception of Sherlock as the canonical stories were published. Stories for which dates could not be found, such as those published in books, were moved to the back of the year.

Each chapter begins with a description of Conan Doyle's activities that year. I tried to keep the essays self-contained, but some events, such as Conan Doyle's longtime relationship with Jean Leckie, span years, and you may need to read the essays in previous books in the series to fully understand them.

The stories were reprinted as accurately as possible. No attempt was made to standardize British and American spelling. Some words have undergone changes over the years — "Shakespere" instead of "Shakespeare" and "to-morrow" for "tomorrow" — they were left alone. Obvious mistakes of spelling and grammar were silently corrected, except in certain stated cases, and long paragraphs were broken up to aid readability.

Acknowledgments

A great effort was made to determine the copyright status of these pieces and obtain permission to publish from the rightful copyright holders. If I have made a mistake, please contact me so that I may rectify the error.

As each volume went to press, I'm reminded again of how many people helped make this series larger and better than I could have done alone. Research assistant Scott Harkless provided rare and crucial stories. Denise Phillips at Hershey Public Library worked hard to acquire the books and articles I asked for. Peter Blau generously shared the fruits of his researches. Charles Press provided me with a shopping list from his *Parodies and Pastiches Buzzing 'Round Sir Arthur Conan Doyle*, and happily filled in the gaps with extremely rare items from his researches.

Then there are the writers whose books led the way: Otto Penzler for *The Big Book of Sherlock Holmes Stories*; Bill Blackbeard for *Sherlock Holmes in America*; Frederic Dannay and Manfred Lee ("Ellery Queen") for *The Misadventures of Sherlock Holmes*; Philip K. Jones for his massive (10,000 entries!) database of Sherlockian pastiches, parodies, and related fiction; John Gibson and Richard Lancelyn Green for *My Evening With Sherlock Holmes* and *The Uncollected Sherlock Holmes*; Paul D. Herbert for *The Sincerest Form of Flattery*; Peter Ridgway Watt and Joseph Green for *The Alternative Sherlock Holmes*; The Sciolist Press, Donald K. Pollock, and the other editors behind *The Baker Street Miscellanea*.

By digitizing the nation's newspapers and making them searchable, The National Library of Australia enabled me to find previously unknown parodies and research their local references so we can appreciate what was going on in New South Wales, Mudgee, and Perth.

Andrew Malec has my thanks as well for contributing his articles on the career of Frederic Dorr Steele and his involvement with the Players Club.

Finally, my love to Teresa, wielder of the red pen and owner of my heart.

☞ **Get the newsletter:** If you want to learn more about my books, my researches and the media I eat, sign up for the Peschel Press newsletter. You'll get an intermittent chatty letter about what we're publishing plus a glimpse behind the scenes at a growing publishing house. Visit either www.planetpeschel.com or www.peschelpress.com and look for the sign-up box.

☞ **Got a review?** If you like this book — or even if you don't — could you leave a word or two at the online book retailer of your choice? I would really appreciate it.

"Life's Journey": An autographed postcard from Conan Doyle.

1925

The end of the world occupied Conan Doyle's thoughts and that led him into an unusual investment: real estate.

This year, he bought a second home for his family in the country, and opened a Spiritualism bookstore in London.

The home was Bignell House, located near Minstead in the New Forest, a land that had been inhabited since Saxon times. The area appealed to Conan Doyle's sense of history, but it was also the source of many happy memories. It was in nearby Portsmouth that he began his career as a doctor, and it was while living alone in a cottage in the New Forest that he finished The White Company *(1891).*

Bignell began life as a thatched cottage and a barn during the reign of George I (1714-1727). Conan Doyle had it renovated with red brick, white plaster, and wooden beams. He expanded its footprint by attaching the cottage to the barn, added modern conveniences such as central heating, and channeled an underground spring to create a waterfall.

Bignell was a refuge in more ways than one. It was a quiet retreat from the bustle of public life and socializing at Windlesham. But there was a second, darker reason for the purchase.

Conan Doyle was preparing for the end of the world. He had been hearing that mediums around the world were receiving warnings from beyond of the coming apocalypse. His personal spirit guide, Pheneas, contacting him through his wife Jean's automatic writing, told him that strong earthquakes and enormous tidal waves would cleanse humanity of the unbelievers. The veil to the next world will fall, he foresaw, and the survivors will build a new utopia.

What to do? Announce the end of the world and alarm the public? But what if it didn't happen? Reluctant to "commit the spiritualistic movement to a prophecy which may not materialize," he decided to say nothing publicly. Instead, he wrote a pamphlet for private circulation among the believers.

Publicly revealed after Conan Doyle's death, "A Warning" described in detail how the world will end in a series of bullet points:

"That the crisis will come in an instant;

"That the general destruction and utter dislocation of civilised life will be beyond belief;

"That there will be a short period of utter chaos followed by some reconstruction;

"That the total period of the upheavals will be roughly three years;

"That the chief centres of disturbance will be the Eastern Mediterranean basin, where not less than five countries will entirely disappear.

"Also the Atlantic, where there will be a rise of land which will be a cause of those waves which will bring about great disasters upon the Americans, the Irish, and the Western European shore, involving all the low-lying British coasts. There are indicated further great upheavals in the Southern Pacific and in the Japanese region."

But every apocalypse has a silver lining. Conan Doyle also foresaw the coming of a "high spirit" who "would command the reverence of all." In short, he said, this would be nothing less than the Second Coming, predicted in Revelations. Only the true believers in the Spiritualist movement will be able, he wrote, "to go forth and devote themselves entirely to the comfort and instruction of the terrified and bewildered human race."

With the end times approaching, building a refuge for himself and his family in the New Forest made sense.

In the meantime, there was Spiritualism work to be done, and this year saw the opening of The Psychic Bookshop near Westminster Abbey in London. The store was something of a family affair. His eldest daughter, Mary, joined the staff, and on some days, Conan Doyle would leave his flat just around the corner and wait on customers. Anyone who wanted to reach the bookstore could send a telegram addressed to "Ectoplasm, Southwest."

A few months later, a museum was opened on the second floor. There, visitors could see Conan Doyle's proof of life after death in the form of paraffin casts of spirits' hands, photographs of ghosts and magical creatures (including the Cottingley Fairies), messages from the spirit world and other memorabilia. They could check out Spiritualism books from the circulating library, and arrange to have their works published through Conan Doyle's press.

But despite Conan Doyle's popularity, visitors stayed away in droves. Four years later, he announced that the venture had failed. After his death, the store and museum moved out of the family's control. It is believed that German bombers destroyed the artifacts during World War II.

Meanwhile, Oscar Slater re-entered Conan Doyle's life. Years before, Conan Doyle had gotten his death sentence reduced to a life term.

Now, Slater smuggled a letter out of prison seeking his help in winning his release. Scottish authorities received a new barrage of letters from Conan Doyle, pointing out that those sentenced to life were released after 15 years. But the authorities refused; Slater had broken the rules in prison. Undeterred, Conan Doyle continued his crusade.

In July, the new Professor Challenger novel, The Land of Mist, began serialization in The Strand. Readers hoping for another rousing adventure saw their hopes dashed. The story centered around journalist Edward Malone, who accompanied Challenger in The Lost World. Now engaged to Challenger's daughter, Enid, he sets out to prove the existence of life after death. He does such a good job that, by the end of the story, even the professor admits "it is incredible, inconceivable, grotesquely wonderful, but it would seem to be true."

As if to demonstrate what readers missed, a silent movie version of The Lost World was released earlier that year. Featuring an introduction by Conan Doyle, it thrilled audiences by showing dinosaurs moving thanks to innovations in stop-motion animation.

The rest of the year was marked by two Spiritualist events. In September, Conan Doyle chaired the International Spiritualist Congress in Paris. His appearances were disrupted by fans who forced their way into the hall to hear him. Conan Doyle had to threaten to leave before the crowds settled so he could deliver his lecture.

On Armistice Day, Conan Doyle lectured before a packed crowd of 5,000 at Albert Hall in London. When he asked who were in touch with their dead to stand up, more than half the attendees did so. "I prophecy that within five years to such an appeal every man and woman in this great hall will arise. We are not testifying to faith, but to fact."

Publications: Psychic Experiences *(Nov.)*.

Conan Doyle's cameo in *The Lost World*.

The Little Dragon of Jade

Edgar Wallace

The 1920s and '30s were known as the golden age of detective fiction, and the detectives who exemplified the era shared similar characteristics. They were well-educated, either from the university or self-taught (or in the case of Holmes, both), and capable of drawing on obscure knowledge. They were aesthete gentlemen, taking pleasure in one or more of the fine arts. If they were policemen, they were generally inspectors from Scotland Yard. The amateurs were wealthy, had plenty of leisure time, or were in professions, such as priest, which allowed them to travel freely. And there was never any hint of sex about them.

Then there was Detective Superintendent Minter of the London Metropolitan Police, created by the prolific Edgar Wallace (1876-1932). Nicknamed "Sooper," he's an elderly, cantankerous investigator who in appearance could have been Columbo's British cousin. A plain-speaking realist, he regards with suspicion the modern methods of detection in favor of keeping your eyes open and never giving up.

"Sooper" first appeared in a series of short stories in the mid-1920s, such as this one from the May 16 issue of The Saturday Evening Post. *Several of them were collected in* The Lone House Mystery and Other Stories *(1929) and reprinted in* The Sooper and Others *(1984). But the best of the small lot is the sole novel* Big Foot *(1927), a bizarre thriller with the trademark weird Wallace touches.*

Sooper? I'm used to it. Naturally the young policemen won't call me that to my face, they'd be ticked off[1] if they did. I want "sir" and "superintendent" from them. Now, over in New York I'd be "chief" to everybody, but in the metropolitan police area "chief" means that herring-bellied[2] deputy-com-

---

[1] The literal meaning is to place a checkmark against a list of items as they are noted. During World War I, it was used in the British military to mean a scolding. War poet and soldier Wilfred Owen (1893-1918) noted in a 1915 letter that "He has been 'ticked-off' four or five times for it; but is not yet shot at dawn."

[2] An insult meaning skinny to the point of emaciation, herring not noted as being a plump fish. The term was originally applied to horses, as in *A Strange Horse-Race* (1613) by Elizabethan writer Thomas Dekker (c. 1572-

missioner and nobody else.

As a detective I'm a disappointed man: I've got no science in me. Pawson, the banker, was telling me the other day that the only way to discover whether a chap is crook or just plain stockbroker is to examine a gland — I forget the name of it — in the middle of his neck. He read about it in a newspaper. He said that another way is to measure his head.[1] Personally, I've never had the time. When I put the stick to a man's head it isn't to measure it.[2] But I admire that kind of detective. There's a book been written about one. He lived up in the West, had an apartment in Baker Street and played the fiddle. An' when he was short of clues, he took a shot of "coke" an' naturally he saw more clues in a minute than a flat-footed policeman would see in a year. This feller always had a doctor around so that you might say that he wasn't as big a fool as he looked.

I've seen the scientific method tried — once! There used to be a sub-inspector of the CID at Scotland Yard named Croomb. He was a sergeant of mine when I was in K Division,[3] a young feller who took police work pretty serious, though he never got a real good case till the Hillsboro Road[4] murder came along. I must say he put his back into that an' did good work. You remember the case — the woman's body in a sack an' nothin' to identify her except she wore odd stockin's? Croomb worked on

---

1632): "The third that came sneaking in was a leane ill-faced shotten-*herring-bellied*-rascall."
[1] A reference to phrenology, a pseudoscience that contended a person's personality, including his character and thoughts, could be discerned by measuring the shape of the skull and irregularities on its surface.
[2] British policemen were armed with a wooden truncheon, 14 to 16 inches long with a ribbed handle.
[3] The basic unit of policing in the Metropolitan Police. London was divided in 23 divisions. K Division covered the East End of London, and included Limehouse, Bow, Poplar, Blackwall, Isle of Dogs, West Ham, Plaistow, Canning Town, North Woolwich, East Ham, Forest Gate, Ilford, Chadwell Heath, Dagenham, and Barking.
[4] A street in the Dulwich area of London's Southwark borough south of the Thames.

the stockin's and got Lebrun, the Hoxton[1] butcher, in the pen, an' eventually on to the trap.[2] It was good work — but, what's the word when a parson starts in to put fancy bits into the marriage service? Unorthodox! That's it! The case got him promotion, which was good, but it got him into the 'rist class,[3] which wasn't so good. He started laboratizin': fixed up a sort of workshop at the back of his house in Camden Road, and he an' his girl used to work there for hours. Her name was Eleanor Fenning, a pretty blond, who had been to college an' held degrees in science.

It's a great thing for any man when a woman believes in him, because women work by a kind of wild animal instinct that's neither sense nor reason. Never played the races with a girl, have you? She doesn't look up form or go pikin' round for tips — she just likes the pretty jackets — the mauve an' cream, or maybe the powder blue with silver trimmin's, an' she plays a twenty-to-one shot that all the clockers say couldn't win unless the others dropped dead; and it comes home alone.[4]

Eleanor believed in Croomb. She got an idea that I was jealous of him and kept him out of promotion. When a woman thinks that way you've just got to let her go right on thinkin' — it's like lettin' Niag'ra fall.

---

[1] A neighborhood in the Hackney Borough of the East End. During the Victorian era, the development of railway travel encouraged residents to move to the suburbs, reducing Hoxton to a slum. While gentrification has taken place since, council housing for the poor still dominates some parts of the area.
[2] He was hanged, the trap being the trapdoor he fell through on the gallows.
[3] Detectives rise through the ranks of Metropolitan Police in this order: third class, second class, and first class detective-sergeants, then second class, first class, and divisional inspector, and then to chief detective inspector.
[4] *Form:* The racing form, which lists the races, the horses, the starting odds, and other information. *Pikin':* Old criminal slang for slinking around. *Pretty jackets:* Racing colors. Jockeys wear colorful silk jackets representing their stable to help tell them apart during the race. *Clockers:* Men who time the horses as they warm up on the track.

She was strong for Eastern stuff. Read Major Laye's *Short Study of Native Crime* and Bissart's — can't think of the title now, but it's got to do with crimes that are committed by natives for religious purposes.[1]

"There are a lot of undiscovered murders, Sooper," she used to say to me, "that are traceable to the rites an' ceremonies of the mysterious East."[2]

"Maybe there is, Miss Fenning," says I, "but there's a whole lot that's traceable to people wantin' the money in the mysterious West."

Some of the stuff she talked about, I didn't understand. In my young days education wasn't so epidemic as it is now. We hadn't anybody at headquarters who could tell you whether a bloodstain came from a mammal or an animal — are they? Well, whatever they were.

Charlie Croomb kept samples of London mud an' could tell you whether a burglar lived in Kilburn or Kew.[3] My own way is to ask him and tell him he's a liar: say that often enough, and he'll spill it. And what does it matter where he lives so long as you've got his fingerprints, an' records can tell you the day of the month he went down for his last conviction?

Real crime an' book crime's different. In a book, the feller that's caught leanin' over the body with a gun in his hand is usually the hero of the piece, and the bird who did the shootin' is the old butler who's been in the service of the family for forty-five years.[4] But in real life, when you find some-

---

[1] These books were made up by Wallace.
[2] Wallace is poking fun at thrillers involving Oriental criminals such as Sax Rohmer's Fu Manchu novels. The trope was so prevalent and obnoxious that Catholic priest and mystery author Ronald Knox (1888-1957) made it one of his ten rules for mystery writers in 1929: "No Chinaman must figure in the story."
[3] *Kilburn:* An area of northwest London near the City of Westminster. *Kew* is in the Richmond upon Thames borough about 8 miles southwest of Kilburn.
[4] Mystery author Mary Roberts Rinehart (1876-1958) is credited with inspiring the phrase — even though she didn't write it — "The butler did it" in *The Door* (1930) in which (*spoiler alert*) the butler really did do it.

body with a gun within shootin' distance of the dear departed, you pinch him and he's properly hung, walkin' to the drop with a firm step an' hopin' everybody will take a warnin' from his drinkin' habits.[1]

It's because we're unscientific in London that out of fifty killings a year we catch twenty-eight an' the other twenty-two die by their own hands. I'm old-fashioned. I don't believe in temp'ry insanity or brain-storms or psycho — whatever the word is. No doctor ever gets in the box[2] to swear that a burglar's not responsible for his actions, and you don't produce brain specialists to explain why the head cashier is ten thousand short at the call-over.[3] It's only when somebody is killed, and somebody else stands up in the dock an' puts himself on God and his country (as they say at trials), that the nerve doctor pulls out his diagrams to prove that the cause of all the trouble is a shortage of grey matter in the anterior cavity of the epiginkium. In the Bible, which is a pretty useful tex'-book, there's nothing about brain-storms an' subconscious urges. When Cain opened the register he did his shooting because he wanted more than he was gettin'[4] — an' that's why

---

[1] Before the condemned man or woman was executed, they were permitted to say a few words. Many sought God's blessing, or apologized for their crimes. But what they lacked in eloquence or contrition was made up by the printer of confessional broadsides that were sold at the execution. For example "The Last Words of James Mackpherson Murderer," who was hung for various crimes in 1700, begins "'I spent my time in rioting, / debauch'd my health and strength, / I pillag'd, plundered, murdered, / but now alas! at length, / I'm brought to punishment condign, / pale Death draws near to me, / The end I ever did project / to hang upon a Tree."

[2] In America, it is called the witness stand. It gets its name from the traditional structure, which looked like an open-topped cube. This has since been replaced by a more stripped-down version with evenly spaced slats below the rail.

[3] To prevent fraud or embezzlement, the day's transactions were recorded in several ledgers that were audited at closing time. The clerks would swap account books and call out the transactions, which were verified by another clerk.

[4] In the book of Genesis, Cain was the first-born of Adam and Eve. He slew

most murders are committed. But in that good book there's quite a lot about wickedness. It's an old-fashioned word that never arises in court, except in the indictment. Right down behind every bad crime you'll find that word if you look for it. But generally it is called something else.

And science can get you all wrong. What respect can you have for the scientific mind when you see it heave a paving-brick through the plate-glass window of a jeweller's shop?

Professor Charles Bigglewood was, in a manner of speaking, a friend of mine. He used to call me "Sooper" for one thing. And I've dined at his house in Clarges Street[1] for another. He wrote books on chemistry an' the human mind. I don't know who read 'em — I suppose there are queer people who buy that sort of junk, but I never met 'em. He gave me a copy of one with his own name written on a blank page, and I tried to read it, but the book was kind of dry. There were no characters in it and no pictures, but the binding was grand. I had it on the shelf of my parlour for years.

I got to know him through savin' the life of his daughter. That sound like a detective story, but all I did was to grab her by the hair just as she was steppin' in front of a motor-car. She was about eight at the time — a nice girl but romantical, even at that age. She said she was glad she wasn't killed, because it would have made the driver feel so bad. Some people are like that. Personally, I'd rather a driver threw any kind of fit than the amb'lance bells should be ringin' for me. That's my nature — egotistical. I took her home. I was a mere inspector in those days an' wore uniform, havin' been fired out of the Special Branch[2] for tellin' my superintendent he was playin' fa-

---

his brother Abel after God accepted Abel's sacrifice but not Cain's.
[1] A very wealthy and fashionable street. It is located in the Mayfair area and dead ends on Piccadilly at Green Park.
[2] A unit of the Metropolitan Police dedicated to intelligence and anti-terrorism activities. It was established in 1883 to battle the Irish Republican Brotherhood, a fraternal group fighting for an independent Ireland. It was renamed Special Operations 12 (SO12) and charged with spying on subversive groups and protecting senior politicians, the prime minister,

vourites. No, it wasn't a question of promotion, only I raided a night club and pinched a lady friend of his, and he wanted the charge withdrawn.

Well, Professor Bigglewood took a view that I'd done something big in scalping his daughter — wanted to give me money, and asked me to dinner, and the Lord knows what. I liked him. He was a pretty nice old man: married his housekeeper late in life — she'd been dead six years when I met him. A clever old boy in spite of his learnin'. Ever noticed how easy these bright scholars fall for a con man? He was an inventor, too — got a process for dealin' with spelter workin'[1] in the Midlands, and bringing him in a whole lot of money every month. He liked good wine — talked about port as if it was human. In appearance he was nearly the double of the late Gen'ral Booth[2] — long, white beard, fierce sort of nose, and white hair. I've sat listenin' to him by the hour wonderin' at his horse sense. He was the only man I ever met who didn't think police headquarters ought to be more scientific.

And he had one hobby — the collection of little idols — Buddha an' Shion[3] an' quaint things like that. One night he

---

and public figures. Author Salman Rushdie (1947-) was protected by an SO12 unit. In 2005, it was announced that SO12 would be disbanded and its functions merged with SO13, Scotland Yard's anti-terrorism branch.

[1] Also called zinc, it is a metal used in the Victorian era to make cheap household goods such as candlesticks, figurines, ornaments, and clock cases.

[2] English Methodist preacher William Booth (1829-1912) was the founder and first General of the Salvation Army. A longtime evangelist who was frequently at odds with the Methodist hierarchy over his desire to travel and preach, he ended up leaving the church. Retaining his belief in Methodist doctrine, he founded a mission in London's East End devoted to helping the poor and most needy. Booth used the Christian Gospel and the Protestant work ethic to attack vice and poverty, frequently against opposition from the alcohol industry, the Church of England, and the press, which portrayed Booth as a money-grubbing preacher who practiced nepotism. But he outlasted them all, and by the time he died in 1912, 40,000 people attended his funeral, including Queen Mary.

[3] *Buddha:* Siddhartha Gautama, a monk, teacher, and sage who lived in

opened a case and took out a little green dragon—made of jade.

"There's a history to that, Sooper," he said. "I bought it from a Chinaman at Tower Hill.[1] Gave him a pound for it. He was found in the river next day with his throat cut!"

"How do you know it was the same Chink?" I asked him, bein' suspicious about coincidences.

"My card was in his pocket. He had told me he had another like it, so I asked him to bring it to me."

I remembered the dead Chinaman. Up at the Yard we thought there had been a Tong fight.[2]

Croomb got to know Bigglewood, too — I can't remember for certain, but I've an idea I introduced him. Never mind about that; Croomb met him, an' once or twice went to dinner with Miss Fenning. Naturally, idols thrilled Eleanor, who wanted to know whether any of 'em had been stolen from a temple when the priest was full of hootch. She got that out of a book. But I reckon that most of his idols came through the usual junk-shops, and that the only body robbed was the professor. Except in one case — the jade dragon. Croomb had his views about this.

---

ancient India between the 6th and 4th centuries B.C. His doctrine was the foundation of Buddhism. *Shion:* An abbreviation of Fkonrskon-Shion, now called Fukurokuju, the god of wealth, happiness and longevity. One of the seven lucky gods in Japanese mythology, he is usually portrayed as an elderly man with a long white beard and an elongated, bald head. He carries a crane and a turtle, both symbols of longevity, and holds a staff with a sacred book attached to it.

[1] One of the oldest areas of London, Tower Hill is located near the Tower of London and between the City of London and the remains of the Roman-built London Wall. Tower Hill hosted public executions of many condemned peers and traitors.

[2] *Tong:* A social group of Chinese immigrants living in the United States, Canada, and Australia (tong is Chinese for "hall" or "gathering place"). Many are benevolent associations that provide support and protection for its members, but some have also been involved in criminal activities. Between 1880 and 1930, tong factions clashed in the Chinatowns of American cities over control of the drug trade, prostitution rings, and gambling dens.

"I've advised the professor to send it to a museum," he said. "In my considered opinion that dragon is a dangerous thing to have around."

From what I heard later it seems that Bigglewood hung on to the dragon.

I hadn't a chance of seeing it, for I sort of lost sight of him for years; every New Year's Day I got a wire or a card from him wishin' me luck in the comin' year, may it be bright an' prosperous, an' the usual stuff. Once or twice he wired from Switzerland, an' I guessed that Amelia — that was his daughter's name — was winter-sportin'. I saw her once or twice bein' driven in the professor's new Rolls sedan — the old man did things in style, had the smartest chauffeur, the fattest butler, and the slickest footman in Clarges Street.[1] I didn't know anything about her bein' married, but Sergeant Cross, who is in charge of Records and reads Births, Deaths and Marriages for his own amusement, brought the cutting to me. She'd married Captain Arthur Helby, DSO, MC,[2] in Derby somewhere. About three months after Records brought me a cutting that made me feel mighty sorry for the girl and her father. It was of a death: "Helby, Captain Arthur Helby, DSO, MC, on October 24th, in Dublin, after a short illness."

That was all. I wrote to the professor, but got no answer, and when I rung up his house in Clarges Street the caretaker told me that the professor had gone abroad with his daughter. The caretaker said that the captain died a natural death, though there was a lot of shooting in Dublin round about that time.[3]

---

[1] A street in the City of Westminster made up of Georgian town houses.
[2] *DSO*: Distinguished Service Order, a military decoration awarded for meritorious acts by officers, especially under fire; *MC:* Military Cross, an award given to officers for gallantry in battle. *Derby:* A city in Derbyshire, a country located in the middle of Britain.
[3] Ireland was entering a new stage in its struggle for independence from Great Britain. After a three-year guerilla war, the Anglo-Irish Treaty was concluded in December 1921 that gave Ireland a limited independence. Northern Ireland's decision to remain in the United Kingdom sparked a new round of fighting that officially ended in May 1923.

The next I heard was that she'd married again — a middle-aged general, and had left for India on her honeymoon trip. This bit of news was in the early editions of the evening papers the very day I saw the professor. I sat down an' wrote a letter to the old man. As a matter of fact, after I posted it I wished I had torn it up, because I didn't want him to feel that I was chasin' him. And that night I met him. I was up west lookin' for the taxi burglar — a man who used to drive a taxi up to the house he was going to "bust."[1] It was a good scheme, because there's nothing suspicious about a taxi loafin' round a residential square. This bird I was looking for had done three good jobs in a month and got away with 'em.

In the ordinary course of duty I called in at Vine Street, an' was talkin' to the inspector, when I heard somebody comin' into the charge-room,[2] an' lookin' up I nearly dropped — for the man in the patrol's hands was Professor Bigglewood! He was in evenin' dress, his top hat was on his head, and he was, to my eyes, dazed but sober. He saw me an' nodded very solemn. I didn't say a word, but just listened to the young officer who had brought him in.

"I was on duty in Regent Street at one-five this morning," he said (we teach young policemen to give evidence to the point), "an' I saw this man take a wooden pavin' block from a pile that was standin' by the roadside. Before I could reach him he had thrown the brick through the plate-glass window of the Ten Per Cent Jewellery Store."

I couldn't believe my ears.

"Are you sure it was this gentleman?' I asked, though it was no business of mine, and I apologized afterwards to the inspector in charge for buttin' in."

"Certain, — sir," says the officer. "He was the only man in sight."

---

[1] Criminal slang for burglary since the mid-1850s.
[2] A room accessible by the public and where a suspect is formally charged with a crime and recorded in the charge book kept there.

The inspector started in to ask the professor his name and address, and Mr Bigglewood answered without any hesitation. He said that he had been to his club, the Learned Societies, in St James's Street.[1] There had been a dinner given by some of his friends in honour of his daughter's wedding. According to the professor's story, all the men at the dinner were the kind who have to be in bed at ten by doctor's orders, and round about eleven he had a whisky-an'-soda in the readin'-room and went to sleep. When he woke up the club was in darkness an' he had to unlock the front door and let himself out. He was kind of bothered, but he wasn't drunk. He was certain of this — half-asleep was the way he put it. He was half-way down Regent Street when he heard somebody walkin' behind him, an' had a horrible feelin' of fear. It was so bad that he grabbed the first thing he could lay hands on — which was a road block. He said he could no more help doin' it than he could help standin' on his feet. He just lammed out with the block, and bing went the window!

The divisional surgeon came in at that minute, which was lucky, for the doctor knew Professor Bigglewood, and naturally he wouldn't certify him as drunk — not that he would have done that in any case. As to the man who was following, the policeman swore there was nobody near.

"I think Mr Bigglewood's theory that he was walking, to all intents and purposes, in his sleep is a sound one," said the doctor and laughed. "You'll have to settle the cost of the shop window with the jewellers, professor," he said.

I could see the old man was upset — who wouldn't be? Suppose you were a high-class professor an' woke up and found yourself in the dock on a charge of smashing a jeweller's window at one o'clock in the morning! The long and the

---

[1] An organization that promotes a profession, academic discipline or art. The Royal Society of London and the French Academy of Sciences are examples of learned societies. *St. James's Street* runs from Piccadilly to Pall Mall and was the home of many notable clubs such as Brooks's, White's, and Boodle's.

short of it was that he was released, and the inspector said he'd send a man down to the shop first thing in the morning and explain how the accident happened.

The professor asked me to walk back home with him; he wouldn't take a taxi — he thought the walk would kind of wake him up. Most of the conversation was on my side; he seemed too rattled to talk. From Vine Street to Regent Street isn't far, but we walked pretty slowly because he was an elderly gentleman. As we turned out of Piccadilly I saw a taxicab drawn up in front of Bigglewood's house, and there was an inspector and a policeman there, an' the inspector was Croomb. He was knocking at the door as we came up.

"Is that Professor Bigglewood?" he said. "Good evening, professor. Is this cab waiting for anybody in your house?"

Bigglewood shook his head; he was still a bit dull. He began feelin' in his pocket for the key, an' after a bit Croomb and I walked round and had a look at the taxicab. It was a new machine, and the engines were stone cold. It had been standing there, according to the policeman, for the best part of two hours.

"Is it — in the way?" asked Professor Bigglewood, who suddenly seemed to wake up from his trance.

"No, sir," said Croomb. "Will you open the door, professor — maybe somebody is inside."

What Croomb thought, and what I thought too, was that maybe the house was being burgled. And, of course, when we wanted to get into the house the professor had lost his key

"Is there anybody in the house?" I asked.

He shook his head and began to search his pockets.

Just at that minute I heard a church clock strike two. We were standing there, all of us looking, or feeling, pretty foolish. I didn't know what to do with the professor, though I had an idea that if I searched him thoroughly I'd have found the key, though naturally it was a delicate matter for a superintendent of police to suggest that he search anybody.

I don't know why I particularly remember that moment:

the dark street with the street lights, and the late traffic passing along Piccadilly at the end; the clear sky overhead, with a few stars showing, and a faint scent of flowers coming from the Lord knows where. I remember Croomb saying:

"You will remember, professor, that I told you the other day about the danger of taxicab burglaries?"

And that's about all I remember. Suddenly me and the taxicab came into collision. My elbow went through the window, and the next second I found myself lying across the steering-wheel with all the breath knocked out of me. I didn't hear any explosion, didn't see any flash. When I tell you that the hood of the car was cut to ribbons by flying glass, and that one of the railings in front of the house was flung fifty feet, you'll have an idea that it was some explosion.

I got to my feet, and the first thing I saw was the professor lying in a heap on the ground. The next thing was the policeman lifting Croomb from the gutter I don't know how the policeman had escaped, because he stood in the path of the explosion, but except that he lost his helmet and had his chin cut by the glass he was none the worse, and Croomb escaped altogether, except that he was knocked out.

I sent the policeman running for the fire alarm, and ordered him to send back the people who were turning into the street to see what it was all about. The front of the professor's house was blown out completely, and so was one of the walls, but fortunately there was a party wall of a house that was untenanted.[1] There was no more fire than a smouldering carpet, and we had that out before the fire brigade came on the spot.

Police reserves were rushed to Clarges Street to keep off the crowd, but long before they had arrived Croomb and I discovered the taxi man. He had been flung against the wall,

---

[1] A solid wall between adjacent homes. A party wall keeps a fire in one house from spreading to another. "Party" in this instance has nothing to do with a fun gathering, but is a legal term denoting the individuals involved in a contract or a lawsuit (as in the legal phrase "the party of the first part").

and he was lying half on a settee and half on the floor, and he was dead. A tall, good-looking fellow he had been — Croomb and I pulled him out into the street, and before the doctor came it was pretty easy to see that nothing could be done for him.

Before he went into the house we had made the professor as comfortable as we could. He was quite unconscious, but as far as I could see there was no bad injury. I thought he was knocked out, as Croomb had been, but when the doctor came he took a very serious view, and they rushed him off to the hospital in the ambulance.

Before the police stretcher got to Clarges Street we made a search of the dead man's clothes, and the first thing I found was a small jemmy[1] in his right-hand coat pocket. It was the newest jemmy I have ever found on a burglar.

"We've got the taxi thief," said Croomb. "I suspected this from the moment I saw the machine outside the door!"

He'd hardly said the words before he made his real discovery. Suddenly I heard him say: "Good God! Look at this!"

In the light of the lantern I saw in his hand the little green dragon of jade!

"Where was it?" I asked.

"In his overcoat pocket," said Croomb, and when we had finished the search we went into the house, to the back room where the professor kept his collection. Only one case was opened, and that was the one, according to Croomb, where Bigglewood always kept the dragon. Nothing else was touched. There were two or three items of solid gold, and one or two things in the room that were worth real money, but the cases had not been so much as opened. Of course, the glasses were shattered by the explosion, and some of them were on the floor.

"It's easy to see what he came for," said Croomb. "The dragon!"

---

[1] Criminal slang for a crowbar or a prybar. Being caught on the street with a jemmy is a sure sign to the police that you're up to no good.

He was quivering with excitement.

"I told the professor the last time I saw him to send that thing to a museum. The thing is as clear as daylight. He came here to pinch the dragon, and took some time in finding it. The door leading to the collection room has been wrecked, so we can't tell yet how it was opened, but I'll bet money that it was 'busted' by a jemmy."

"How did the explosion happen, inspector?" I asked him. I always believe in asking questions: you sometimes get an idea from the answer. Quite a lot of people get their education either that way or by contradicting what other people say.

"There was a gas-stove in Mr Bigglewood's study. It may have been leaking, or it may have been left on by accident. The man must have come into the room and heard me and the constable talking on the street. We'd been here a quarter of an hour. Either he lit his match to light a cigarette or to find his way out — there's no sign of an electric torch[1] here — and the room blew up."

I sort of scratched my head at that.

"Maybe he couldn't smell the gas?" I suggested.

"He might smell the gas and never dream there was any danger," said Croomb a bit sharply, and I didn't argue with him.

The professor died without regaining consciousness about four o'clock in the morning, and as I was busy all the forenoon I didn't get any chance of seeing Croomb. I don't think it would have been much use my talking, even if I had.

I have never been quite sure whether Croomb or Eleanor was the official press agent, and it was not my business to in-

---

[1] A flashlight, invented by Conrad Hubert (1855-1928), a Russian inventor and businessman who changed his name from Akiba Horowitz after arriving in America. He founded the American Electrical Novelty and Manufacturing Co. and sold a flashlight promoted as "Ever Ready." In 1905, Hubert renamed his company American Ever Ready. Eventually, the Ever Ready name was applied to his batteries, now called Eveready, and the company is now called Energizer Holdings Inc.

quire; but certainly the late editions of the evening papers smelt like Eleanor.

"Green Dragon Clue in Taxicab Mystery," was one headline, and "The Vengeance of the Chinese Dragon God" was another. On the whole I guess it was Eleanor the public had to thank, for she was strong for the mysterious East.

There was a double inquest; one on the taxi-man, whose name was Rolls and who lived at Notting Hill;[1] another on the professor. Rolls wasn't well known; he had only been living in his present lodgings for a month. There were no papers to identify him, and beyond a few things that I had collected and locked up in my room in Scotland Yard, no kind of clue whatever. The jury returned a verdict of accidental death in both cases, and the green dragon was handed round to the jury and the Press-box, and pretty nearly everybody in court, and for the next week all the papers published articles on the Mysterious East, and how bad it was to go monkeying with Chinese religion.

The long and the short of it was that Croomb got a step in promotion. When I saw the deputy commissioner the day after the inquest he told me that he thought it wasn't much credit to me that a junior officer should have taken the case from right under my nose and made a success of it.

"In fact, Sooper," he said, "I can't help feeling, after reading the minutes of this case, that our department must be brought up to date. We need more science, a larger and wider perception—"

And all that sort of stuff.

Croomb and his young lady got married on the strength of his promotion. I went to the wedding and to the party they gave after. What I missed was the little green dragon. I thought it ought to have been put on the invitation cards, and maybe done in sugar on top of the cake.

The deputy was sore with me — and naturally. I didn't

---

[1] A neighborhood in West London that's had a long association with artists since the 1870s.

tell him all I might have told him. He said it was my business to come to him as soon as I found the strip of sponge-platinum and the bottle of cyanide.¹ Perhaps he was right, though I'd told the Chief Commissioner and the Home Office pathologist, who's got more science in the fingers of his left hand than most people I know. We knew Rolls had been poisoned, because we found the poison in Bigglewood's pocket, and the old pathologist, he found the rest by careful investigation. And we knew that the taxi-driver's name wasn't Rolls at all, because I took his fingerprints and turned them up at the Yard, and found his name was Williams, alias Helby — well, here's the story:

Helby was a crook, a man of good education, who used to take jobs as chauffeur in a family where there was a chance of pickings — he did two terms of light imprisonment for theft and larceny. And then he came into Bigglewood's service and got acquainted with the girl. The first thing the old professor knew about the affair was when he got a wire that Helby had married the girl at a Midland registrar's office. He had been married before, but a little thing like that didn't worry Mr Helby.

The old man, to save his face, published the notice of the wedding to "Captain Helby." I've got an idea that this young scoundrel had held some sort of commission in the war.

Anyway, Bigglewood had to pay out to keep his new son-in-law, though he couldn't hope to give Helby all the money he wanted. And then, after a few years, the first Mrs Helby turned up, about the same time as Arthur was arrested for burglary in Dublin. With the fear of a charge of bigamy hanging over him, Helby sent a message to London, having milked the professor as dry as possible, to say that he was dead.

The fake was worked from Ireland, and the young widow, who couldn't have been very sorry after the life she had lived,

---

¹ *Sponge-platinum* is a fine platinum powder. Because gas molecules could bond to its surface, it was used in self-lighting lamps, ovens, and stove burners.

went back to her father, and eventually married General Carslake. I discovered that the "dead man" had been doing three years for burglary, and that he came out of prison two months or so before the death of the professor.

He managed to hire a new taxi, and got a licence under the name of Rolls. He may or may not have been burgling in London. All that I know is that the jemmy we found in his pocket was bought by an old gentleman with a white beard the day of the explosion.

Helby would have lain low, only he heard about the forthcoming marriage. This put an idea into his head that he might blackmail the old man, and the night before the wedding Helby turned up in Clarges Street (I could have produced the professor's servant to prove this, but I didn't) and in all probability asked a big sum as the price of his silence.

The old man was as keen a student of human nature as I've ever met — the fact that he put the dragon and the jemmy in Helby's pocket proves that — and he planned the murder of the blackmailer with the care of a scientist — I'll never again say anything against science. It's perfectly true that he did hide in the club till it was shut, that he let himself out and made his way down to Clarges Street, where Helby was waiting for him. He doped him with cyanide of potassium in a glass of port. As soon as Helby was dead, he laid a strip of sponge platinum on the table, turned on the gas fire and went out. Sponge platinum is not a new one on me — I use it every morning to light my gas-ring. The moment coal gas gets at this mineral it turns it white hot, and that's what happened when the room was full of gas and how the explosion occurred. That piece of sponge platinum was almost the first thing I found when I got in the room.

When the murder was done. Bigglewood went out of the house, got to Regent Street by a back way, and, as soon as he saw a policeman, put a brick through a window, expecting to be locked up for the night. He was alibi-hunting, and it was bad luck that I happened to be in the station when they pulled in.

No, sir, we didn't want any scandal. The Home Secretary didn't want it, and the Chief Commissioner didn't want it. Sooner than have scandal, they gave Croomb his promotion. Drop in one night on him and his wife and hear the tale of the little green dragon of jade. And don't laugh, or you'll be giving me away.

Edgar Wallace, 1930.

Sherlock Holmes Splits Hairs—

With apologies to Sir Arthur Conan Doyle for having borrowed the services of two famous gentlemen

By
GEORGE C. HENDERSON

George C. Henderson

Illustrated by "Holpert"

For some reason, author George C. Henderson (b. 1891) chose to write the news story for the Aug. 15 issue of Collier's *in the form of a pseudo-pastiche, perhaps as a way of conveying the amazing ways science was becoming useful in police work.*

Capt. C.D. Lee of the Berkeley (Calif.) Police Department did exist. His work on classifying hair fibers was part of a broader effort under Police Chief August Vollmer (1876-1955) to improve policing. Vollmer was among the first to take advantage of new inventions, such as using motorcycles and cars. He also created a school to train officers, required college degrees for officers, and hired female police officers.

Henderson was a West Coast newspaper reporter who also wrote seven novels, many of them Westerns. His sole non-fiction work was Keys to Crookdom *(1924), a dictionary of criminal slang that popularized words such as bootlegger, burglar, and bum steer. The artist who signed himself "Holpert" could not be identified.*

"Oh, Watson," cried my friend Sherlock Holmes as I entered the laboratory in Berkeley, Cal. "Come here a moment, will you?"

My friend's manner showed more excitement than I had observed since our arrival in America.

"This is Capt. C. D. Lee. You remember, Watson, how I used to deduce a man's residence and tastes from the ash of his Trichinopoly cigar?[1] That was nothing, I assure you, Watson, to what Captain Lee has just done."

Holmes has amused himself by studying American slang. Turning to the pleasant-faced, middle-aged man he said:

"Show him your stuff,[2] Captain."

"It is a science of hair identification," Lee told me. "Mr. Holmes has been good enough to express his interest. I told him to bring me a hair — a single hair — of any sort he chose. He has brought me a hair from the head of a boy eight to fifteen years old of Scandinavian or German descent."

"Absolutely right," said Holmes crisply. "The son of that couple who came on from Denver on the train with us, Watson, and are now stopping at our hotel across the hall. What was their name — Larssen? Exactly."

At Holmes' suggestion I made a few notes from which I transcribe this account of Captain Lee's methods — one of the most important of our contacts on this American tour.

Lee washes the hair with chemicals, removing all grease and dirt, and places it under a microscope that magnifies 750 diameters.[3] He turns on a powerful light underneath the hair.

---

[1] A Trichinopoly cigar in *A Study in Scarlet* led to Holmes' admission that he had made a special study of ashes and can identify any brand of tobacco at a glance. He did not, however, deduce the man's residence nor his tastes. Trichinopoly is a cigar made from tobacco grown near present-day Tiruchirappalli in India. It was a cheap cigar and crudely made — basically a cylinder with the ends cut off instead of tapered — and one of India's major exports during the Victorian Era.

[2] The word stuff has been used to mean an unspecified material, thing, or activity for a long time, but it was only in the 20th century that "show your stuff" entered the language. The earliest the phrase appears is in an ad in a 1908 issue of *Popular Mechanics*, in which vendors at the St. Louis Electrical Show were encouraged to "Get in now and show your stuff to the buyers of the Great Southwest." By 1925, the phrase was showing up in *Boy's Life* magazine as a euphemism for displaying your talents.

[3] An archaic way of expressing how much to zoom in on an object. In this case, it means that the image should be 750 times as long and 750 times as wide as the object. Since at 250 times, the hair will appear as a thick branch, 750 times provides an even more detailed view of the follicle.

The hair is transparent, but there can be distinguished a saw-tooth edge marking the outer cuticle, then a mass of cells colored slightly with the granules of pigmentation, and finally, in the center, a pith.

No other animal has hair like man except the monkey. Even the monkey hair can be distinguished by its smaller diameter. Lee's collection of scores of magnified photographs of various kinds of hair shows the marked differences. The hair of a deer has no well-defined pith. The hair of a sheep, a cat, a squirrel, or a mouse appears like a strip of backbone or line of vertebrae. A rabbit's hair resembles an ear of corn. The hair of a dog has an effect of large dark splotches on a gray background.

The next step is to photograph the hair, much magnified.

Comparative size indicates the sex. The hair Holmes had brought for testing was larger than the hair of a girl of eight to fifteen years. The photograph showed that the pith had only begun to develop, indicating either youth or senile old age. The color and size together showed that it must be the hair of a boy, not a graybeard. By the size of the pith, the age could be checked as between eight and fifteen.

Determination of nationality is less sure. Lee is now working to reduce this to exactness. He was only able to tell us that slight variations in the cross sections of hairs are now being charted. These variations are marked between the races. A cross section of the hair of a North American Indian is round; of a Negro, elliptical.

Captain Lee told Holmes of three instances in which hair identification had been useful. I remember that it saved a man wrongly suspected of robbery of a street car and, in an another instance, verified a taxicab driver's story that he had struck a man a fatal blow only in self-defense.

"Make a note, Watson," said Holmes, as we took our departure, "that only the bald man is safe. And not he, if he uses hair tonic."

Sherlock Among the Spirits

Anonymous

Conan Doyle's conversion to Spiritualism in 1917 made him a figure of fun, but that criticism was largely muted when it became clear many families who had lost their sons and fathers in the war found comfort in it. But as memories of the war faded, it seemed like the world turned its attention back to the living and looked to the future.

Conan Doyle continued his crusade, however, and he became a lightning rod for skeptics, especially after he publicly supported the Cottingley Fairy photos in 1920.

A month after Conan Doyle's The Land of Mist, *with its conversion of Professor Challenger to Spiritualism, started its serialization in* The Strand, *this counter-attack appeared in the Aug. 15 issue of* G.K.'s Weekly. *Its authorship is unknown, but it may be by the magazine's founder, Gilbert Keith Chesterton (1878-1936). The rotund intellectual was a multi-talented writer and artist, writing more than 80 books, hundreds of short stories and thousands of essays. He was also a social critic and an effective apologist for Christianity, particularly after he converted to Roman Catholicism. His greatest fictional creation was Father Brown, the amateur detective who solved mysteries using intuition and his insights into human nature.*

Chesterton has another connection with Holmes. An amateur artist, he drew 19 illustrations for a never-published edition of Holmes stories. They were reprinted in 2003 by the Baker Street Irregulars.

The Spiritualist Séance, which my friend Conan Doyle had induced me to hold in my old rooms in Baker Street, was just over. It had been a tremendous revelation. The medium, Dr. Magog,[1] whom I assumed from the first to be a charlatan

---

[1] This subtle dig plays off the fact that Magog appears several times in the Bible as a nation that is the enemy of Israel and God. In Revelations, a freed Satan will lead the nations Gog and Magog to attack "God's people," only to be defeated by a fire from heaven. Christians refer to seeing Gog and Magog as a sign that we're in the last days before the Apocalypse and the second coming of Jesus Christ: "We are only in the midst of that great battle of 'Gog and Magog,' which is to ultimate in the final and complete destruction of *all* wrong" (*American Spiritualist Magazine*, vol. 3, 1877).

(for my training had been strictly scientific and rational), because of his long white hair and beard and his Lithuanian name, astounded me with the accuracy of his suggestions. He even converted Sir Arthur's other friend Dr. Challenger, whom readers of the *Strand Magazine* may remember as having discovered a world of prehistoric animals, whose manners and demeanour he seemed to share. He had begun by having grave doubts, which he expressed by hurling the table to the end of the room and dancing on several enquirers after truth; but halfway through the proceedings, he burst into sobs that shook the building.

I could understand his feelings. The medium mentioned things that could only be known in the innermost domestic circle; such as a knock given to a girl when she was a child, now recalled by the spirit of her brother killed in the war. Sometimes this intimacy was even distressing; as in the picture called up before us of a girl sobbing in a remote chateau in France, and the gloomy admission by a young man present that the memory moved him to remorse. Perhaps the most remarkable case was that of the spirit of a daughter who told her father not to neglect his appearance from grief at her death, seeing that the Shining Ones liked to see him in a single eyeglass and spats.[1] Now the man in question was indescribably shaggy and shabby, but he admitted that he had indeed been thus adorned in happier days.

I was brooding on these things after the others had left, when I heard a step on the stair that told of one of them returning. Dr. Magog himself hurriedly re-entered the room, saying: "I had forgotten my hat. Interesting occasion, wasn't it?"

---

[1] *Single eyeglass*: Better known as a monocle, it was a lens attached to string or chain that was attached to the clothing to keep it from being lost. *Spats*: A cloth or leather shoe covering that protects the instep and ankle from the weather. Originally called spatterdashes or spatter guards, they were worn by soldiers as part of their field uniform before moving to civilian wear. The white models look very stylish and draw attention to the man's elegant footwear and dancing abilities.

"You absolutely amazed me," I answered.

"You have often told me so, my dear Watson," he replied.

I sprang to my feet and stood stiffened with incredulous stupefaction, for I had caught a note of something more marvelous than any psychical marvels.

He seated himself languidly and removed the white wig, showing the unmistakable frontal development of the greatest detective in the world. "If you had used my methods, Watson," he said, "you would have known that a man never forgets his hat except when he is wearing a wig. It was a deplorable lapse. Well, you see, I converted Challenger."

"A wonderful achievement," I said, "The discoverer of the prehistoric world."

"A very appropriate occupation Watson," he said. "I should say Dr. Challenger's powers of scientific observation were just about equal to noticing one of the larger Plesiosauri a few yards off.[1] With a little more attention to minutiae he might even see a mammoth on the mat."

"But how on earth did you manage it?" I asked. "How did you know of that nursery incident, for instance?"

"The girl was good-looking and healthy and she had false teeth. More probably she had them knocked out; and who should knock them out if not her brother?"

"And what about the eyeglass and spats?" I demanded.

"I have myself written a little monograph on 'The Monocle of Crime,' and we saw something of its devastating effect when we looked into that little problem of the Haunted Hat Peg. The man had different markings in the two eye sockets, in a way only produced by the single eyeglass. Did you ever know a shabby, unshaven man wear a single eyeglass? His beard bristled like that of all men who were once clean shaven. I guessed the spats; but I was careful only to say that the

---

[1] A order of apex predators that swam in the oceans from roughly 66 million to 203 million years ago. They were short- and long-necked warm-blooded creatures with four long flippers whose bones were discovered in the early 19th century. They ranged as adults from 5 to 50 feet long.

higher intelligences would like to see them. There is no accounting for taste."

"And how did you know," I asked, lowering my voice, "that the young man had broken the heart of a lady in a chateau?"

"He hadn't," replied Sherlock Holmes, "but I could see by his face he would be the last man to deny it. Rather too obvious, Watson. Will you pass me my violin?"

Cover of *The Land of Mist*, British edition, 1926

Intelligence Service

Z. 4.999

Illustrated by "RVG"

Translated by Bill Peschel

In 1066, the Duke of Normandy crossed the English Channel with his army, and, as William the Conqueror, became the first Norman king of England. England has never forgiven France ever since. For centuries, this rivalry played out on numerous battlefields, and it wasn't until the rise of a unified Germany that the two antagonists put aside most of their differences in the face of a common enemy.

But an alliance doesn't necessarily mean friendship, and the two nations remain united in their bemused contempt for each other. Take this story, for example, published in the Dec. 13 issue of Le Matin ("The Morning News") of Paris.

Whitechapel,[1] 5:49 p.m. Behind the docks, the light from the electric globes glitter on the small street like diamonds in

---

[1] A neighborhood in London's East End. Its location near the docks on the Thames made it a popular place for immigrants. The Jack the Ripper murders took place there in the late 1880s.

the thick fog.

Strong smells of gin and rotted grains rose from the sheds whose feet bathed in the Thames. In the middle of the stream that cuts the street, a woman in a feathered hat waits for the statuesque policeman to escort her to the night court.

I enter the small pub. To keep from being noticed, I disguised myself as a Hawaiian general. I place on the table my cocked hat, my chewing gum and the secret code of the British Admiralty I just bought at the nearest bookstore.

After a second the man entered. He was dressed in a checkered Inverness cape,[1] and he puffed scrolls of smoke from the blond tobacco in his briar pipe. He also carried, I was to learn later, very compromising documents. The man's light blue eyes were piercing and disturbing. They searched the room until they stopped on me.

"I know you," he said with a Scottish highland accent. "You were born in Belleville,[2] as evidenced by your mountain shoes; your father was an arthritic metal smelter; because you have your ears widely spread, you have failed twice obtaining your bachelor's degree; and you like cherries soaked in *eau-de-vie*."[3]

I was amazed; he had just dissected my life like a bitter almond. I looked at him, stunned.

"Are you determined to work with us?"

"Yes, sir," I replied.

---

[1] A weatherproof sleeveless coat with an added short cape from which the wearer's arms emerge. It was developed in Scotland in the 1850s and underwent modifications in the length and design before it reached its final form. Although Holmes typically wore an Ulster coat in the books, he was portrayed with the showier cape in Sidney Paget's illustrations.

[2] The French word for "beautiful town" is used by at least 10 places in France, as well as a fictional location for the French animated movie *The Triplets of Belleville* (2003). In this case the narrator is probably from the Paris neighborhood on the east side of the city. It was founded as an independent municipality (called a commune) after the French Revolution, and was annexed by the city in 1860.

[3] Literally translated as "water of life," it is a colorless fruit brandy.

"Let's speak in French," said the man with a strange smile. He lowered his voice. "Let me introduce myself. I am Sherlock Holmes."

"The Great Detective."

"Simply 'The Detective' will do; the smartest man in Britain, presently chief of the Intelligence Service of His Majesty's Army. Your country concerns us. France is secretly rearming and, as the vulture flies, London is too close to Paris. We need vital information about your strategic points."

"How much do you pay?"

"One thousand pounds down and another thousand pounds upon delivery."

"Done. What do you desire? I have on me the number of soldiers who guard the Elysee Palace,[1] the plunger from a rapid-firing "680", and a model of the Republican Guard's regulation boots."[2]

"We know all that; we need more important military intelligence." The man spoke in a low voice. As he whispered these grave words — I must confess — he nervously pricked his left forearm with a Pravaz syringe[3] and with his right foot

---

[1] It has been the official home of France's president since 1848, but before that its history mirrored the fortunes of the French royalty. Designed in the French classical style and built in 1722 for an aristocratic family, it was bought by King Louis XV for his mistress Madame de Pompadour. The monarch sold it after her death in 1773 to the court's banker, one of the richest men in France, for his use as a country home. In 1787, it was sold to the Duchess of Bourbon, who named it the Élysée Palace, after the Elysian Fields, the equivalent of heaven in Greek mythology. After the French Revolution, the palace was confiscated and turned into a business offering food, drinking, dancing and gambling. In 1808, it was sold to Emperor Napoleon Bonaparte, and after his final downfall after the battle of Waterloo, it was returned to the Duchess of Bourbon, who sold it to Louis XVIII. The most notable event in the palace since then occurred in 1899, when 58-year-old President Félix Faure died of apoplexy while having sex with his 30-year-old mistress.

[2] A tool used to regulate the explosion time of a shell after firing. An explanation for the "680" could not be found.

[3] Charles Gabriel Pravaz (1791-1853) was a French orthopedic surgeon and

beat the march of the First Scottish Grenadiers.¹

"I want to know," he said, "where is the Eiffel Tower. Then, I want to know where I can find the Opera railway station. Finally, I need to know what the cannon sounds like at the Palais-Royal.²

"Good God!" I said, my teeth chattering, "you're not pulling your punches! What you're demanding is not simple."

"Take it or leave it, but I advise you to take it, because if you leave, my poor arthritic son, there is a good chance that you'll finish your days in the lowest dungeon in the Tower of London."³

"I accept, but you must pay me the advance."

"Here!" He handed me a thousand pounds in sixpence coins.⁴ By the time I counted my money, he vanished, or

---

inventor of the hypodermic syringe.

¹ A non-existent unit. There may be Scotsmen in the Grenadier Guards, a long-serving infantry regiment in the British Army, but no specific unit by that name is on its roster.

² *Eiffel Tower:* Probably the most famous symbol of Paris, the tower was considered a failure by artists and intellectuals when it was built for the entrance to the 1889 World's Fair. More than 7 million people visit it every year. It is named for the engineer and designer Gustave Eiffel (1832-1923). *Opera*: A railway station in the 2nd arrondissment of central Paris. Named for the Place de l'Opéra Square. Nearby lies the Palais Garnier opera house, the home from 1861 to 1875 of the Paris Opera. Apart from its architectural and musical merits, it is also known as the setting of the novel by Gaston Leroux (1868-1927) *The Phantom of the Opera* (1910). *Palais-Royal:* A former royal palace located next to the Louvre in the city's 1st arrondissement. It was built for Cardinal Richelieu (1585-1642) in 1639 and became royal property upon his death. It is now used by the Ministry of Culture and the Constitutional Council.

³ A castle located on the banks of the Thames in central London. The White Tower was built by William the Conqueror in 1078. More buildings and two concentric rings of walls and a moat were finished by the late 13th century. The Tower has served as a mint, an armory, records office, a prison (1100-1952), and is currently the repository of the Crown Jewels of England. During the 16th and 17th century, it imprisoned nobles, some of whom were later executed for treason.

⁴ A coin from the old British monetary system. It is also called a tanner or half-shilling (since a shilling is 12 pence). Worth about a pound today,

maybe he metamorphosed. Because from that moment on, my steps were dogged by an Italian organ player from Barbary playing Toselli's serenade night and day.[1]

I was part of the "Intelligence Service." To reflect the important role I was going to play, I virtuously swallowed a cocktail, a cocktail mixed from equal parts shame and pride.

I crossed the English Channel and rented near my field of operation in Paris a boiled-egg shop to convince my neighbors that I was an honorable merchant. I stuffed my display with fake eggs and hired accomplices: two nurses for the cannon of the Palais-Royal, a paratrooper for the Eiffel Tower, and a fake naval officer whose uniform was similar to that of the employees of the subway.

Dressed in their colorful coats, my henchmen reconnoitered their targets. Meanwhile, I enjoyed the high life at the expense of the Intelligence Service. I had mistresses, a sedan, washable gloves and vermeil cigarette holders.[2]

In the end, my fun became the ruin of me.

Holmes' advance represents a substantial fortune. It's also a substantial weight, since £2,000 in half-shillings weighs 500 pounds.

[1] A popular piece of classical music, better known as Serenata "Rimpianto" Op.6 No.1. Enrico Toselli (1883-1926) was an Italian concert pianist who performed all across Europe. His elopement with Archduchess Louise of Austria in 1907, a few years after she deserted King Frederick Augustus of Saxony, caused a scandal. Their marriage, however, ended in divorce in 1912.

[2] *Sedan:* A passenger car that has three compartments for the engine, passengers, and cargo. The name is derived from a sedan chair, a box with poles front to back that was carried by porters. The word was first applied to vehicles in 1912, although they existed as early as 1899. *Washable gloves:* While the properties of goatskin used to make chamois gloves make them washable, advances in tanning and treatment of other hides led to the advertising of gloves that could be washed in gasoline or warm water and soda. *Cigarette holders:* When women took to smoking in greater numbers after 1900, this fashion accessory was invented to keep falling ash off their clothes (hence the unusually long lengths), reduce staining of the fingers, gloves and teeth, cooled the smoke and kept the lips from tearing the thin paper. Men took to them as well but preferred the shorter lengths.

One fine morning, Sherlock Holmes appeared in Paris. We met in the shop, where I updated him about our operations. The paratrooper could not reach the Eiffel Tower because of the demolition work at the Exposition Internationale des
Arts Décoratifs,[1] the fake officer had been bottled up for eight days at the Madeleine,[2] and the nurses were deafened by the Palais Royal's cannon and I had to drive them to the hospital.

The most intelligent man in the United Kingdom looked at me angrily, then suddenly bursting into a mad laugh, he whistled in a beautiful key. Two French agents entered the store and dragged me to the depot.

As if failing in my mission wasn't bad enough, it turns out Sherlock Holmes was in cahoots with the Pointed Tower.[3]

---

[1] The style known as Art Deco debuted at the International Exhibition of Modern Decorative and Industrial Arts in Paris. From April to October 1925, more than 16 million people visited the 15,000 exhibitors from 20 nations. It was a celebration of Modernism in art, design, and architecture. The Eiffel Tower could be seen from the exhibition, especially after the Citroen company decorated it with 200,000 lights that displayed patterns of shapes, circles, the signs of the zodiac, and the company's name.

[2] A subway station in the 8th arrondissement of central Paris. It is one stop west of the Opera station. Although it bears the same name as the traditional small cake that inspired Marcel Proust to write *Remembrance of Things Past*, the subway stop was named for the L'église de la Madeleine, the Neo-classical church consecrated in 1842 to Mary Magdalene.

[3] [Original footnote] La Tour pointue (The Pointed Tower) in French slang means the Préfecture de police de Paris, 36, quai des Orfèvres (police headquarters in Paris) because of the pointed tower above it.

The Rollo Boys with Sherlock in Mayfair; or Keep It Under Your Green Hat

Corey Ford

Illustrated by Gluyas Williams

There were always books written to appeal to children, such as The Swiss Family Robinson *(1812)*, Tom Brown's Schooldays *(1857)*, Little Women *(1869)*, and The Adventures of Tom Sawyer *(1876)*. But it took the appearance of cheaply printed and cheaply priced "dime novels" to launch the genre of boys' adventure stories, where youthful enthusiasm, imagination, and cleverness were championed. Heroes such as Frank Merriwell, Frank Reade Jr., Tom Swift, and the Rover Boys were sunny optimists who built fabulous machines, explored exotic parts of the world, and defeated bullies and villains.

These stories were the target of Three Rousing Cheers for the Rollo Boys, the first book by humorist Corey Ford (1902-1969). In each chapter the boys embarked on a different adventure where silly things happen. For example, in one story, after the boys and their sweethearts are shipwrecked on a desert island, Ford describes what happened next:

> "'What shall we eat, though,' complained Dolly. She had no sooner spoken than a second wave carried up a table and a full set of dishes, and rapidly spread places for seven, handing each of the castaways a French menu as it departed down the beach. 'Dat old devil sea,' muttered Captain Blossom, as a third wave rolled apologetically up the beach with some butter, which the second wave had apparently forgotten. And he continued to shake his head and mutter as more waves drifted in after supper and washed the dishes."

In the chapter below, Ford introduced the boys to two popular literary figures: Sherlock Holmes and Michael Arlen, the author of the best-seller The Green Hat *(1924)*. An Armenian by birth, Arlen (1895-1956) emigrated to Britain where he launched his literary career with his romances about Britain's Smart Set, the young generation who passed through the war years unscathed and had time and money for idle frivolities.

The Green Hat told the short, tempestuous life of Iris March, the doomed last member of an aristocratic family, who recklessly drove a yellow Hispano Suiza luxury car and sported a green cloche hat. The novel shocked readers with its frank discussion of sex — at least frank for its time — which included Iris' declaration that she wanted sex and didn't care much who she did it with. Her life of joyous abandon was marred by Gerald March, her alcoholic brother, and her first husband, "Boy" Fenwick, who committed suicide "for Purity" — in particular his bride's lack of same. In the end, she dies tragically in an auto accident.

The story was illustrated by Gluyas Williams (1888-1982), an American cartoonist whose skilful depictions of the sophisticated wealthy class appeared frequently in *The New Yorker*.

"My dear Rollo Boys," said Sherlock Holmes, as he lounged over the test tubes in his long purple dressing gown, his pipe clamped between his teeth and the visor of his detective cap pulled down over his eyes, "I am seeking to ascertain the chemical elements of Purity." He held up two empty test tubes to the light, shook them, and poured the contents into a glass globe. "I should say they are about two parts of fiction to one of truth," he concluded slowly, examining the glass globe, which was empty, "and the rest merely impotence."

The three Rollo Boys were seated about the fire in their dressing gowns, the visors of their detective caps pulled down over their eyes, and their pipes clamped between their teeth. Silence fell over the little room, picking itself up again and rubbing its shins with an ill-concealed oath as it limped through the door.

Outdoors the windows were being washed by an autumnal rain, named Tony.

"You may have wondered that I should have sent for you to come here," said Sherlock Holmes slowly, as he emptied the contents of the globe and stirred the remaining vacuum reflectively. "But perhaps you can tell me what is needed."

"I should say, well, about a pony of brandy,"[1] murmured

---

[1] American slang for one fluid ounce of spirit, smaller than a shot of liquor

Tom Rollo absently, with one eye on the contacts of the globe.

"It is in connection with the strange mystery of the Mayfair Suicides," explained the detective, ignoring the fun-loving Rob's remark as he drained off the vacuum and threw it away leaving only the hole in space where the vacuum had been.

"You probably read in the *Evening Standard* this morning that one 'Boy Fenwick'[1] was found lying in the courtyard of the Hotel Vendôme, dead of a shattered reputation. He had fallen, it appears, from his bedroom window on the third floor. Iris March, his beautiful young wife, had been asleep, had suddenly awoken, if there is such a word, to a sharp feeling of solitude, had happened to look out at the dawn. ..."

"What came next?" gasped Dick Rollo.

"*Four trailing dots!*" hissed Sherlock Holmes, and removed the hole, leaving only the space.

"The Sign of the Four!"[2] cried Harry; and the three Rollo Boys stared at each other in horror. "But why—why—?"

Sherlock shrugged. " 'Boy died,' she said, 'for Purity!'"

And so saying, he seized the contents of the space where the hole had been which had been left by the vacuum, removed the contents, removed *that*, and held the result up to the light. "I have discovered *Purity!*" he cried.

"But you have nothing there!" ejaculated Tom.

"Precisely," laughed Sherlock Holmes diabolically, as the doorbell rang. "But if I am not very much mistaken, and I have never been mistaken except in the following cases," naming them, "this is the very lady now of whom we were speaking. It always is," he added by way of explanation, as he drew aside the window curtains and pointed to the long, low, empty battle chariot before the door, like a huge yellow insect, open as a

---

(1.5 oz.). Bartenders who use pour spouts in their bottles measure their pours by counting out loud so each word could be clearly understood. For a pony, they count to four; for a shot, to six.

[1] As noted in the introduction, he was the husband of Iris March who killed himself "for Purity."

[2] A reference to the second Sherlock Holmes novel published in 1890.

yacht, it wore a great shining bonnet, as supplied to his Most Catholic Majesty. (Ed. Note: It was an automobile. Ans.)¹

"The lady is tall, not very tall, but short, her face is small as a lady's handkerchief provided she hasn't a cold, wearing a light brown leather jacket, and as they would say in the England of long ago — she is fair. To be fair, to be sad . . . why, is she intelligent, too? And always her hair dances a tawny, formal dance ... may I have the next? I promised Lord Eggleston. But ... on her cheek, under the shadow of a Green Hat which she wears bravely, *pour le style*."²

"My God, Sherlock!" cried Dick, amazed by the man's extraordinary powers of deduction, "how can you tell all that?"

"Oh, I read the book," snapped Sherlock Holmes, as the door opened and our visitor entered.

"I've always wanted," said the voice of the Green Hat. One could not see her face, because the full moon does not rise over El Dorado till Thursday. One murmured thus and thus. She murmured: "You know, vaguely. ..."

"Of course, vaguely," said Sherlock Holmes. She sat in the deep wicker armchair. People named Elmer always sit in deep wicker armchairs. Superficially; but, then, God help us all! "I wonder." Who said that?

"Who said what?"

"I wonder."

"Perhaps you are right," she replied; and her hand smelled dimly of that scent whose name I shall now never know. She too belonged then to the scent-whose-name-I-shall-now-never-know School. "Why?" she said. "But, really ... "

She looked at him through a pair of opera glasses, upside down, and then she wound her watch, but one did not know. One never knew. Even if one wrote it ... Or even why ...

"Women," he said, "are—"

---

[1] Abbreviation for answer. This sentence is a good example of Arlen's writing style, which came to be called Arlenesque. Ford will continue to poke fun at Arlen's style for the rest of this story.

[2] A French phrase meaning "for the style," or to be stylish.

"You are not a bad woman, Iris March. You are just bad grammar."

"Of course, *women*. But —"
"Then how should I say 'women' — ?"
"You should make a dash after them," suggested fun-loving Tom merrily.
"Am I," she cried suddenly, "real? I must know. Am I thus,

or else thus? Do I wear this hat for the style (*pour le style*)? Am I — style? *His style?*" She shuddered. "Am I vacuity, or Mencken,[1] or both?" Her eyes were spoonfuls of the Mediterranean. *"Do I exist?"*

The clock struck twelve. What of it?

"You are not a bad woman, Iris March," said Sherlock Holmes kindly. "You are just bad grammar."

Chrysanthemums bloom in September; and they say that the Americans will "tell the cock-eyed world." Phut! one never knows. People with prominent left ears — *qu'est-ce que c'est que ca!* (what is it that it is that that?[2]) — one prefers turnips.

"Boy died," she said, "for Purity. And there's Gerald. ..."

"My God! Not Gerald. ... "

" ... " she replied, and was gone. Phut!

"The Sign of the Four!" gasped Dick, as the Rollo Boys stared at each other in horror. "We are not a moment too soon!"

"To the rescue!" cried Sherlock Holmes; and, seizing their magnifying glasses, the Rollo Boys set out in hot pursuit.

CHAPTER NINE

As swiftly as possible (which is not any too gosh-darned swift) the Rollo Boys and Sherlock Holmes advanced down their intricate maze of twisted phrases, similes, and winding allusions, trying to find their way through the mystery of Mr. Arlen's style. Now and then their eyes watered as a loose adjective whipped their faces; and once Dick caught himself in the nick of time from stepping into a deep insinuation directly in his way. On both sides little bypaths lured them from their

---

[1] H.L. Mencken (1880-1956) was an acerbic journalist and cultural critic. At this time he edited *The American Mercury* magazine and wrote columns for *The Baltimore Sun* newspapers. *Vacuity* means empty space or empty-headedness.

[2] The phrase is an idiom that means simply "what is that?". Since an idiom is a group of words whose meaning cannot be deduced by translating the individual words (such as feeling "under the weather" or "missing the boat," Ford was having fun by literally translating it.

main course, but they continued resolutely ahead, reading neither to the right nor to the left. Once a deep chasm between two chapters loomed before them, and they only crossed the gap by grasping at a hidden meaning. Once a break in the narration yawned at their very feet. Once Dick yawned himself. ...

"Pray God we are not too late!" prayed God Sherlock Holmes as they followed down the trailing dots to the little group that stood clustered about the open window of Gerald's bedroom, on the third floor of Shepherd Market.[1]

"It's awful," said one. "You see ..."

"Exactly," said the lady of the Green Hat. "And he —"

"Quite," replied one; for Gerald was not. "Gerald died," explained the lady of the Green Hat, as Sherlock Holmes and the Rollo Boys arrived at a run and stared at the open window at the sidewalk below, "for Purity!"[2]

---

[1] Not a residence as implied in the story, but a square in the Mayfair area of central London. A popular location for writers and artists, Shepherd Market was Michael Arlen's home, and he set much of *The Green Hat* there.

[2] The characters in *The Green Hat* debate what purity is and what it meant to Boy Fenwick, who killed himself in Dauville, France, by leaping from a window. What it means is never explicitly said; one character says "That might mean anything, and so of course we all took it to mean the worst thing as regards Iris." While this may seem unusual to modern readers, this gives you an idea of the distance between what was publishable in our time versus the years following World War I.

For those who don't want to plow through *The Green Hat*, here's a section from Chapter Three in which the narrator discusses purity with his friend, Hilary. It is not only a succinct summary of the situation, but there is an unexpected shout-out at the end:

"It seemed to me that it was, to say the least, rather hasty of a young man to die 'for purity' in connection with a girl of twenty. Hilary, in two thousand years we have discovered only one caddish way of getting to Heaven, and Boy Fenwick, like many "idealists," has taken it.'

"'You probably don't realise,' said Hilary, oh so reasonably, 'the depths of sudden despair — in decent people.'

"'But I thought we were discussing human beings!' And, as regards human beings, one couldn't help thinking that a girl who had confessed that her lover had died 'for purity' was purer than the lover who had not been able to live for it. Boy Fenwick's death had an air of getting away with

Well! but one can count to ten. You Americans would say: "It is a wow!" She was saying: "... and in the heart of the dandelion a tiny little rose." There is one for you. For that matter, there is one for Burbank. "Who?" asked Holmes.

"Hilary ..." she replied wildly, "and Guy ... and Napier ... and old Sir Maurice ..."[1]

"The Sign of the Four!" gasped Dick, and the Rollo Boys stared at each other in horror.

"Cripes! all of them?" ejaculated Tom.

"Hark!" cried Sherlock Holmes; and all the Rollo Boys pricked their ears except Harry, who had had his ears pricked by an old gipsy woman when he was a baby.[2]

From afar came the mysterious punctuation: "... . ..."

"S O S!"[3] gasped Holmes, and the Rollo Boys set out in hot pursuit.

CHAPTER NINE[4]

There was a rhythm. There was syncopation. It had a beat,

---

rather a good thing. He had destroyed the girl by exalting himself — for purity! How did boys come to have the infernal conceit of setting themselves up as connoisseurs of purity? And he had taken care to leave his corpse in such a position as best to foul the fountains of his young widow's womanhood. Sir Arthur Conan Doyle ought to speak to him about it."

For those who don't want to read *The Green Hat*, your editor included, it is revealed that after Boy, madly in love with Iris, finally marries her, he discovers he has syphilis, a sexually transmitted disease for which (in 1925) there was no safe and effective treatment. It wasn't until 1947 that penicillin was proved to treat the disease.

[1] These are all characters from *The Green Hat*.
[2] In the 1920s, the popularity of ear piercing declined in favor of clip-on earrings. It seemed like only sailors and gypsies pierced their ears. For a long time, anyone who wanted their ears pierced had to go to their family doctor or hold "piercing parties" at home. It wasn't until the later part of the 20th century that commercial outlets appeared that offered piercings.
[3] Holmes is incorrect. In Morse code, the international distress signal is three dots, three dashes, and three dots. Contrary to popular belief, the letters do not mean "save our ship" or "save our souls." It's simply a code word that is easy to remember and to send.
[4] [Ford's footnote] No; it isn't an error.

like a policeman. Instant, unforgettable, unforgivable, it throbbed like a sore thumb. There were many green dresses: red, blue, pink. The women had white oval faces, small breasts, black eyes, thin arms, and husbands named George. Everyone's husband is named George; and there you are. Or there. I see you, behind the clock.

"Quick!" hissed Holmes. The King of Spain was eating salted almonds.

Silently the three Rollo Boys and the detective drew on the red and green checkered pants, the bright gold epaulets and cocked hat, the long blue beard and spectacles; and thus completely disguised as head waiters they wandered unnoticed toward that table ... (which table? How should I know; listen what he's saying. I know, but Mama — Ssssh!)

Hilary said: "Life is, life being what it is, life ..."

Sir Maurice started: "We are the damned victims —"

Guy and Napier said nothing. They were somewhere else. They were never in Buffalo either.

"— of a literary style," finished Guy; and Napier said thus and thus.

They walked arm in arm to the window. Everyone walks arm in arm to the window, or goes to the Boston Symphony and wears dress shields.[1] "Iris ..."

"The Sign of the Four!" croaked Dick, as the Rollo Boys stared at each other, slightly bored as a matter of fact.

"We die," announced the four, standing on the window sill, "... you first, Hilary? After you, Guy. No matter ... 'for Purity!'" They lit a cigarette. ...

"We are getting warmer!" gasped Holmes, mopping his brow as the Rollo Boys set out once more in hot pursuit.

CHAPTER NINE[2]

"Iris ..." rose to their lips. "That car's gone mad!" They

---

[1] Replaceable moisture-absorbing pads that were applied to clothing to wick away sweat. They act as an alternative to antiperspirants, and are very useful in an era where laundry had to be washed by hand.

[2] [Ford's footnote] Just go with the flow.

swept headlong around the corner. "Iris!" Holmes sobbed. "Stop her, Arlen! Stop her! Not that —"

She poised on the sill of the third-story window. "I die," she said, "for Purity —"

"Not at all," smiled Mr. Arlen. "There has been no murder."

"For purity of what?" shrieked Tom.

"For purity of grammar," she replied, as she held her nose and jumped. People yelled. ... The Rollo Boys were on the sidewalk and Holmes stooped and picked up the Green Hat. Beneath it on the sidewalk there was only a great, jagged, dripping stain ... only a mixed metaphor. ...

"Michael Arlen!" cried Dick, leaping into the swarm of eager parodists, humorists, and newspaper columnists who had already gathered about the nonchalant novelist in their midst. "Wanted for the murder of those Charming People!"

"Not at all," smiled Arlen suavely, as he elbowed his way through the rapidly increasing crowd of imitators and burlesquers, and set off in the direction of Southampton. "There has been no murder. All good Arlen characters when they die simply go to America!"[1]

---

[1] Ironically, Arlen himself will move to America during World War II. He had been living in France with his family since 1928, but moved back to Britain when war broke out in 1939, where he wrote newspaper columns and published a novel and joined the Civil Defense. Objections were raised to his appointment in the House of Commons because he was a Bulgarian

"Three rousing cheers for the Rollo Boys!" shouted the relieved citizens at Mayfair, tossing their green hats in the air and cheering lustily. The cheers were given with a will; and the contents of that will, and how it affected the fortunes, not only of our young heroes, but also of the author and his publishers, will all be related in the next volume of this series, to be entitled:

"And Here Let Us Say Good-by; or, Beer and Light Winesburg."¹

And here let us say Good-by.

Good-by.²

Time magazine cover featuring
Michael Arlen, 1927.

---

and his novels were vaguely objectionable. Arlen responded by resigning and moved to America, where he lived until his death in 1956.

¹ A reference to *Winesburg, Ohio*, a popular 1919 short-story collection by Sherwood Anderson (1876-1941). *Light Winesburg* is a reference to the Prohibition-era law that allowed retailers to obtain a license to sell beer and light wines (the latter less than 14% alcohol).

² Ford is aping the traditional way most Rover Boys adventures ended.

1926

This was another quiet year in Conan Doyle's life, spent mostly at home and notable for the variety of publications. It would prove to be the last great burst of literary energy before the end.

March saw the publication in book form of The Land of Mist, in which Professor Challenger embraced Spiritualism. Reviewers were not happy with the book's emphasis on convincing readers of spiritualism over story. This was followed in June by The History of Spiritualism, a two-volume work. By this time, the value of Conan Doyle's name had dropped among book publishers, and he had to partially finance its printing.

Meanwhile, on the other side of the Atlantic, a meeting of singular importance to the future of Sherlock Holmes took place in New York City. A journeyman writer for the Saturday Review of Literature met an English printer and discovered a mutual affection for the stories. Over drinks, they quizzed each other on their knowledge of the canon, an echo of the game the writer had played with his brothers and friends as a boy. His interest in Holmes revived, Christopher Morley (1890-1957) will go on to write the forward to the collected Holmes stories in 1930 and found the Baker Street Irregulars in 1933.

As the summer ended, Sherlock Holmes returned to the public for one last series of stories. While they would appear in The Strand, as usual, they would first appear each month in the U.S. magazine Liberty, starting with "The Adventure of the Three Gables" in September, followed by "The Adventure of the Blanched Soldier," "The Adventure of the Lion's Mane," and "The Adventure of the Retired Colourman."

On Halloween, the magician Harry Houdini died of complications from appendicitis. A week before, as part of a demonstration before some college students after a show, he had received several strong blows in his midsection. Despite the increasing pain, he refused to seek medical attention. Even when his fever spiked and a doctor advised he go to the hospital immediately, he refused until after the day's show. Conan Doyle wrote a gracious letter to Bess calling her husband "a fine and honest man" and expressed regret "that shadows grew up between us." He hoped that Houdini would contact him from beyond, and while the magician had given Bess a code he would use to send a message, none ever appeared.

In December, Conan Doyle took on another challenge to his detecting skills. A young mystery writer, Agatha Christie (1890-1976), had left her home one night and vanished. A police search of the local area, including its ponds, came up empty. Newspapers nationwide picked up the story, and speculation centered around her husband, Archie, who had left the home that evening to spend the weekend with friends. Crime novelist Edgar Wallace told the papers he suspected that Christie had left home to spite someone who had hurt her.

After a week, the chief constable for Surrey approached the man who, years before, had been made an honorary deputy-lieutenant of the county. But instead of investigating the case, Conan Doyle turned to what he called "psychic science." Obtaining a pair of Christie's gloves from her husband, he turned them over to Horace Leaf, a psychic who specialized in psychometry, the ability to gain impressions from objects. Conan Doyle reported that Leaf had deducted that Agatha was involved, that she was alive and would be found within a few days, and that water was somehow involved.

Eleven days after her disappearance, Agatha Christie was found at a hydro spa in Harrogate, Yorkshire. Conan Doyle was pleased and suggested that the British police should turn to psychometrics for help. As for Christie, she said nothing about her disappearance, or Conan Doyle's "help," for the rest of her life. We know more about her opinion of Holmes. In her second mystery novel, Murder on the Links (1923), Hercule Poirot bests his French rival who emulates Holmes' methods. Three decades later, Hercule Poirot declares in Mrs. McGinty's Dead (1952), "I have my methods, Watson. If you'll excuse me calling you Watson. No offense intended. Interesting, by the way, how the technique of the idiot friend has hung on. Personally, I myself think the Sherlock Holmes stories grossly overrated."

Publications: Holmes in Liberty: "The Adventure of the Three Gables" (Sept.); "The Adventure of the Blanched Soldier" (Oct.); "The Adventure of the Lion's Mane" (Nov.); "The Adventure of the Retired Colourman" (Dec.); **Other:** The Land of Mist (March); History of Spiritualism (June; 2 vol., with Leslie Curnow)

A Disciple of Sherlock Holmes

Maurice Morelo

Illustrated by Henri Monier

Translated by Bill Peschel

While Holmes doesn't appear in this story, reading his stories inspired Maurice Morelo's hero to follow in his footsteps. Little is known about Morelo except that he was a journalist who wrote for Le Petit Parisien *("The Little Parisian") where this story appeared in the March 16 edition.* Parisien *was a popular French newspaper since its founding in 1876. But during World War II, it advocated collaborating with the occupying Germans, a position which forced its closure in 1944. Henri Monier (1901-1959) was a cartoonist and book and magazine illustrator.*

A brooding man in worn clothing was Narcisse Barsanufe. He did not attract the attention of passers-by on the streets of Paris, and no one suspected that this petty bourgeois[1] with a pathetic appearance aspired to become a famous detective.[2]

For the time being, he collected tickets in a tiny cinema, a job that he considered very inferior to his capacities, and here is why.

Watching crime movies, in addition to breathlessly reading the novels of Conan Doyle and Gaston Leroux,[3] fired Barsanufe's

---

[1] A term drawn from Marxist philosophy to classify a group of semi-autonomous peasants and shopkeepers. Marxism theorizes that this group represents a threat to the working class because it identifies with the elite bourgeois and emulates their values. In French literary society, a petty bourgeois was a figure of fun and contempt, obsessed with money and status and hypocritical about morality.

[2] Not surprising if you consider that his first name was drawn from the narcissus flower. In Greek mythology, Narcissus fell in love with his reflection in a pool of water, inspiring Sigmund Freud (1856-1939) to use his name to define narcissistic personality disorder, characterized by an abnormal need for admiration and feelings of self-importance.

[3] The French writer (1868-1927) is best known for the novel *The Phantom of the Opera* (1910). Leroux also wrote seven novels about reporter and

brains with theories on the observations and deductions that, in the course of judicial investigations, the bloodhounds should put into practice if they are to achieve success.

So our man, thoroughly possessed of these techniques, believed himself capable of surpassing all the Sherlock Holmes and all the Rouletabilles of the earth.

Unfortunately, he had few opportunities to test his skills, so he resolved to tempt fate.

One evening, he walked into his wardrobe, took a wallet containing his modest savings, and hid it in a place where no one would discover it.

Then he went to bed and his sleep became populated with fabulous dreams.

When he awoke the next day, he ran to his closet, saw the disappearance of his wallet, and exclaimed in despair and conviction: "I am robbed!"

He immediately ran to the local commissary to tell him of his misfortune, and boasted with a knowing air that he was making a great effort to discover the author of the misdeed.

Returning to his apartment, Barsanufe lay flat on his stomach, according to the rules of his art, to meticulously measure the footprints left on the floor of his apartment. From the examination of these footprints, he concluded that the thief was wearing a size 41, that the heel of his left shoe, a little worn, denoted a precarious situation of his owner, and that it measured 1.64 m (Size 41 X 0.04 (?) = 1.64 m).[1]

Closely examining the ground with a magnifying glass, he discovered a reddish hair of a clear tint. This hair told him that it belonged to an almost bald individual of the race called redhead. A butt jammed into the corner of the chimney made

---

amateur detective Joseph Rouletabille, of which his most famous was *The Mystery of the Yellow Room* (1908), the first locked-room mystery and still worth reading today.

[1] Morelo is simply poking fun at how a detective could arrive at absurd conclusions from precise measurements, as you'll see in the next paragraph.

it clear that the burglar was a smoker who was over forty years of age (size 1.64 m + size 41 = 42.64, i.e., 42 years, 2 months and 4 days). Moreover, he was a very skilful climber, as there was no sign that the locks were picked on the apartment and the cupboard.

Barsanufe easily deduced from these observations that the individual was none other than himself, and this observation filled him with joy, for he had just made a rigorous demonstration of the indisputable value of the methods used by him to discover the thief.

It was now time to find the wallet.

By following the footprints from their point of departure, that is to say, from the threshold of the apartment, one could determine exactly the path traveled by the burglar. The latter, without any hesitation whatsoever, which proved he had perfect knowledge of the apartment, had crossed the antechamber, then the dining-room, and went directly to the mirrored cupboard in the bedroom.

From this place, the footsteps moved away in the direction of a black cabinet with no exit that served as a storeroom.

Inside, a chair brought into this small room proved that the person had to use it to reach a board below a coat rack. Barsanufe climbed the chair and put his hand on the wallet placed there by the malefactor who, doubtless disturbed in his operations, had paused in his work intending to come back and finish the job at the first opportunity.

The wallet being found, Barsanufe did not pursue his investigations further, but, happy with the complete success of his experiment, he hastened to the commissary of police to inform him of the result.

"Monsieur," said Barsanufe, with an air of great importance, "I discovered my thief."

"Ah! Ah! Very well, I congratulate you on your insight. And who is it?"

"It is myself," he affirmed, not without pride.

"Perfect, perfect! Then I have only one duty to fulfill: In the name of the law, I arrest you!"

Le Petit Parisien's front page for March 16, 1925.

A Strange Suicide

Pierre Henri Cami

Because humorist Pierre Henri Cami (1884-1958) published "The Adventures of Loufock-Holmes" in 1926, we accepted that as the place to print this story. It wasn't until we began researching it that we discovered that some of these stories were published earlier. "A Strange Suicide," for example, was found in the July 1921 issue of Inter-America *magazine. This was usual, because the magazine published translated articles from Mexico, Central America, the Caribbean, and South America, presumably for its largely North American readership. The reason why was explained in a note from the editor: "This supposed incident was sent us by an Argentine friend. It was taken from an Argentine newspaper or magazine, but the sender neglected to indicate the source. We therefore translate and publish it, without being able to give due credit." Which just goes to show, that wherever Sherlock Holmes travels in the world, his doppelgangers follow close behind.*

SCENE I

A DEAD MAN THAT SPEAKS

The scene is laid in the consulting room of LOUFOCK-HOLMES.

THE UNKNOWN VISITOR (*entering*). Señor: I have come to submit to your brilliant deductive talent my mysterious and inexplicable situation. For the last ten years I have practised the profession of an executioner of sardines.

LOUFOCK-HOLMES. An executioner of sardines?

THE UNKNOWN VISITOR. Yes; as executioner in a canning factory. I was appointed to decapitate sardines before putting them in the tins. From seeing heads fall I became neurasthenic.[1] I resolved to commit suicide. Before continuing my story, permit me to ask a question: Am I visible to the naked eye?

---

[1] A medical condition first used in the 1830s that is characterized by headaches, insomnia, and exhaustion. Considered to be caused by depression or emotional stress. Because Americans were considered particularly prone to it, the condition was nicknamed "Americanitis."

LOUFOCK-HOLMES. Perfectly visible. As for the rest, it is very natural.

THE UNKNOWN VISITOR. You will not say that it is natural when you know that I have been dead for about two hours.

LOUFOCK-HOLMES. What did you say?

THE UNKNOWN VISITOR. I say that this morning I carried out my plan of committing suicide. With the aid of a strong rope I hanged myself from the ceiling of my dining-room at number 6, Calle de Tombe-Issoire.[1]

LOUFOCK-HOLMES. Since you are here, that is impossible.

THE UNKNOWN VISITOR. Nevertheless, it is true. At this very moment I am hanging in my house, and, at the same time, I am present here.

LOUFOCK-HOLMES. All this is very strange. I am going to hasten to your domicile to ascertain for myself whether it be true that you are hanging from the ceiling of your dining-room. I should say at once that you have been the victim of a hallucination. You will wait here in the company of my faithful pupil.

SCENE II

THE ABSENT-MINDED SUICIDE

The same surroundings.

LOUFOCK-HOLMES (*returning*). You were right, señor. Your body is, indeed, hanging from the ceiling of your dining-room.

THE UNKNOWN VISITOR (*horrified*). Then . . . who am I? Who am I?

LOUFOCK-HOLMES. Calm yourself. On the way I made my deductions. Without a doubt, you are the spirit of the body hanging in your house. You rematerialized immediately after

---

[1] An old road in the 14th arrondissement of Paris that leads to the ancient part of the city. A section of the vast ancient catacombs used as a municipal ossuary in the late 18th century runs under the street.

your suicide, and you have assumed the appearance and dress of the body that you have just abandoned. However, my attention was attracted by one detail.

The Unknown Visitor (*with eagerness*). What detail?

Loufock-Holmes. You are wearing black boots, and the body hanging in your house has on yellow boots.

The Unknown Visitor. Yellow! You said yellow?

Loufock-Holmes. Yes; yellow. I have come to the conclusion—

The Unknown Visitor. Go to the devil with your conclusions! Now I understand it all! I am an assassin!

Loufock-Holmes. An assassin?

The Unknown Visitor. Yes. I lived with my twin brother. Apart from our boots, we resembled each other in a startling manner. Then the question is simple enough: instead of putting the rope around my own neck, I made a mistake and—

Loufock-Holmes. You passed it around the neck of your señor brother.

The Unknown Visitor. Yes. I mistook my twin brother for myself. Thinking to hang myself, I hung him. How absent-minded I am!

Pierre Henri Cami self-portrait.

LORD CAMEMBERT SMUDGED?

Holmes Deduces Spirit Pictures

EVERYTHING IS DISPROVED!

"Doctor Watson" (Earle Ennis)

Illustrated by Jimmy Hatlo

While the controversy over the Cottingley Fairies inspired several parodies poking fun at Conan Doyle's incredulity, it was not the only case to do so.

During his lectures, Conan Doyle typically displayed a series of photos showing mediums manifesting spirits caught by the camera. One of them was sent to him by Lord Combermere. It had been taken in 1891 in the library of Combermere Abbey, the family home in Cheshire. The timed exposure was long, and the photographer left in the middle of it. When the photo was developed, a faint human shape could be seen sitting in one of the chairs. On the back of the photo, someone wrote "The Ghost of Combermere Abbey." This photograph was taken of the Library by Miss Corbet, on Dec. —, 1891, on the afternoon of the funeral of Wellington Henry, 2nd Viscount Combermere. The figure in the chair on the left of the photograph (legless) is supposed to be a likeness of him."

The photo was one of many in his lecture, and Conan Doyle merely drew the audience's attention to it and moved on. But displaying the photo angered Lord Combermere's nephew, A.A. Campbell-Swinton (1863-1930), the Scottish electrical engineer best known today for figuring out the theory behind television decades before its invention. He did not take kindly to airing the family ghost in public, and a barrage of letters and articles debating the matter appeared over the next six months.

Not to be outdone, reporter Earl Ennis decided to have a go at identifying the ghost, with the help of a horrible pun, in this story from the April 30 edition of the San Francisco Call. *Before entering journalism, Ennis (1885-1951) was involved in the burgeoning radio field. As the owner of Western Wireless Equipment Co., he became the first to broadcast from an airplane in either 1910 or 1911. At the same time, he also broadcast the heavyweight prizefight between Jim Jeffries and Jack Johnson. After failing to invent an "aeon relay" to transmit conversation over long distances, he moved to newspapers, spending 40 years at California newspapers.*

Illustrator Jimmy Hatlo (1897-1963) created the long-running single-panel strip They'll Do It Every Time, *which was written by readers' contributions. He was also known for creating* Little Iodine, *a female forerunner to* Dennis the Menace.

> LONDON, April 30.—A. A. Campbell-Swinton, a consulting engineer and scientist, who is a nephew of Lord Combermere, says he has inspected the photograph exhibited by Sir Arthur Conan Doyle, England's most prominent spiritualist, and which purports to be a spirit picture of the late Lord Combermere and charges it to be a fraud.
>
> "What is supposed to be a spirit," said Campbell-Swinton, "looks more like a smudge. To say it bears any likeness to Lord Combermere is ridiculous."

As usual I found Sherlock Holmes sitting cross-legged on the floor of his Baker Street lodgings entirely surrounded by ciphers, cryptograms, navy shag and cross-word puzzles.[1] He

---

[1] *Navy shag:* A type of tobacco that Watson preferred. Also called Player's Navy Cut, it was a mild Burley leaf from Virginia. The name was inspired by the sailors who would cure the leaf with a combination of rum, molasses and spices. *Cross-word puzzles:* While examples of crossword-like puzzles have been found as early as 1873, it wasn't until 1913, in the *New York World* that the first modern puzzle appeared. Their regular publication in newspapers over the next few years sparked a fad for them. In 1924, the first book of puzzles was published. It sparked a national fad that grew until the New York Public Library complained puzzle fans were monopolizing dictionaries and encyclopedias "so as to drive away readers and stu-

was smoking violently and playing Rubenheimer's *Melody in Q* with one finger on a ukulele. His greeting was characteristic.

"Ha! Watson," he exclaimed. "You have been playing polo, your grandmother was a Beauchamp, and the price of eggs has gone up. What do you know about smudges?"

I was amazed, even though I was used to his remarkable powers.

"Nothing," I confessed, knowing that was what he wanted me to say so he could explain himself.

All Smudged Up, as It Were

"Ah!" he said, rubbing his hands. "I thought so."

He jumped to his feet and took a photographic plate from a drawer and handed it to me.

"What do you see on it?" he demanded.

"A smudge," I said promptly.

"What kind of a smudge?" asked Holmes, his eyes gleaming.

"It looks like a giraffe or a necklace," I said, "or a big cheese."

Holmes closed the door and locked it. Then he pulled down the shades. As I watched, he got down on all fours and crawled over to me and whispered in my ear.

"Watson," he said. "That is the picture of a soul!"

I was dumbfounded.

"Whose?" I asked.

Mar-r-rvelous! But Whose Soul Is It?

"That," said Holmes mysteriously, "is what I have been hired to find out."

"But you have a theory," I said. "Whose soul is it that looks like a big cheese?"

He nodded violently and filled three of his pipes simultaneously.

---

dents who need these books in their daily work."

"Lord Camembert,"[1] he said softly and twiddled his fingers.

It was inconceivable. I said so.

"Look again," said Holmes.

I did. This time the smudge resembled a growing tree or a dried abalone in winter.[2]

"It has changed," I said. "It seems longer."

Holmes chuckled with diabolical glee.

Quick—The Needle! It's Peggy Joyce

"Quite a likeness, eh?" he laughed. "Wonderful," I said. "But who is it?"

"Peggy Joyce," he replied. "The woman of mystery."[3]

---

[1] Camembert, of course, is a creamy cheese made from cow's milk that originated in Camembert in northern France.

[2] One of 56 species of a shelled marine snail. In many species, the interior of its shell is highly iridescent and valuable for decorative objects. Dried, it is considered a delicacy, used in soups or braised and eaten like steak.

[3] Peggy Hopkins Joyce (1893-1957) was an actress, model, and dancer known for her lavish lifestyle that included many affairs, numerous engagements, six marriages to wealthy men, and many newsworthy scandals. Born Marguerite Upton in Virginia, she appeared on the vaudeville stage by age 15, and within three years had left the stage and married a millionaire. The marriage was annulled when he learned she was 17. With the settlement money, she attended school in Washington, where she married her second husband in 1913. She performed in the Ziegfeld Follies, divorced husband #2 and immediately married husband #3. She divorced him the next year in a highly publicized trial, but kept his name and $600,000, her jewelry, and a lifetime annuity. Between 1920 and 1925, she was in the press for blowing a million dollars in a week on a shopping spree, had numerous affairs, and reappeared on stage in Earl Carroll's Vanities. She also married for a fourth time in 1924, declaring "this is the first time I have ever been truly in love." She would divorce him in 1926. For nearly 20 years she stayed single until 1945 when she married consulting engineer Anthony Easton. Her final marriage, which lasted until her death, was to retired bank teller Andrew Meyer (1953), although there is some doubt about whether she divorced #5 first. While Holmes proclaimed her "the woman of mystery," the bigger mystery is why all these wealthy men married her.

"But she is not dead," I protested. "How can you have a picture of her soul?"

Holmes laughed so loudly the ormolu clock[1] fell off on its face and positively refused to tick.

"That's what the Duncan Sisters[2] wanted to know, but I wouldn't tell 'em."

"Marvelous," I exclaimed. "How were these spirit photographs taken?"

Holmes showed me. He took a piece of paper. In the exact center he made a pinhole. Then he handed me the paper.

"Look through the hole and tell me what you see," he commanded.

I did so. "Nothing!" I said, after a moment.

"Ah," said Holmes. "That it is. That is exactly it. Wonderful, isn't it?"

I admitted that it was.

Yea, Truly, the Boy Is Clever

Borrowing my cocaine needle he cleaned his pipestem

---

[1] A bronze mantle clock gilded with finely ground gold. The process used highly heated mercury that emitted fumes that poisoned the craftsman. Many of them did not live beyond 40.

[2] A musical comedy team consisting of Rosetta (1894-1959) and Vivian Duncan (1897-1986). In 1923, their performance in *Topsy and Eva*, a musical comedy based on *Uncle Tom's Cabin*, made them stars.

thoughtfully.

"You know, Watson," he said, "some folks do not believe in smudges. For myself—I agree with Bud Corrigan.[1] You can't tell a soul by the company it keeps. The little affair of the czar's taxicab taught me that. This is simple. I have here the soul of Peggy Joyce on a plate. Therefore ..."

"She is soulless?" I suggested.

"Capital, Watson, capital," said Holmes, slapping me on the back.

"But Lord Camembert — is he also . . . ?"

Holmes shook his head and threw the canary out of the window to note the time it took for it to hit the ground in comparison with the strokes of Big Ben's clapper.

"No," he said, and to this day I believe he meant it.

Before my eyes he smashed the plate. He must have seen my surprise.

"I have saved two souls," he said.

Nor would he ever tell me what it was all about. But always afterward when he saw a smudge his spirits rose.

Detail from the Combermere Ghost photo.

---

[1] Unfortunately, a search of digitized newspapers (not just California, but across the country) and books from the period resulted in no identification of Bud Corrigan.

The Adventure of the Missing Hatrack

Frederic Dorr Steele

Illustrated by Frederic Dorr Steele

On the courthouse steps in Boston, American Mercury editor H.L. Mencken (1880-1956) sold a copy of his magazine and was arrested. Inside the magazine was a story called "Hatrack." It was about a part-time prostitute who services the church-going men in her small town. The story contained no curse words or unsavory descriptions, and there was nothing glamorous or salacious about Hatrack, who was given that nickname for her Olive Oyle-like physique. But because "Hatrack" offended the New England Watch and Ward Society, the magazine was banned in Boston, and later by the post office.

That's just one backstory behind "The Adventure of the Missing Hatrack," by Sherlockian illustrator Frederic Dorr Steele. The other story involves the Players Club, a social group founded in New York City in 1888 by Edwin Booth, the popular actor and brother of actor and Lincoln assassin John Wilkes Booth. Steele was a longtime member of the club, known for his skill with a pool cue and given the nickname "The Little Giant." He was also the editor of the Players Bulletin magazine, in which this story appeared in its Oct. 15 issue.

"The Adventure of the Missing Hatrack" is a curious mix of inside jokes about its members, combined with a fun poke at the censorship battle that became another skirmish for free speech in the U.S.

Steele (1873-1944) was an artist and freelance illustrator who worked for many of the top magazines. But to Sherlockians, he's best known as the American Sidney Paget. Basing his Sherlock on stage actor William Gillette — who made a career out of portraying Holmes on stage — Steele illustrated the stories that later appeared in the U.S. editions of The Return of Sherlock Holmes and The Casebook of Sherlock Holmes.

It was on an evening in October 1926, that Mr. Sherlock Holmes made one of his rare visits to The Players.

Many years had passed since the great man had come to

Gramercy Park,[1] and the faithful John McDonald at the door did not at once recognize the tall, spare figure looming before him in the fading light.

"What name, sir?" he asked.

For answer Holmes silently handed him the familiar fore-and-aft cap.[2]

"Can it be — Mr. Holmes?" gasped McDonald in an awe-stricken whisper. Overcome by his agitation, he sank on a bench. The hall boys, coming to his assistance, saw that his hair was quite white.

Ten minutes later Sherlock Holmes was seated at his favorite table in the southwest corner of the grill-room.

"All is as usual, Watson," he said genially. "It is indeed good to be back again in these dear surroundings, which your touch has made more beautiful than ever."

"You do me too much honor, Holmes," I replied. "As Chairman of the House Committee I try to—"

Holmes interrupted. "I observe you have added the wielding of the cue to your other accomplishments."

"Holmes, you are astounding!" I said. "I rarely play pool, but it is true that I did play just a frame or two today. But how could you know?"

"Elementary, my dear Watson, elementary. A faint but distinct odor of Lillian Russell talcum powder aroused my suspicions, and they needed no further confirmation than the little blue chalk-mark near your left shoulder."[3]

---

[1] A private park in the Gramercy neighborhood of New York City, established in 1844. Access to it is limited to the neighboring residents who pay an annual fee to get a key to the gate.

[2] Conan Doyle never described Holmes wearing the iconic deerstalker cap. It was up to illustrator Sidney Paget to depict Holmes sporting it (along with the Inverness cape) in "The Boscombe Valley Mystery" (1891). The look was adopted by William Gillette for the *Sherlock Holmes* play, which in turn was imitated by Steele in his illustrations. As its name implies, the cap was worn by hunters, and the long brim at each end was designed to shed water.

[3] Russell (1860/1861-1922) was one of the most famous actresses and sing-

"My dear Holmes, it is marvellous."

"Attention to detail, Watson, is—"

Suddenly the insistent peal of a bell was heard from an upper floor. Holmes' austere face broke into one of its rare smiles. "I am glad to hear that my friend Marcosson has returned."

"You are right again," said I in astonishment. "He is even now entertaining the Pope and Premier Mussolini in the private dining room."[1]

"How restful this old room is!" Holmes resumed. "And is it not a pity that crime and madness can lurk in so peaceful a spot! I had hoped, my dear fellow, to spend a few completely idle hours here, listening to the innocent prattle of my actor friends, but it was not to be. Certain important persons have asked me to look into some strange events here. Books have mysteriously disappeared from the library and reappeared in unexpected places. A story called 'Hatrack' has been brutally cut out of a magazine. No man's private copy of *La Vie* is safe.[2]

---

ers of her time, celebrated for her buxom beauty and talent, for being married four times, and for being the mistress of wealthy businessman Diamond Jim Brady (1856-1917). She was also not shy about making money off her name by endorsing products such as Coca-Cola and a line of beauty products marketed as "Lillian Russell's Own Toilet Preparations." She and her manager could be careless at times, such as when her signature appeared below the statement: "I have taken three bottles of Lydia Pinkham's Compound and feel like a new man." She was among the first celebrities to endorse a politician, endorsing Theodore Roosevelt in 1912 alongside *Sherlock Holmes* actor William Gillette.

[1] Isaac Marcosson (1877-1961) was a magazine editor and author. He was also noted for his interviews with famous men and women, which makes it appropriate that he would sit down with Pope Pius XI (1857-1939), in his third year of his papacy, and Benito Mussolini (1883-1945), in his fourth year as Italy's prime minister.

[2] La Vie Parisienne ("Parisian Life") was a sophisticated risqué literary humor magazine. While the contents were relatively mild, it published illustrations of scantily clad women in tasteful poses, which was enough for General John J. Pershing to warn U.S. soldiers from buying the magazine. This didn't stop them from taking home copies of the magazine after the war. After the war, postal authorities banned the magazine at least once from being sent through the mail.

A man named Banning has appealed to me for protection; the poor fellow is beside himself."¹

He paused and lighted his briar.

"And that is not all. A person called Girardot has been seen talking in low tones with a waiter and pointing to a plate of food.² The word 'poison' was overheard. There are sinister forces at work, Watson. I am told that Frank Warrin, the solicitor, has lost a pound and a half through worry.³ My friend Allen McCurdy has begged me to look into the case. Indeed I expect him to meet me here."⁴

At this moment that individual appeared and joined us at table. The great man greeted the newcomer kindly, and McCurdy, his brow knotted with anxiety, plunged at once into the recital of his suspicions.

"The Hatrack is not the only thing, Mr. Holmes!" he said vehemently. "Can you explain to me why George Middleton persists in playing Kelly?⁵ You can't tell me the money power

---

¹ Kendall Banning (1879-1944) was a poet and magazine editor who had his share of run-ins with the censors. As editor of "Snappy Stories," a pulp magazine aimed at a male readership, he fought the Boston Watch and Ward Society — the same group that banned "Hatrack," for a story he published. As part of his campaign, he privately published in 1926 a collection of innocuous nursery rhymes with censorious black boxes placed over words at random.

² Etienne Girardot (1856-1939) was a stage and film actor. He played Lord Fancourt Babberley in the first U.S. production of *Charley's Aunt* in 1893. The suggestion of murder predates by a few years Girardot's role as the coroner in the Philo Vance movies starring William Powell.

³ Frank Lord Warrin (b. 1883) was a New York City lawyer who in 1918 acted as a technical advisor to the Americans during the peace negotiations at the end of World War I.

⁴ A club member renowned for his ability to make a masse shot, a trick shot that makes the cue ball spin around a ball. He was also a disputatious member who, according to a book about the club: "could always be relied upon to take the opposite side to your own in any proposition." There's no doubt that it's him in Steele's illustration, knocking the table in front of Sherlock and shouting "Tell me that, Mr. Holmes!

⁵ A playwright, director, and producer, Middleton (1880-1967) was instrumental in forming the Dramatists Guild to renegotiate an agreement in

isn't behind him! This trivial game is only a cloak to conceal some damnable plot. Doesn't his mind keep wandering from the game? And how about those trips away for a rest? How do we know what is going on in Bermuda? And why does Paul McAllister wear those whiskers?[1] Tell me that! Why does A. E. Thomas try to pass himself off as Augustus Thomas?[2] And Owen Meech![3] Does anybody believe that is a real name? Why does Oliver Herford have no telephone address?[4] Why, I say,

---

which the theatre managers received 50 percent of the stock and picture rights for any plays they produced. In January 1926, 131 dramatists agreed to form a closed shop and draft an agreement to present to the producers. Middleton was known at the club as "Desperate" George after an incident at the pool table. During a game, seeing his ball trapped and with a big pot at stake, he closed his eyes and left it to chance. His blind shot won the match. When he was asked how he figured out the right shot, he admitted: "I took a desperate chance." *Kelly:* Kelly pool was a popular game in the first half of the 20th century, and it was played often at the Players. Also called "pea pool," it is played with the standard set of 16 pool balls and 15 smaller numbered markers called peas or pills. The peas are placed in a opaque bottle and each player secretly draws one pea. The number on it is the numbered ball they must sink to win the match.

[1] An American film actor (1875-1955) who appeared in 37 movies between 1913 and 1940, including *Beau Geste* (1926), *She's a Sheik* (1927), and *Noah's Ark* (1929). As the story implies, he had an impressive beard.

[2] Augustus E. Thomas (1857-1934) was a playwright best known for being among the first playwrights to base his plays on American history. He also directed five movies, including *The Jungle* (1914), based on Upton Sinclair's notorious 1906 novel.

[3] A stage actor known for his character roles in Shakespearian plays. In real life he had an abstracted air which led to one memorable incident in the pool room. Absorbed in looking up a number in the telephone book and sensing the presence of a strong light over the table, he proceeded to lay the book down on the table's green felt in mid-game. The players were too astonished to object. They were also curious: Would his conscious mind surface and realize where he was? The answer: No. He found the number, picked up the book, and left the room.

[4] English artist and writer (1860-1935) whose family emigrated to the U.S. in 1876. His work appeared in magazines such as *Life, Harper's Weekly, The Masses,* and *Punch.* He was also noted as a wit. When the Episcopal priest Bishop Henry Potter (1834-1908) lamented that his nephew had married an actress, Herford reassured him saying "I wouldn't bother about

"TELL ME THAT, MR. HOLMES!"

does John Phillips wear rubbers?[1] What does Russ Whytal conceal in that umbrella that he carries on pleasant days?[2] If you keep your eyes open you will see three men who call themselves Drew, Denny and Schmidt huddled together.[3] What, I ask you, is the subject of those conferences? Why did Cy Nast spend all that time digging in walls and monkeying with the electric wires?[4] I tell you there are things going on

---

it, Bishop. You know actresses happen in the best-regulated families."

[1] Magazine publisher (1861-1949) who co-founded the muckraking *McClure's* magazine that published Ida Tarbell's expose of the Standard Oil trust and Conan Doyle's short stories and articles. "Rubbers," it should be noted, refers to a type of latex overshoe that is worn over the dress shoe and not what you're thinking.

[2] Actor and playwright (1860-1930)

[3] John *Drew* (1853-1927) was considered the leading matinee idol of his time. He is also the uncle of John, Ethel, and Lionel Barrymore, which makes him Drew Barrymore's great-great uncle. He was also the third president of the club. George K. *Denny* was an actor and one of the club's directors. Arthur P. *Schmidt* (1846-1921) was a music publisher.

[4] Cyril Nast (1879-1966) was advertising manager of New York Edison Co. He was the son of cartoonist Thomas Nast (1840-1902).

that we don't know anything about!'

During this tirade Sherlock Holmes sat quietly, his deep-set eyes bent on the Gramercy stew as though to penetrate its inmost secrets.[1] "These singular incidents of which you have told me," he said at length, "whose meaning is so baffling to the simple mind of the actor, artist or literary man, are plain enough when—"

At this moment a tall, raw-boned stranger stalked into the room leading a small ferret-like animal.

"Mr. Brian Hooker, I believe,"[2] said Holmes, extending his hand in greeting. "It is good of you to respond to my summons, and I note that you have brought the animal with you."

"Anything to oblige!" drawled the stranger, with the rich twang of the Connecticut Yankee. "Yes, sirree. I guess no keener or stauncher cheese-hound can be found in all New York."

"I thank you, Mr. Hooker," said Holmes affably. "My purpose will be disclosed without great delay. Clearly, gentlemen, the time has come for action. John, bring me the latest copy of *La Vie Parisienne*."

With the magazine clutched in his talon-like hand, Holmes led the way down to the billiard room, which was now deserted save for two weird figures. One of these sat in semi-darkness on a high chair and when addressed as "Dick"

---

[1] A dish from the Gramercy Tavern and Beer Hall that operated at 129 East 18th St. for more than 150 years. It is now occupied by Pete's Tavern. It is not the same as the Gramercy Tavern that opened on East 20th Street in 1995.

[2] Poet, lyricist and librettist (1880-1946). His 1923 translation of Edmond Rostand's *Cyrano de Bergerac* was used by José Ferrer (1912-1992), who won a Tony award in his 1946 Broadway version of the play, and an Oscar in the 1950 film adaptation. His affection for the free-lunch counter at the club was well-known and led to his nickname Cheese Hound. One afternoon, a member walked in with a letter demanding to know where Hooker was. A fellow member said, "I will arrange it," lifted the cover of the cheese plate, and placed the letter there. No sooner had he replaced the lid when Hooker came down the steps, marched to the bar, and lifted the lid on the cheese plate.

"No stauncher cheese-hound can be found in all New York."

moaned slightly.[1] The other stood in a corner near the water

---

[1] Elevated chairs, akin to tall bar stools with arms, are a common feature of pool rooms. They allow for spectators to sit high enough to watch the action on the table. Of the 14 members named Richard in 1926, the strongest candidate by far is newspaper editor Richard Lloyd Jones (1873-1963). When he was editor of the *Tulsa Tribune,* he hired his cousin Frank Lloyd Wright in 1929 to design his new home, which contains a billiard room. His admiration for Lincoln would later lead him to help preserve the Lincoln farm in Hodgenville, Ky., as a national historic site.

Also telling is that the longtime member was referred to as "Dick" in a long anecdote — the only one involving a Richard — in the club's 50th anniversary book. When Jones was 14, he stayed with a friend in Chicago. Edwin Booth was performing in a play, and since he was a friend of the family,

pitcher and silently regarded the party.

Holmes proceeded to a small table on which lay a plate of partially consumed cheese. Lifting the cover, he picked up a fragment of the substance and rubbed it vigorously on the fresh and lovely magazine.

"Really, Holmes," I protested, "as Chairman of the House Committee[1] I fail to understand —"

"You always fail to understand, my good Watson," said Holmes with a touch of asperity, as he placed the magazine on the table beside the plate. "We will now return to the grill-room and await developments.[2] And, Reggie," he added, addressing the silent figure, "keep your eyes open!"[3]

Richard attended the performance. That day, he woke up early. A statue of Abraham Lincoln by sculptor Augustus Saint-Gaudens (1848-1907) had been installed recently in Lincoln Park, in a ceremony attended by 10,000 people, including the president's grandson, Abraham Lincoln II (1873-1890), who later died from a blood infection caused by a cut on his arm.

According to the book:

"It was a beautiful bright morning and the Park was deserted. Dick looked at the statue for a time. As he turned back along the path he had come by, he heard the click of horses' hoofs on the entering road. A carriage rolled up and halted. A man alighted and walked toward the tall bronze figure. He stopped midway and gazed at it for some time. Then with bared head went nearer and looked up into the face of Lincoln long and intently; bowed his head awhile, Dick said, as if in prayer; finally took a flower from his coat and laid it on the pedestal at Lincoln's feet.

"As he walked back to the carriage he turned around once, with hat in hand and arms half extended — a sort of gesture of appeal. Then slipped into the carriage and drove away, leaving the place deserted save for the hidden boy in the shrubbery who was thrilled by what he had seen. For he knew the man was Edwin Booth."

[1] The group charged with overseeing the club's operations.
[2] A room in the basement containing tables where food can be served, as well as a pool table where Mark Twain played with the club's co-founders.
[3] Probably Reginald Bathurst Birch (1856-1943), whose illustrations of Little Lord Fauntleroy in the 1886 novel by Frances Hodgson Burnett started a fashion craze that condemned boys to wearing ringlets, black velvet suits adorned with lace collars, and matching knee pants. *The Players' Book* celebrating the club's first 50 years recalls him "at 82 or 83, still erect and slender, still the perfect pattern of the boulevardier, with immaculate

For perhaps three hours we sat waiting in tense silence. There was no sound in the dimly lighted grill-room. Hourly, August, the sturdy watchman, passed silently through the house, carrying his heavy black weapon. Holmes, his nerves as always under iron control, gave no sign of emotion save that from time to time he rose and hurled a plate through the window on to the piazza.[1] I made no comment on this, for by custom considerable latitude is allowed to our honorary members.

At last there was the faint sound of a footstep on the floor below, followed by an ugly tearing or ripping. Like a tiger Holmes sprang from his chair and was the first to reach the downstairs room. Prostrate beneath the table lay the unfortunate magazine. It had been brutally attacked and its mangled innards streamed out on the floor.

"You know my methods, Watson," said Holmes, briskly. "The miscreant has evidently risen to the bait, but I fear he has taken alarm and fled. Quick, Hooker, the cheese-hound!"

The trembling animal sniffed at the cheesy remains and strained at its leash, barking furiously. Holmes' voice rang out sharply. "Now we shall see what man or devil can have done this thing. Release him!"

With a mighty bound the hound sprang toward——

[The next installment of this gripping mystery serial will not appear in an early issue.]

---

manners, waxed moustache and Inverness coat, and still to be seen now and then at the bar, but always, always standing, awake or asleep, not infrequently the latter.

[1] The word has two definitions that could apply here. It could be either the balcony that runs across the front of the club, or Gramercy Park across the street.

The Ape of Agate

Anonymous

School magazines were a popular source of Holmes parodies. Maybe because at that age boys first encounter the great detective, and on those of a certain temperament it leaves a lifelong impression. It helps that the stories, as we've seen, are full of easily replicated tropes that can be bent in any direction — dramatic, humorous, self-referential, or topical — as the writer chooses.

This story appeared in the November issue of The Comet, *the school magazine at Rugby, one of England's oldest public schools.*

The great detective sat in his chair, puffing away contentedly at his "six-shooter."[1] He was clad in a dressing gown, with slippers which contained his tobacco as well as his feet. Round him was a galaxy of moustaches, beards, wigs, greasepaint, lip-stick, and all manner of devices. At a moment's notice he could transform himself completely.

The telephone bell whirred: the great detective at once clapped on a beard, adjusted a voice-alteration machine, gave a few deft touches with the lip-stick, and turned to the instrument.

"Ha — what? — yes — yes — ha! — no — today you say? — yes — at 10 a.m. Ha — see that the room is not touched. I will be round in a minute."

He turned, remained for a minute deep in thought, his back to the window, so that he failed to see the face of a Chink convulsed with fury that for a fleeting minute was pressed against the pane; then he touched a concealed bell

---

[1] A check of slang dictionaries, newspapers, and books from the period show no connection between smoking pipes and the slang name for a revolver. There is now, however, a six-shooter pipe marketed today for marijuana smokers. According to one website, a worker at Jim Henson's Creature Shop built the pipe in 1999 using the company's machine shop. He acquired a patent on the design and has been selling the product ever since.

with his foot; almost at once a shaggy-looking animal ambled into the room.

"Prystwatusaletexclazxturvel," jerked out the great detective. At once the animal straightened himself up, and we behold the great detective's boy assistant in disguise.

"Well, chief?"

"His most august and royal highness the Maharajah of Chung-lo has been found murdered in his rooms at the Hotel Magnificent. There are no fingerprints apparently — nothing. But no criminal on earth ever succeeded in not leaving a clue: I have always succeeded where the police have failed. Get ready, lad, and come."

In two minutes, armed to the teeth with revolvers, knives, chloroform bottles and shillalahs,[1] they descended by the great detective's private tube-line to the hotel. Many was the crook, posted to watch the great detective's comings and goings, that had been puzzled by this private line.

Arrived at the hotel, a burly policeman barred the great detective's entrance to the suite. "No one allowed in, sir." The great detective flicked back the lapel of his coat; at once the limb of the law salaamed.[2]

"We must first find the motive," hissed the great detective. He beckoned to the native servant to come closer, and bade him tell all he knew.

"Massa, de baas' agate stone hab been stolen. De baas he bring it from Injia, and de dam Chinks, dey steal it."[3]

---

[1] A cudgel made from a hardwood such as oak or blackthorn.
[2] Presumably the great detective had his badge on the underside of the lapel. *Salaamed:* A salute that accompanies saying "Salam," the Arabic word for "peace." Depending on the country and the relationship between greeter and greeted, the gesture can involve a handshake with the right hand, placing the right hand over the heart, brief kisses on the cheek or kissing the elder's ring.
[3] An example of ethnic humor in which the black butler is speaking in a stereotypical manner drawn from slavery, from calling any man addressing him as "Massa" (for "Master"), mispronouncing words such as "India" ("Injia"), and using fractured grammar.

"Ha," snarled the great detective.

Then for an hour dead silence reigned in the room — silence broken only by the hard breathing of the detective, as he crawled hither and thither; stopping a minute to jot down a note on his shirt cuff, and then on again. One or two articles that he picked up he carefully sealed up in an envelope.

At the end of an hour he got up, sat down, and for five hours smoked shag. Just as the room was becoming totally uninhabitable, the chair gave a convulsive lurch as the great idea struck the detective.

"A paper, a paper," he roared. In a minute he was tearing it open. A second sufficed. "What a fool a man can be," he bellowed, jammed on his hat, and made for a taxi.

"The Zoo; and £10 if you do it in two minutes." In one min. 55 secs, the car drew up outside the Zoo, leaving a cylinder or two behind it in Piccadilly Circus.[1] Throwing down a note, the great detective rushed through the barrier and made straight for the monkey-house.

There he found what he expected: a sickly monkey. Without a second's delay he applied his pocket stomach pump, and there was the agate.

Later that night, the great detective was sitting by the fire with his assistant. "Well, chief: tell me how did you get on the trail? I confess I'm beaten."

"Well, my boy, in that room I found a cigarette end of a sort that can only be got out of an automatic machine at the Zoo. I saw in the paper that the Maharajah of Chung-lo paid a visit to the Zoo yesterday. Evidently he suspected something, and so concealed the stone in a monkey. His murderers did their foul deed in vain, and I think the police will get them, now I have given them the clue."

---

[1] A major road junction in London's West End where Piccadilly Road intersects with Regent and Glasshouse streets, Shaftesbury Avenue and Leicester (pronounced Lester) Square. The American equivalent would be Times Square in New York City. The word circus is derived from the Latin word meaning "circle."

The Scarlet Pimple

Anthony Armstrong

George Anthony Armstrong Willis (1897-1972) was a Canadian-born British writer and journalist who had several stories adapted for radio and movies, such as Ten Minute Alibi *(1934)*, The Man in the Road *(1956), and* The Man Who Haunted Himself *(1970). This Sherlockian take on* The Scarlet Pimpernel *appeared in the November issue of* Gaiety *magazine.*

The third day of Nivôse in the year I of the Republic.[1]

A small room in the Rue de Cordeliers, Paris, and two men crouched over a tiny fire.

Citizen Tinquier-Fouville, warming his hands, gnashed his teeth in rage as he spoke:

"At last shall we catch that accursed Englishman, the Scarlet Pimple. This time he cannot escape."

"I am not sure," replied the other slowly, taking snuff. This last speaker was the famous Citizen Shovealong, the life-long enemy of the Scarlet Pimple.[2] Though soberly dressed,

---

[1] During the French Revolution, the calendar was replaced with one that removed all references to royalty and religion and fell in line with Enlightenment principles of rationality. The year was reset to the Roman numeral I and began on the autumnal equinox at the Paris Observatory. There were 12 months divided into three 10-day weeks, with five or six days each year placed at the months at the end of each year. The day of rest was moved to the tenth day of the week. *Nivôse*: Derived from the French word for "snowy," was the fourth month and started between 21 and 23 December and ended between 19 and 21 January.

[2] A play on Citizen Chauvelin, the enemy of the Scarlet Pimpernel. In the 1903 play and 1905 novel by Baroness Orczy (1865-1947), the wealthy Sir Percy Blakeney portrayed himself as a foppish idiot, even to his French wife Marguerite. During the French Revolution, he became the Scarlet Pimpernel, naming himself for a flower *(Anagallis arvensis)* and rescued French aristocrats sentenced to death. The French envoy, Chauvelin, blackmailed Marguerite into helping him unmask the Pimpernel. She discovers that the Pimpernel is her husband, and tries to stop the envoy from carrying out his plot. Baroness Orczy, who was an honest-to-heaven de-

and actually the owner of a dirty pocket-handkerchief — the only one in Paris — which had more than once earned for him the epithet of "aristo," he was as relentless and cruel as any of them.

"The trouble is, Citizen, is that he is so clever," went on the first, picking his teeth now that he had finished gnashing them. "He can impersonate anyone, what?"

"H'm," replied Shovealong, and took some more snuff.

The other grasped his arm,

"That's enough— " he began.

"This snuff? Well, what about it?"

"*That is enough,*" I said. "It will go to your head. We must keep cool tonight."

Reluctantly the other disposed of his snuff-box; then carefully dusted his handkerchief and returned it to his sleeve.

All was pitch dark, save where five flaring lamps lit up the guard-room, and a tavern, blazing with light, resounded to the din of ribald laughter. A bright full moon looked down upon this scene of debauchery. But otherwise all was pitch dark.

Two cloaked figures sat in the shadow of a lamp-post. They were chilled to the bone and wet to the skin, also masked to the eyes and armed to the teeth.

To these two came up a third man.

"Are you there, Citizen Shovealong?" he asked.

"Yes," answered Shovealong, snuffing snuff as if he could never snuff enough, "and so is Citizen Tinquier-Fouville. Has anyone in disguise with forged papers tried to pass out of the gate, Citizen Wathot?"

"Not a single one. No one at all suspicious has passed, save an old man with a large beard who spoke with a foreign accent,

---

scendant of Hungarian aristocracy, was the first to create the hero who keeps his identity a secret, the forerunner of Zorro, The Spirit, Batman, and Superman. She is also rare among writers for marrying a man who not only supported her — he co-wrote *Pimpernel* — but they stayed happily married for nearly half a century.

and said he was going to put flowers on his mother's grave in the cemetery outside; and a carrier with a cartload of hay."

"Are you sure it *was* hay?" asked Shovealong with his customary shrewdness.

"Oh, quite, Citizen. The man told me it was for a sick horse he had at Barency.¹ That's how I knew it must be hay, for otherwise he would not be taking it to a horse. *Que voulez-vous*, Citizen?" ²

"Did you see their papers? Were they forged?" put in Tinquier-Fouville suddenly.

"No, they had both left them at home."

"*Nom d'un Dunhill!*³ How do they expect us to tell whether papers are forged or not when they leave them at home? Tut, tut, most careless! Well, resume your watch, Wathot; you are doing very well; let not even a mouse through without careful scrutiny. Arrest everyone you think may be the Scarlet Pimple in disguise."

Ten minutes later came a terrible uproar, and the two Citizens sprang to their feet. In the dim light cast by the five lamps, the tavern and the full moon, Wathot was seen to approach with a group of prisoners.

"What is the matter, Citizen Wathot?"

"We have arrested the famous Scarlet Pimple," announced Wathot in triumph. "At least we have arrested four of him, so the chances are four to one that it is really him — I should say *he*."

Citizen Shovealong sat down suddenly and took some snuff.

---

¹ In "A Question of Passports," a short story from *The League of the Scarlet Pimpernel* (1919), Barency was a village outside Paris that supplied cabbages and potatoes to the city. The Pimpernel was able to smuggle six condemned aristocrats out of the city with stolen passports under the eye of revolutionary Jean-Paul Marat (1743-1793).
² "What do you expect?" spoken with mild exasperation.
³ Pseudo-French that directly translates as "name of Dunhill." Dunhill is a cigarette brand introduced in 1907 by tobacconist and inventor Alfred Dunhill (1872-1959).

"I don't quite follow," he said faintly. "Your reasoning. . . ."

"Well, this one," went on Wathot, pointing to the first, "speaks English like a cursed aristo; we heard him."

He pushed the man forward, who replied, as the Citizen said, in unmistakable English.

"Garn! 'Oo are you a-shoving?"

"The *new* 'aristos,'" explained Wathot. "But these next two must assuredly both be him — them — *he*; because they were both heard to say "Damn!" . . . And this last one I don't know much about, but I arrested him to keep my hand in. The Scarlet Pimple's disguises are so wonderful he might be any of them — or all of them."

"Who are you?" Tinquier-Fouville asked the last man.

"Holmlock Shears," replied the other.

"Holmlock Shears! But dash it, man, you've no business here. Your article doesn't begin till next month!"

"No," replied the great detective calmly, "but the author left this lying about close to the rough copy of the next article, and so I slipped across to help you."

"Well I never!" swore the Citizen with one of his rough Paris oaths.

"None of these men is the one you seek," went on the great detective calmly. "The Scarlet Pimple is much too clever an impersonator for that. He has even impersonated *me*."

"Well, where is he? Who is he?" put in Shovealong.

Holmlock Shears drew himself up to well over his full height.

"*You!*" he cried, pointing full at him.

For a moment Citizen Shovealong stood absolutely still. He was overwhelmed — astounded — dismayed. That anyone should accuse him of being his own lifelong enemy! The man whom he had been pursuing unsuccessfully through volume after volume![1]

---

[1] Baroness Orczy wrote several Pimpernel sequels, including two short-story collections, as well as spin-off novels about the French aristos Pimpernel rescued, his ancestors, and even one in which Sir Percy comments

Then the true cleverness of the Scarlet Pimple dawned on him, and he realised that the great detective must be right. The Scarlet Pimple had been impersonating him all along, and he, fool that he was, had not known it. He had been tracking him here, there, and everywhere, mocked at, defeated at every turn, only to find he was he himself and not himself at all. . . .

He took a dose of snuff to conceal his mortification, and then arrested himself in triumph.

Holmlock Shears returned swiftly to his own article, just in time for the fair copy.[1]

Baroness Emma Orczy, author of *The Scarlet Pimpernel*.

---

on modern-day England of the 1930s, *The Scarlet Pimpernel Looks at the World*.

[1] The final version of the manuscript, written or typed neatly so the typesetter could read it. The author's working drafts are traditionally called "foul papers."

The Reigate Road Murder

Anthony Armstrong

In the previous story, "The Scarlet Pimple," Holmlock Shears admitted he popped over from his story that wouldn't appear until the December issue of Gaiety. *True to his word, here it is.*

I make no excuse for putting the following before the public, for the simple reason that the incidents narrated form the only occasion when my famous friend, Holmlock Shears, ever found himself at fault over a case.

I remember we were sitting in our room in Baker Street, one wet afternoon, occupied in our usual fashion — I with a pencil trying to write some further memoirs, and Shears playing the violin behind an impenetrable cloud of blue smoke — when a lady was shown into the room.

She was tall and of medium height, with dark light hair, a mouth and two eyes. She wore a macintosh, face-powder, and a worried look, and advanced upon me from the doorway.

I dodged — not without difficulty, owing to my wound received at the battle of Maiwand[1] — and speaking from cover, asked her what she wanted.

"Murder has been done," she gasped. "Where is Mr. Holmlock Shears? I do not see him."

I pointed silently to the smoke cloud from which issued the strains of Mendelssohn's *Lieder*. Each strain was, of course, disguised to as to prevent Mendelssohn[2] recognising his own property.

---

[1] The Battle of Maiwand on July 27, 1880, was a major battle in the Second Anglo-Afghan War that ended in an Afghan victory. The "real" Dr. Watson was also wounded at Maiwand, pensioned off, and returned to London, where he met Holmes as related in *A Study in Scarlet*.

[2] It's doubtful that Felix Mendelssohn would have cared considering he died in 1847. His most famous composition is *Lieder ohne Worte*, (*Songs Without Words*), solo piano pieces so popular that critics underrated them, one opining that "It is not true that they are insipid, but they might as well be."

"He is inside there," I said proudly.

"Will he speak to me?"

I walked across and knocked on the edge of the smoke cloud.

"Lady to see you, Shears"

Mendelssohn's *Lieder* — what was left of it — changed abruptly to "I Don't Love Nobody,"[1] played with the back of the bow and one cuff-link; three strings snapped; the smoke barrage drifted away; and Holmlock Shears was revealed to our sight.

It is totally unnecessary for me to describe in any way my well-known friend; his tallness, his leanness, his long fingeredness, and his pointed eyes. I need not weary the reader by mentioning his hawk-like nose which gave him such an air of alertness, and will pass over any reference to his chin, and to his hands, mottled with chemicals, spattled with nicotine, and measled with pricks from his hypodermic syringe. There is no need for me to describe — but by this time I have done it.

"You are married," suddenly flashed my companion, glancing at her left hand. "This afternoon you used face-powder."

"However did you know?" gasped the woman, recoiling in amazement at this sudden remark, and though I had had ample previous proof of Shears' superhuman powers of observation and deduction, even I was overcome with wonder.

"Now what is it you want with me?" he went on. "You'll have to be quick, because I'm only allowed two pages."

"There has been a murder at my house in South London. It's nothing serious — only my husband; but I should like, just as a matter of interest, you understand ..."

---

[1] It may be coincidence, but several records with that title were recorded by black singers: in 1923 by Ethel Finnie and Edna Hicks, in January 1924 by Clara Smith, Lena Wilson, and Virginia Liston. By the way, there are two techniques for playing with the stick side of the bow. *Col legno* (Italian for "hit with wood") involves striking the strings like a drum, while with *col legno tratto* ("with the wood drawn"), the stick is drawn across the strings. Players who fear damaging the bow this way are advised to keep a cheaper bow on hand for this purpose.

This technique appears in Mussorgsky's *Night on Bald Mountain*, Mozart's *The Turkish Concerto,* and the Mars segment from Holst's *The Planets.*

"One minute. I suppose Scotland Yard are there and have no clue and are completely baffled?"

"Oh, yes, we got all the usual procedure over at the beginning and now they've gone away. But it is all most puzzling, for not only can we not find the murderer, but we can't even find the corpse. I am sorry to trouble you about such a little thing."

"To a great mind nothing is little. I will come at once." His eyes flashed swiftly over her. "It is raining," he said quietly, just as if it were the most commonplace remark in the world.

"Wonderful!" I ejaculated, while our visitor stood staring at him in amazement, which small incident I have only included to show the abnormal analytical power possessed by the great detective. In a flash he had deduced the above from her streaming macintosh[1] and wet umbrella, whereas ordinary people would have looked out of the window.

Half an hour later we were in the very house where the dastardly crime had been committed. Shears was faced with the stupendous task of not only discovering the murderer, but also of discovering the corpse. But he was at once busy. He examined with a pocket lens the road outside, the path inside, the aspidistra[2] in the front parlour, and everyone who happened to pass him — myself twice included — talking the whole time about Cremona fiddles[3] and uttering little cries of self-encouragement.

Springing upon a small pile of grey dust in the hall, he

---

[1] A raincoat made from rubberized fabric, invented by Scottish chemist Charles Macintosh (1766-1843).

[2] A house plant commonly found in English boarding houses and middle-class homes. Better known as the cast-iron plant, due to its ability to thrive despite neglect, it became so identified with English respectability that George Orwell (1903-1950) used it as a symbol in his novel *Keep the Aspidistra Flying*. Coincidentally, Orwell also wrote a Holmes parody reprinted in the 1915-1919 volume.

[3] The city of Cremona in northern Italy has long been known for its craftsmanship, particularly in musical instruments. Probably its most famous luthier is Antonio Stradivari (1644-1737) whose estimated 500 surviving violins are among the most sought-after in the world.

scrutinised it closely.

"There are one hundred and fourteen different kinds of cigar and cigarette ash, my dear Watnot," he began. "I have written a monograph on the subject. This ash is the ash of a Trichinopoly cigar[1] ... No, I'm hanged," he broke off suddenly, "it isn't after all. I don't know what it is. Why can't they always smoke Trichinopoly cigars?" he went on petulantly. "They have always done so far, and between you and me it is the only one I really know."

But despite this serious setback, such was his amazing cleverness that within ten minutes he had formulated his theory about the murder. Summoning our hostess to the parlour, he began, "This is a very simple crime. The murder was committed by three men; one with a squint to the right, one with a squint to the left, and one without a squint at all. One of the three was smoking a Trichin — no, was just smoking — and had a short while before purchased something for one shilling and elevenpence three farthings.[2] They rode cycles and carried the corpse away in the direction of Reigate."[3]

"By heavens, Shears, this is wonderful!" I ejaculated.

"Not at all, my dear Watnot; very elementary. Pass the hypodermic syringe."

---

[1] A cigar made from tobacco grown near present-day Tiruchirappalli in India. It was a cheap cigar and crudely made — basically a cylinder with the ends cut off instead of tapered — and one of India's major exports during the Victorian Era. A Trichinopoly cigar in A Study in Scarlet led to Holmes' admission that he had made a special study of ashes and can identify any brand of tobacco at a glance.

[2] For centuries, the British monetary system was a unique system in which the basic unit was the pound, which was divided into 20 shillings, each of which was divided into 12 pence (also called a penny), and that was divided into four farthings. Hence, 960 farthings made up a pound. Amounts were expressed using up to three numbers representing pounds/shillings/pence. One shilling, 11 pence and three farthings would be written as 1/11¾. Great Britain's currency was converted to the decimal system on Feb. 15, 1971.

[3] A town in Surrey, England, about 22 miles south of London. Formerly a medieval market town, today it is primarily the home of commuters traveling to London for work.

"But you amaze me. What ..."

"An intrinsically simple case of plain deduction with one or two instructive points. I reasoned thus. Our hostess here tells us that there has been a murder. Therefore a murder has been committed. There is no body. Therefore it has been taken away. So far, so good. But by whom, and how? By the murderers, who were three in number, and carried the corpse away on their bicycles; for there are three bicycle tracks on the Reigate road outside, and, moreover," he emphasises his words with his forefinger, "moreover, all exactly parallel, such as could only have been made by men carrying a rigid body laid across the handle-bars between them. I have already sent off my band of ragged urchins from Baker Street to follow up the tracks and tell the men they are wanted on the telephone. That little subterfuge will fetch them back so that in half an hour we may expect to have them under lock and key."

"Marvellous!" I murmured feebly. "But the squint..."

"Elementary, Watnot, elementary. The two men on the outside carrying a body between them must each have had a squint inwards in order to be able to do it. Or if they hadn't they will have by now. As regards the article purchased for one and elevenpence three farthings, that follows simply on the finding of the cigar ash. That cigar the man was smoking could only have been given him instead of the farthing change ..."

He broke off suddenly as a voice was heard outside, and our hostess rushed to the door.

Shears sprang to his feet.

"What is it?" he asked.

"Thank Heaven, the mystery is solved!" cried the lady triumphantly. "It is my husband alive and well. He was not murdered after all. He has just returned from a ride on his tricycle!"

Shears lit his pipe in baffled anger and disappeared in a cloud of blue smoke, drawing the violin, his last bow, and the hypodermic syringe after him.

The Marriage of Sherlock Holmes

Gregory Breitman

Translated by Benjamin Block

This story is probably the most risqué tale told during Conan Doyle's lifetime. It was daring not so much for the implication of Holmes and Watson courting the same woman, but for where it was published and by whom.

It was published in the December issue of Beau: The Man's Magazine, *owned by Samuel Roth (1893-1974). The respected poet and Greenwich Village bookstore owner started four literary magazines, including* Beau, *that tested the boundaries of copyright and obscenity laws. The material was fairly mild at first, such as Benjamin Franklin's "Advice to a Friend on Choosing a Mistress." What got Roth into hot water was publishing chapters from James Joyce's* Ulysses *without the author's permission. Then he pirated an edition of* Lady Chatterley's Lover, *for which he was arrested in 1929 and imprisoned. When he challenged his conviction for selling a magazine containing literary erotica and nude photos, the Supreme Court opinion in* Roth v. United States *(1957) changed the definition of obscene material that could not be protected by the First Amendment.*

All this was in the future. As for this story, little is known of its author, except that Breitman (1873-1943) emigrated to the United States from Russia in 1923. His translator, Benjamin Block, was a Russian native who also translated works by science-fiction writer V. Orlovsky, the novelist Maxim Gorki, and poet Vladimir Mayakovsky.

"Is that you, Watson?"

Doctor Watson briskly entered Sherlock Holmes' cabinet and pressed warmly the extended hand of the host.

Sherlock shifted his pipe from one corner of his mouth to the other and pointed out the armchair to his friend. Doctor Watson seated himself opposite the host and said:

"Sherlock, you have not changed a wee-bit! Think of it! We have not seen each other for three months, yet, as soon as I put my foot across the threshold of your apartment, you recognized me immediately!"

The famous detective did not smile, but an effort to do so was quite evident. Perhaps he only stirred his pipe, and the movement of his lips suggested a gentle smile.

"Who else, beside you, my dear friend," he began, "would have come into my apartment and freely groom his hair before the big mirror, without even inquiring about me from the servant-maid? Every person possesses some subjective nuances of manner which accompany him wherever he goes and expose themselves unconsciously. Don't we recognize people by their gait?"

Watson, without doubt, was pleased silently with his friend's explanation. He leisurely lit his cigar and when his head at last became enveloped in clouds of grey smoke, he asked carelessly:

"My friend, you are married?"

Holmes raised his eyes at his friend, only to meet the latter's cynic glance; either was pretending to look less surprised than the other, as if some play was hidden in it. Holmes replied:

"You have reached your conclusions because of the new order in my house, the odor of perfume and a lady's apparel hanging on the clothes-rack in the antechamber?"

"Not at all, Sherlock, I haven't even noticed that," calmly retorted Watson, "but I judge by the smooth, unmistakable marriage ring on the fourth finger of your left hand. To be sure, Sherlock, you never cared for trinkets!"

Holmes brought up the palm of his left hand to his face and for several minutes thoughtfully examined the gold ring on his finger.

"You are right, my friend," he murmured, "this is — the proof, sure proof for any detective. Yes, I am married."

"What on earth has come over you, Sherlock," inquired the doctor somewhat sympathetically, gazing reflectively at his friend.

Sherlock Holmes took out the pipe from his mouth and after having ascertained that the fire had burned out completely, he then remarked:

"One unsuccessful adventure, Watson!"

"Poor Sherlock!" sighed the doctor compassionately. A brief but serious silence followed. Holmes was meditating and Watson was waiting.

"Watson," at last began the famous detective, "as you know, I was always wont to report to you all my adventures; at all times I feel the need to share with someone my observations and impressions; my thoughts work much faster then, and during a conversation I may arrive at a more practical decision much easier than during the process of thinking."

"If that be the case, my friend," fired back the doctor, "I very much regret that we have not seen each other for such a long time, still I presume, that, had there been someone for you to have a heart-to-heart talk with, your situation would not have become so sadly complicated."

"Why do you suppose that I am unhappy in my marriage, Watson?" curiously rebutted Holmes, as sparks of fire seemed to be playing in his eyes.

"Only because of my conviction that such a serious and self-existing person like yourself can never be satisfied with married life, whatever supernatural qualities your lovely consort may possess. It is mainly up to you, not to her. Coupled life, especially with a woman, is a thing unnatural, as much as love without a woman is unnatural. Matrimony, in its present form, is — a savagery, a survival of barbarism and ignorance, a violation of the nature of the modern human being, an impurity of some sort ..."

"And, most of all it is a great inconvenience," concluded Sherlock Holmes. "Life begins to resemble a piano, onto the strings of which a cane with a golden head has been stuck. Absolutely incompatibility."

"What a misfortune it is for mankind that the woman is denied the ideal franchise with the man!" remarked the doctor bitterly.

Sherlock spoke slowly: "I would gladly bear her name, carry out all household duties, make her the head of the family, just to be given the means to reckon with a definite quantity, only to know with whom I am dealing!"

"You are right, Sherlock; the psychic life of the woman is utterly inconceivable to the man, while the woman proper is always a puzzle to him. In that alone lies the nature of her relationship to him. Since Creation there was not, nor will there be, such a man who could understand a woman. Not because there were not and there will not be any erudite and perspicacious men, but simply because it would be almost as supernatural if there were a man who could understand the languages of dogs, birds and jack-asses ... "

"Why, then, does a woman understand a man so well," asked Sherlock sighing.

"Because this is one of the peculiarities of her nature. She was thus created by God," quickly and assuredly asserted Watson. "It is one of her inborn qualities, without which she is — a weakling, a defective, like a cat without whiskers and special pupils, a dog without his scent, a hedgehog without his prickles. This is the weapon she employs in her struggle for her existence and against the man ... "

Watson began to reek with perspiration; he took out his handkerchief and wiped his high forehead. Sherlock lit his pipe and puffed away at it till a thick, gray smoke enveloped him fully. Then, as if speaking to himself, he said:

"Most remarkable! During my life I had fought with all possible criminals, such criminals that police the world over refused to mingle with. I caught the most ingenious swindlers, cleverest thieves, brave robbers and beastly murderers. I traced the most amazing crimes, conceived the secrets of the most complicated adventures and unfolded them. I had dealt with prisoners, bullies, halfwits and maniacs ..."

Watson's face bubbled with astonishment, and stretching himself out to a comfortable position, he interrupted his friend:

"Only your wife you cannot catch!" he shouted.

The pipe in Sherlock's mouth began to tremble as if someone had struck it. A minute later the famous detective made the following reply:

"My good friend, Watson, I love you so, that I know not what to answer you!"

A stifled reproach was heard in the detective's voice. Watson grasped his hand and flared up in ardent exaltation:

"My dear teacher, whatever has come over you? You seem to have forgotten your first and main principle: to regard everything subjectively and seriously! I fail to recognize you, Sherlock!"

"I am not at all sure whether she has committed any crime at all."

"Then, you are jealous, Sherlock!"

"No, not jealous, but suspicious. I have sufficient proof to sustain my contention, I alone am aware of it. To another man she would seem an ideal wife, true and loving. It does not seem as if she had many male acquaintances. She does not spruce herself up or receive letters from anyone, nor does she mention any names in her sleep; in a word, she conducts herself superbly."

"What do you want from her, then?"

"To know to whom she is betraying me!"

"Are you sure about it?"

"You, Watson, if anyone else, should know me at least a little bit!"

"Forgive me, Sherlock! But what is it, namely, that makes you suffer?"

"I am not suffering at all, Watson, I am merely interested. Two arts have met in collision: hers and mine. My nature, however, does not tolerate a concrete secret."

"Of course! But, on what do you base your assumption, Sherlock?"

"I am certain, for instance, that she is taking someone home before she returns to the house. The individual she is riding with is a man and lives not far from here. Judging by your raised eyebrows, you are deeply interested in the affair. Very well, then. I have observed her through the window several times when she was returning from an appointment. She never sat in the center of the seat, but always on the right-hand side. I conclude, therefore, that at her left-hand side sat her escort who, undoubtedly, left the cab before. That her escort is a man is evinced by two outstanding incidents: First, that he sat at her left-hand side; second, that my wife never paid the driver. Consequently, he must have been paid off before, by a man, of course."

"The observation, in all probability, is correct!"

"Then, after the appointment, my wife usually brings home with her the odor of his perfume and cigars. One thing, Watson, you must admit, that I am endowed with a very keen, almost dog-like scent, and I can very easily discern the difference between a cigar and a pipe. Besides, you know well yourself that tobacco smoke assails the nostrils of the non-smoking neighbor more readily than the smoker himself."

The detective filled up his pipe with fresh tobacco; lighting it, he puffed away at it for a brief moment. Then, he stretched and straightened up his back awhile and continued:

"As you see now, I possess a sufficient supply of watchfulness and observation; both of us are engaged in a definite, silent, but stubborn struggle. My wife, for instance, knows well that not until I bear witness of her actions will I utter a single syllable of rebuke to her; I am too serious a man for that. Her general behavior toward me is beyond reproach; neither do I suspect nor feel that she has grown cold toward me; she pretends not to be bored in my company; on the contrary, she is very kind, sweet and amiable. Yet, I have on hand some well-founded material which proves to me that it nothing but make-believe on her part, that she is playing a very subtle game — which must end some day."

"Still, I believe she will come out of this unmarred," remarked the visitor somewhat sadly, "unless you get her in the very act, when it will be impossible for her to prove. or to deceive you any longer; when all roads leading to it will become blocked. Otherwise, it is very difficult to test a woman; you cannot subject her love to an examination. She can make-believe and simulate as much she desires. It is not like us men; we are — mere mechanisms in the process of love."

"You are perfectly right, my friend; but my profession and art have forced me to discount all the time the views on love and women you have just propounded, and which so opportunely coincide with my own convictions, may I not, therefore, take the liberty of asking you, who is deceiving you, my friend?"

Watson doubtless became confused, but succeeded in retaining the composure of his mind. He met Sherlock's keen look with real fortitude, and discharging heavy clouds of smoke, he charged back, slowly, but very emphatically:

"This is a groundless accusation, Sherlock. I merely expressed my views and convictions. They bound me to nothing whatever."

"Perhaps! Yet, I firmly believe that they come to one only through personal experience, and their origin, I may say, is without doubt, the same as mine. But, whereas you are an admirer of concrete facts, I shall permit you to avail yourself of my material with regards to your case."

Watson's face became flooded with color. He was silent, holding the cigar tight in his mouth.

"The fact of the matter is, my friend, that it is more than three months since you have hidden yourself away, and although you have not left London, you have severed all connections with me. That happened for the first time during our uninterrupted friendship. I presume you were not sick nor have had any discord."

"This, if you like, is a thought, but not a reason. I might have been very much occupied."

"Just as I thought it was; you were very much occupied with your *party*. Tell me, Watson, since when is it that you began to spruce, wear such cravats, frizzle your hair, and in general — employ methods of rejuvenation? The odor of your perfume is such as I have met in café-chantants only.[1] Besides,

---

[1] A type of outdoor café in France where popular music was played for the public.

where have your streaks of gray hair disappeared to? And why this white flower in your coat-lapel? I remember, you never gave a snap for all that. And that gold tooth in your mouth, you didn't have it before! All this, my friend, forces me to fully presuppose that a woman is at the bottom of it all.

"I admit that your presumption is not without substantial logic, but it is no proof by any means, Sherlock."

Watson overcame his confusion, but refused to yield.

"I shall now unleash my last reserves, Watson," continued the detective unperturbed. "About a month ago, when I was tracing my wife, I found myself, much to my surprise, near your house. Thinking of you, I decided to step in and share with you my affairs. Alas, friend, you could not receive me!—because there was a woman in your apartment. I confess, however, never before have I met a female in your house, with the sole exception of your servant-maid who, on that occasion revealed the secret; she was fetching up to your room freshly bought candies, fruits and flowers. Oh, Watson, how I wished I could share with you then my frame of mind ... I, perhaps, would not have been married now!"

"But that happened only about three weeks ago, Sherlock!" remarked Watson in surprise.

"Yes, and I was married only a week ago. Till then I was busily engaged in an unsuccessful search for my competitor. A strong depression of mind suddenly possessed me and I became doubtful of my suspicion and art and ... put on this ring ..."

A concentrated silence ensued. Finally, hard-pressed and silenced, the doctor meekly brushed away the ashes from his cigar and confessed naively.

"You are right, Sherlock, I am in love!"

"What happened then, you have parted with your sweetheart?"

Watson's face turned dead white suddenly.

"What makes you think so, Sherlock?"

"I judge by the sadness and disappointment you have expressed about women, and most of all, by the fact, that you have come to me. I presume you were overwhelmed with the desire to have a heart-to-heart talk with someone; you felt lonesome, and your first thought, undoubtedly, was about me, your old, reliable friend. Why, you look awfully bad, Watson! I see you have not shaved for several days. I heartily congratulate you, my dear friend, upon the loss of your woman!"

"You are terrible, Sherlock," declared Watson, and continued sullenly, "why, I am experiencing now a silent heart-tragedy. I have been searching her for the last ten days, but, alas;—as if the earth itself had swallowed her! I have availed all the methods of sleuthing you have taught me, but without success. Her trail ends itself somewhere in this neighborhood. Having strayed down here, I ran in to have a chat with you and forget myself a bit."

Sherlock puffed away at his pipe with great effort, as if vexed by it, and after a short pause, he began with a grimace of anxiety on his face:

"The more searches I conduct, the more convinced I become of how dangerous and deceitful the art of a detective sometimes is. What horrid, strange and incomprehensible concurrences of circumstances there are in our life — concurrences that create a full picture, an illusion of truth, which at the end turn out to be nothing but falsehoods and myths. How many people have been sent to the jails, hard-labor prisons, to the gallows, because of such mistakes of the courts of justice!"

"Why do you say that, Sherlock?" exclaimed Watson, amazed at the sudden change of subject. He took the cigar from his mouth and remained agape for awhile, unable to determine whether his friend was merely joking or speaking in earnest.

"Don't be surprised, Watson," calmly continued Sherlock Holmes. He concentrated his eyes on the edge of his fuming pipe, "even though it may sound unpleasant to you. Haven't we agreed and concluded long since, that everything in this world is possible, is natural and has its organic reasons? Well, then — only an hour ago you tried to convince me that I should regard the affair with my wife objectively and abstractedly. And so, my friend, I am following your kind advice. But, have you considered, at least for a brief moment, this very strange coincidence, that, when I have been looking for my wife, traces have brought me to your house, and when you have been searching for your sweetheart, her traces led you straight to me? Of course, this is a mere coincidence, one of those coincidences, which usually cause the mistakes of the courts. On the other hand, the very circumstance which brought us together today is misleading us.

"Now, supposing I were not acquainted with you. I would even then, beyond all doubts, have entered your house, not in a friendly way, of course, but by means of direct detective indication. Presently, you have come to me also by means of detective indication, although, if I were not your friend, you would have been here just the same. And during our conversation I caught the odor of your handkerchief, when you were wiping your forehead, and recalled immediately the redolence of that unknown man's perfume my wife always brings with her after she returns from her rendezvous. Besides, I have already told you that she also brought with her the smell of cigars; indeed, you are smoking cigars. ..."

Watson availed himself of the chance when Holmes stopped to fix the ashes in his pipe and turned to the detective:

"You are right, Sherlock, and presently you will convince yourself how curious and amusing the pranks of sleuthing sometimes are. In order to prove to you that my case has nothing to do with yours, I shall relate to you briefly the history of my romance, the beginning of which you know, without any doubt."

The latter made a move, seated himself more comfortably in his armchair, and with an unperturbed expression, prepared to listen to his friend's love affair.

"Surely, you remember, Sherlock," began Watson after he lit up a new cigar, "our last adventure about three months ago, after which we first met to-day. Perhaps, you have by now forgotten that charming young lady with the golden tresses and celestial eyes — the girl that kissed our hands and begged us to save her father, whom the agents of the king's police were about to seize and arrest. Your genius then manifested itself in its full glory; in half an hour you put the police to shame and made them confess to the rude mistake they had committed. They suspected the poor gentleman, a cashier of the Trade Bank of England, of embezzlement of two thousand pounds sterling, while, as you directly pointed out, it was stolen by his assistant, who lost the money on the stock exchange."

"I remember, Watson," confirmed Sherlock through his pipe, "the investigation was brief, but beautiful. Yes, I remember that well."

"But I doubt whether you remember the statement the charming young lady had made — about her going to business every morning at 10 a.m. I confess, Sherlock, the young lady has made a powerful impression on me. I fully agree now with those individuals who claim that love is an infectious disease, more obstinate than malaria. Promptly at 10 a.m., the next morning, I was at her house and walked her over to her place of business. Thank God it was a long way off and I had plenty of time to enamor myself, more and more, with her exquisite charms. I have been escorting her to her place of business every day.

"Sherlock, I was infinitely happy. All this time she filled my life with love, caresses and sweetness; she respected my principle never to marry, never to bind my fate with another, nor to surrender my liberty and comfort. Suddenly, about ten days ago, she disappeared. I have not found her yet, and while searching for her, false traces have brought me to you, my dear Sherlock. I believe, however, that it was the instinct, rather than the track, that led me here; I must have just felt the need of some counsel from a man like you."

Sherlock Holmes for several minutes sat with eyes shut.

Then he took the pipe from his mouth, placed it on his knees, and only then did he look up to his guest.

"I remember," said he, "that I could not forget that girl with the golden tresses and celestial eyes. Nor have I forgotten when she had remarked about her going to business at 10 a.m. in the morning, the exact hour when I am eating my breakfast. But you apparently have forgotten, that the very same charming girl added also that she is returning from business at 4 p.m., at the time you are accustomed to have your dinner. And, if you, my friend, were wont to escort her every day to the office, then, I was escorting her every day from the office to her house. I also have succumbed to the fever of love. In my case, my friend, it ended in a catastrophe: I married her, sparing you from such a fate."

Watson was all white and deeply shaken by the phlegmatic[1] confession of his friend, whose malaise was evinced by the quivering pipe he now held in his hand and with which he beat against his knee in order to mask his emotions. Nothing interested him more now than his competitor, upon whom he riveted an obstinate look of his dark, gray eyes. Both were silent.

It is not, any easy venture to guess what the outcome would have been of their, unusual, stiffened silence, but presently they heard a sound that set both of them to tremble and an unforeseen shadow of uneasiness spread over their faces. That brief moment was nothing short of horror. Both host and guest were aghast. They were ready to run. But fate had decreed that each look into the other's eyes and, that assimilated look brought light into their hearts. Lacking roads of retreat and exits out of the situation led them into a silent agreement. And when the door flung open and into the room briskly entered Mrs. Holmes, the two chums sat like statues, true to themselves, and returned to their school of life.

---

[1] A personality that is cool, unemotional and stolid. It is derived from the four humours, the medieval theory that proposed four personality types: sanguine (enthusiastic and social), choleric (extraverted and logical), melancholic (introverted and anxious), and phlegmatic.

Mrs. Holmes indeed was very charming. Beside the golden tresses and celestial eyes, her round face, with its soft and delicate colors and shades, seemed almost enameled; it gleamed with moral chastity and cheerful indolence; a sort of elegant naiveté, which combined both that which is childish and feminine into one beautiful smile and look.

Smartly dressed and childishly cheerful, she stopped suddenly, as if rooted to the spot, and after a second of thoughtful gazing at the two friends, she smilingly extended her hand to Watson, exclaiming in her sweet elastic voice:

"Ah, Mr. Watson! ... I know you! ... My husband has spoken to me a great deal about you. Besides, I actually could not forget you since the first moment I met you. I had dreamed ever since I married my Sherlock, to become acquainted with you more closely. Sherlock had told me a great many fine and interesting things about you, Mr. Watson."

"Poor Watson is in a quandary," explained Sherlock calmly, "he was left flat by a woman whom he was madly in love with and, on whose account, he forgot everyone in this world, even me — his bosom friend. He should be appeased, don't you think so, Mary? I wish you would take upon yourself this task."

"Poor Mr. Watson," sincerely exclaimed Mrs. Holmes as she shot a cunning glance at the sad and silent doctor, who sat in his armchair with downcast eyes.

Sherlock Holmes by now completely regained his composure and watched, not without pleasure, the transpiring scene. He intended, apparently, to carry on his intrigue against his wife, but presently the latter noticed the strange turns of mind on the part of the men, and a flash of suspicion flit through her eyes and face.

The spark of animation the young lady brought in with her into the room was suddenly extinguished, and all at once, a weird silence, which none seemed willing to interrupt, filled up the whole room. Mrs. Holmes began to feel the grip of danger, but could not yet compute its proportion.

Finally, Watson could hold out no longer. Determination

glowed in his look; the instinct of self-preservation was abetting his desire to put an end to this tormenting situation from which, it seemed, there was no way out. His voice sounded dull; he was staring into the distance: —

"Stop that; Mary, Sherlock knows it all. ..."

Mrs. Holmes turned white at once and tears appeared in her eyes.

"You did not act fairly, Mr. Watson, not in the least gentleman-like!" was all she was able to utter.

Watson instantly jumped to his feet as if someone had struck him. His voice quivered now, he was unspeakably agitated.

"Ah, my dear Mrs. Holmes," he exclaimed plaintively, "please do not condemn me; is it my fault that your husband is a great detective?"

During Watson's brief complimentary praise to the detective, the latter attentively puffed away at his pipe, and having inhaled a goodly portion of smoke he spoke in his usual tone:

"Most important of all is that this mystery has at last been brought to a satisfactory conclusion; the whole affair has been cleared up in all its details. I can make you rejoice but at a single fact, my darling Mary, that during my long career as a detective, I have not tackled such an enigma."

Mrs. Holmes somewhat regained her self-possession. Hearing, at last, her husband's words, she dropped slowly on the edge of the sofa and began:

"Act as you like, Sherlock, but I have not deceived you. When you and Mr. Watson displayed so much interest in me, by saving my father, my whole being became filled with affection for you; the two of you became so dear to me that I began to feel a strong penchant for your society — the society of both of you.

"That was at the beginning. I was at a loss then, not knowing for whom to show my preference. Were the two of you to come to me together, it would been much easier for me to decide on either one of you. But right then you two parted, and each one separately made a different impression upon me.

"In the beginning, when we first met, I did even suppose that you, Sherlock, had any intentions of marrying me. You proposed marriage to me only three days before our wedding. And because of that, am I to blame that Mr. Watson proved himself to be more ardent and willing than you were, Sherlock? Both of you were aiming at one and the same object, but, through different roads. Still, Sherlock, I have not deceived you, just I have not deceived Mr. Watson, yet, you two have made me suffer. You are — men and, therefore, you cannot conceive the heart of a woman when it is filled with gratitude; it begets all sorts of feelings and sufferings. When you proposed to me, I left Mr. Watson immediately, because, to you, my dear, I had already given away myself, my freedom and the right over my feelings. You may do as you please, Sherlock, but it would have been far more proper on your part, had you informed me of your intentions beforehand, rather than occupy yourself with investigations that permeate our relationship with a spirit of strife and enmity. Sometime in the future I shall relate to you how I strove against your art and I hope that you will extol my contriving spirit, my dexterity and ingenuity."

The young woman grew silent, encouraged by the address she had delivered, and darting a glance at the men, a shade of crimson unwillingly passed through her cheeks; a current of delight and appeasement filled up her heart. The two friends exchanged furtive glances, and it seemed that, in another second, they would begin to smile.

"It is quite a different task to fathom a woman's heart and soul," at last spoke up Watson, with a nonchalant shrug of his shoulders.

"And a hopeless one!" concluded Sherlock Holmes, as he pressed heartily the hand of the doctor.

Tha Grate Fur Koat Mistery

Albert J. Bromley

Some styles of popular humor were products of their time. Such is the case with dialect humor. After the Civil War, when immigration brought together peoples who all sounded funny to each other, humorists such as Petroleum V. Nasby, Mark Twain, and Finley Peter Dunne told stories in broad accents. Another such humorist was Albert J. Bromley (died 1948), who was a well-known contributor to the Chicago Tribune. *He published two collections,* Snowshoe Al's Bed Time Storries (and Uther Times) *(1926) and* Tha Return uv Snowshoe Al *(1927).*

Rex Homes, tha famus detektiff, sat at his desk cuttin' out paper dolls. Doctor Hotbun, his boozum frend an' kumpanion, sat neer him oiling a slingshot. A nock kaim at tha door.

"Let him in, Hotbun," sed Homes, as he rolled up his sleeve an' shot a pint uv Tanlac[1] inter his forearm.

"How do yew know it's a 'he'?" sed Hotbun, startin' fer tha door.

"Because," sed Homes, "I kin smell likker frum here."

"Wunderfil" exklaimed Hotbun, throwing wide tha door. A beeootifil yung lady entered.

"O, sir—" she begun.

"Say no more, yew are in trouble!" sed Homes.

"How do yew know?" sed she, bewilderdly.

"Because," sed Homes, "yew have a black eye."

"Marvillous!" yelled Hotbun.

"Fer tha past 2 weeks," sed tha yung lady, "I have bin going with a handsum yung fella—"

"Send it in tuh Doris Blake,"[2] sed Homes, as he jammed a

---

[1] Patent medicine sold as a stomach remedy and "system purifier." A mix of wine, glycerin, and bitter herbs, it's 15.7 percent alcohol packed a punch.

[2] Before Dear Abby, there was Doris Blake, who dispensed advice to the lovelorn, along with beauty tips and weight-loss advice, in the *New York Daily News* and 44 other newspapers. In reality, Blake was Antoinette

ounce uv opium inter his pipe an' lit it with a blow-torch.

"Well, enyhow," sed tha beeootiful yung lady, "about 2 hours ago he wuz lookin' at my fur koat—"

"Yew are a waitress!" exklainied Homes.

"Wunderfil! Marvillous!" howled Hotbun.

"And," kontimied tha fair visiter, "all at wunce he batted me in tha eye, wrapped sumthin' up in a bundle an' disapeered. Wen I looked fer my fur koat it wuz gone."

Homes paced tha floor fer several minits. Then, rollin' up his sleeve, he shot a quart uv Kastoria[1] inter his wrist an' sed with a air uv finality:

"Tha yung man took yer koat!"

"Marvillous! Wunderfil!" exklaimed Hotbun.

They went ter tha neerest pawn shop an' recovered tha koat. Tha Uncle[2] told them it wuz brot in about a hour before.

"He has took a train an' left town!" sed Homes. "We will wire all tha neerby sities tuh—er—uh—by tha way, wot wuz tha yung man's occupaishun?"

"He wuz a poet," sed tha beeootifil yung lady.

"Whyinell didn't yuh say so?" sed Homes. So he went ter tha neerest resturant an' got his man.[3]

Donnelly (1887-1964) who also wrote one of the first diet books, *How to Reduce: New Waistlines for Old* (1920). A Life magazine profile in 1941 described her as "a frowsy, gentle, jittery, earnest and overworked Irish-American woman of some 50 years who takes care of her responsibilities as an adviser of youth quite seriously and believes that woman's best place is where she, Antoinette, spends least of her time, i.e., in the home."

[1] Fletcher's Castoria, a laxative marketed for children. It was created by Dr. Samuel Pitcher (1824-1907) and sold as Pitcher's Castoria. It was changed to its new name when in 1871 Charles Fletcher (1837-1922) bought the rights to the formula. Castoria was one of the first products sold through mass advertising from the 1870s through the 1920s.

[2] Slang word for pawnbroker, presumably because a relation would be the most likely person to loan you money. They were also called in Britain "father's brother" or an "avuncular relation." An especially prosperous pawnbroker could be called a "big uncle" or small-time business owner a "wee uncle."

[3] Poets were particularly poor so it would make sense the first thing he would do was fill his belly. They don't call them starving artists for nothing!

1927

This year Sherlock Holmes closed out his career, as far as Conan Doyle was concerned. There was story #59, "The Veiled Lodger," that appeared first in the American Liberty *magazine in February, and #60, "Shoscombe Old Place" in April. In June,* The Case-Book of Sherlock Holmes *gathered the final dozen stories. Breaking with tradition, Conan Doyle contributed a brief forward that conveyed in gentlemanly prose his distaste for his immortal creation:*

"I've written a good deal more about him than I ever intended to do, but my hand has been rather forced by kind friends who continually wanted to know more. And so it is that this monstrous growth has come out, out of what was really a comparatively small seed."

To a doctor's ear, the phrase "monstrous growth" makes Holmes sound like a tumor.

As if to stamp 'finis' on Holmes' remarkable career, Conan Doyle agreed to pick the top dozen stories for The Strand, and award a prize to the reader who guessed correctly. After consciously rereading all of the stories — a tedious task, he found — he set to work. First, he dropped the last dozen stories as less familiar to readers — he would have picked "The Lion's Mane" and "The Illustrious Client" otherwise. He boiled the top six down to "The Speckled Band," "The Red-Headed League," "The Dancing Men," "The Final Problem," "A Scandal in Bohemia," and "The Empty House." After much consideration, he rounded out the list with "The Five Orange Pips," "The Second Stain," "The Devil's Foot," "The Priory School," "The Musgrave Ritual," and "The Reigate Squires."

He submitted his list to The Strand with a memo explaining his decision, and that was the last word from him about Holmes.

In the meantime, there were spiritualism matters to attend to. In March appeared Pheneas Speaks, a collection of messages received through Jean Conan Doyle's automatic writing. Alongside the apocalyptic warnings from Pheneas — an Arabian who lived in Ur before the time of Abraham — there were comments from other spirits, including Conan Doyle's son, Kingsley, and even an editor of The Times of London, who died in 1879. He reported that in the afterlife, there was no need for editors or newspapers: "We know everything. It is like wireless in the air."

Meanwhile, the climax in the Oscar Slater case was reached in July. Through Conan Doyle's Psychic Press, a Glasgow journalist by the name of William Park published The Truth About Oscar Slater. The book rehashed the points Conan Doyle made in 1912, but also revealed that the paid companion to the elderly murder victim had been pressured by police to identify Slater. In the coming months, more stories showed that the police deliberately framed Slater for Marion Gilchrist's murder. Five days later, the secretary of state for Scotland ordered his release. After 18 years in prison, Slater was a free man.

But Conan Doyle's satisfaction was short-lived. After he was found not guilty in a new trial, Slater received £6,000 in compensation. Conan Doyle expected Slater to pay back his supporters who supplied the money for a new trial. Conan Doyle alone contributed a thousand pounds. Slater saw otherwise. Conan Doyle thought Slater acted dishonorably and told him so. When Slater died in 1948, the local newspaper identified him as "Reprieved Murderer, Friend of A. Conan Doyle."

Publications: Holmes in Liberty: "The Adventure of the Veiled Lodger" (Jan.); "The Adventure of Shoscombe Old Place" (March). The Case-Book of Sherlock Holmes (June). **Other:** Pheneas Speaks (March).

Conan Doyle attacked the case against Oscar Slater in newspaper articles such as this one.

The Return of Donan Coyle

"Sugatel"

Nothing is known of the author of this parody that appeared in the March 18 edition of the Bellshill Speaker. *The newspaper was published in a small mining town in Lanarkshire, a county in the central Lowlands of Scotland.*

Heddlock Phones, the great detective, was sitting by the fire in his chambers, clad in a draggled and ash-stained dressing-gown, puffing great clouds of acrid smoke from a huge pipe. By his manner, his friend, Dr. Swotson, who was reading a newspaper at the other side of the hearth, knew that no case in particular was occupying his thoughts, but that the mighty brain behind the high forehead was merely seeking something worthy of its attention. At last, it found it.

"The bane and vice of this age, my dear Swotson," remarked Phones, "is the amount of superfluous verbiage it produces. It says too much. Nothing is left to the imagination; and naturally, the imagination suffers."

"What makes you think so?" asked Swotson, ever eager to catch at the gleams of wisdom the great master of deduction was wont to send forth.

"Well," said Phones, "take the newspaper as a typical example. The specimen of that strange product of our age which you have just lowered to your knee affords a good illustration. Even at this distance I can read one of the head-lines—

A Private Still

"Below it there seems to be about thirty lines of ordinary letter-press. Superfluous, my dear Swotson! Quite unnecessary! Even a man with your alleged scientific training can see what I mean. The expanded account is merely a pandering to laziness. It is a waste of time, energy, ink and paper. If only head-lines were printed, consider what a saving it would be. The head-line, correctly chosen, tells all that need be told.

"Take the one in question. A reporter has evidently come across one of these stories of disappointed ambition which abound so much in pathos, and teach us to be thankful for what few of our aspirations we have attained.

"I can picture the whole tragedy. Twenty years ago, a young fellow in the bloom of youth, and with the enthusiasms and aspirations of his years, joined an infantry regiment of the line.[1] He had heard that will and ability were bound to go far; and, if even in his wilder dreams he did not dwell too much on the possibility of his having a marshal's baton in his knapsack,[2] he at least looked forward to the day when he might retire from His Majesty's service with a high non-commissioned rank — a splendid example of the type to whom callow subalterns[3] cry with relief, 'Carry on, Sergeant-Major.'

"But he discovered that promotion in peace time is slow and anything but sure. In war, his regiment was always drafted away from the seat of operations, or arrived too late to let its members vindicate their worth.

"Our private was consistently unlucky. If he was ill, the doctor could find nothing wrong with him, and reported him

---

[1] A type of infantry that was organized into two to four ranks of soldiers. This formation maximized the unit's firepower, and distinguished it from infantry units such as skirmishers, militia, light infantry and foot guards. Although technological advances such as machine guns made line tactics obsolete by the end of the 19th century, many regiments retained their line infantry designation.

[2] A reference to Napoleon's maxim that "every French soldier carries a marshal's baton in his knapsack." Instead of an army ruled by aristocratic officers — marshals were generals who received a baton for meritorious service — Napoleon favored promoting soldiers from the lower ranks who showed promise.

[3] A junior officer in the British Army. They were the equivalent of second lieutenants in the U.S. Army. Because they were young men of little practical experience, the smarter ones relied on the sergeant-major — the highest rank a soldier could reach without becoming an officer — to guide their decisions.

for malingering. If he had one over the eight[1] to celebrate a comrade's marriage, death, or accession to the rank of fatherhood, someone in authority was bound to see him.

"On parade, his was the tunic which refused to sit straight, his the buttons that refused to shine, his the rifle barrel in which the floating speck of dust persisted in alighting.

"His honesty was put down as hypocrisy, his human weaknesses as vice. Thus, after a score of weary years of striving, he found himself the possessor of an undistinguished discharge — a disillusioned man, and 'a private still.'"

"Ye—es," said Swotson, rather doubtfully, "but—"

"Now tell me," interrupted Phones, "am I not right, and have I not made a better job of the account than the reporter fellow?"

"Perhaps," answered Swotson, "perhaps. But you see, Phones, the paragraph you refer to is the account of a case of shebeening.[2] The man was selling proof spirit at three-and-six a bottle.[3] The fine was one hundred guineas."

---

[1] British military slang for being drunk, based on the assumption that a man can drink eight glasses of beer. Recorded as early as 1925, this implies that beer was weaker than it is now.
[2] Operating an illicit bar where untaxed alcohol was sold. The word is from the Irish *sibin*, meaning "illicit whiskey." This may also have been the source of the word "shebang" as in the idiom "the whole shebang."
[3] Under the old coinage, a bottle was sold for three shillings and six pence. A guinea is a coin worth one pound plus one shilling (or 21 shillings). The name was derived from the Guinea region in West Africa, where the gold was mined. Its value fluctuated between 20 and 30 shillings until it was fixed at 21 shillings in 1816. While the coin was replaced by the paper pound note that year, guineas continued to circulate. The fine of 100 guineas, or £105, would be worth in 2018 about £6,000 ($7,600).

The Velvet Blotting Clue

Anonymous

Illustrated by Eric Fraser

As we've seen in previous volumes, Holmes was used to sell safes, razor blades and dubious medical treatments. This example is unique in that it told a story, spread over four pages in the May 11 issue of Punch, *with illustrations by Eric Fraser, with the solution requiring the reader to hold the last page up to the light! The advertiser, Robert Craig and Sons, was a Scottish paper manufacturer that was incorporated in 1898. Its 800 to 900 employees turned out a variety of colored papers. It also specialized in blotting paper. Sold in pads, it was placed on desks and tables and used to absorb excess ink before it could stain the top. Because it could receive the impression of a pen or pencil, it was a trope in mysteries stories for the detective to examine blotting paper to see if a clue had been impressed into it.*

Illustrator Eric Fraser (1902-1983) was noted for designing the dust jackets for the Everyman's Library series in the 1960s and the Folio Society edition of J.R.R. Tolkien's The Lord of the Rings *(1977).*

"Mr. Holmes!" cried the elderly lady who had burst so unceremoniously into our little flat in Baker Street, "he's gone — vanished! Oh, what shall I do? I knew they would, and now they have!"

With a gesture of admirably concealed ennui, Holmes motioned me to provide a chair. Then he bent on her the penetrating gaze that has probed to the heart of so many a tragic mystery.

"I presume, madam," he said at length, "that you refer to Professor Wilfred Bulkeley, the eminent Egyptologist. You are Mrs Bulkeley, of 19 Cranford Gardens, West Kensington."

I drew in a sharp breath of astonishment. This was incredible! Was there nothing he did not know?

"I had the honour," Holmes continued inexorably, "of dining at your house last Tuesday. I never forget my hosts. Professor Bulkeley, then, has vanished. Excel!— too bad, I mean,

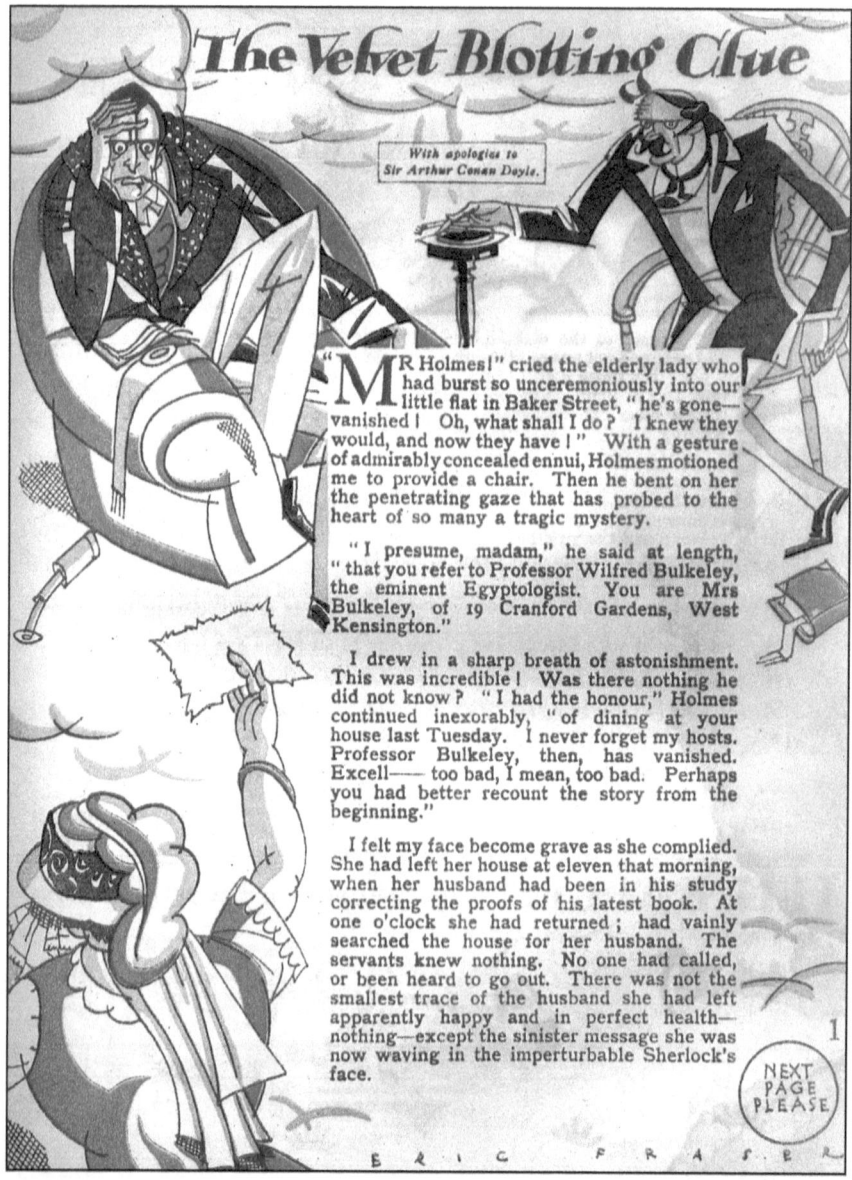

The Velvet Blotting Clue

With apologies to Sir Arthur Conan Doyle.

"MR Holmes!" cried the elderly lady who had burst so unceremoniously into our little flat in Baker Street, "he's gone—vanished! Oh, what shall I do? I knew they would, and now they have!" With a gesture of admirably concealed ennui, Holmes motioned me to provide a chair. Then he bent on her the penetrating gaze that has probed to the heart of so many a tragic mystery.

"I presume, madam," he said at length, "that you refer to Professor Wilfred Bulkeley, the eminent Egyptologist. You are Mrs Bulkeley, of 19 Cranford Gardens, West Kensington."

I drew in a sharp breath of astonishment. This was incredible! Was there nothing he did not know? "I had the honour," Holmes continued inexorably, "of dining at your house last Tuesday. I never forget my hosts. Professor Bulkeley, then, has vanished. Excell—— too bad, I mean, too bad. Perhaps you had better recount the story from the beginning."

I felt my face become grave as she complied. She had left her house at eleven that morning, when her husband had been in his study correcting the proofs of his latest book. At one o'clock she had returned; had vainly searched the house for her husband. The servants knew nothing. No one had called, or been heard to go out. There was not the smallest trace of the husband she had left apparently happy and in perfect health—nothing—except the sinister message she was now waving in the imperturbable Sherlock's face.

NEXT PAGE PLEASE

1

too bad. Perhaps you had better recount the story from the beginning."

I felt my face become grave as she complied. She had left her house at eleven that morning, when her husband had been in his study correcting the proofs of his latest book. At

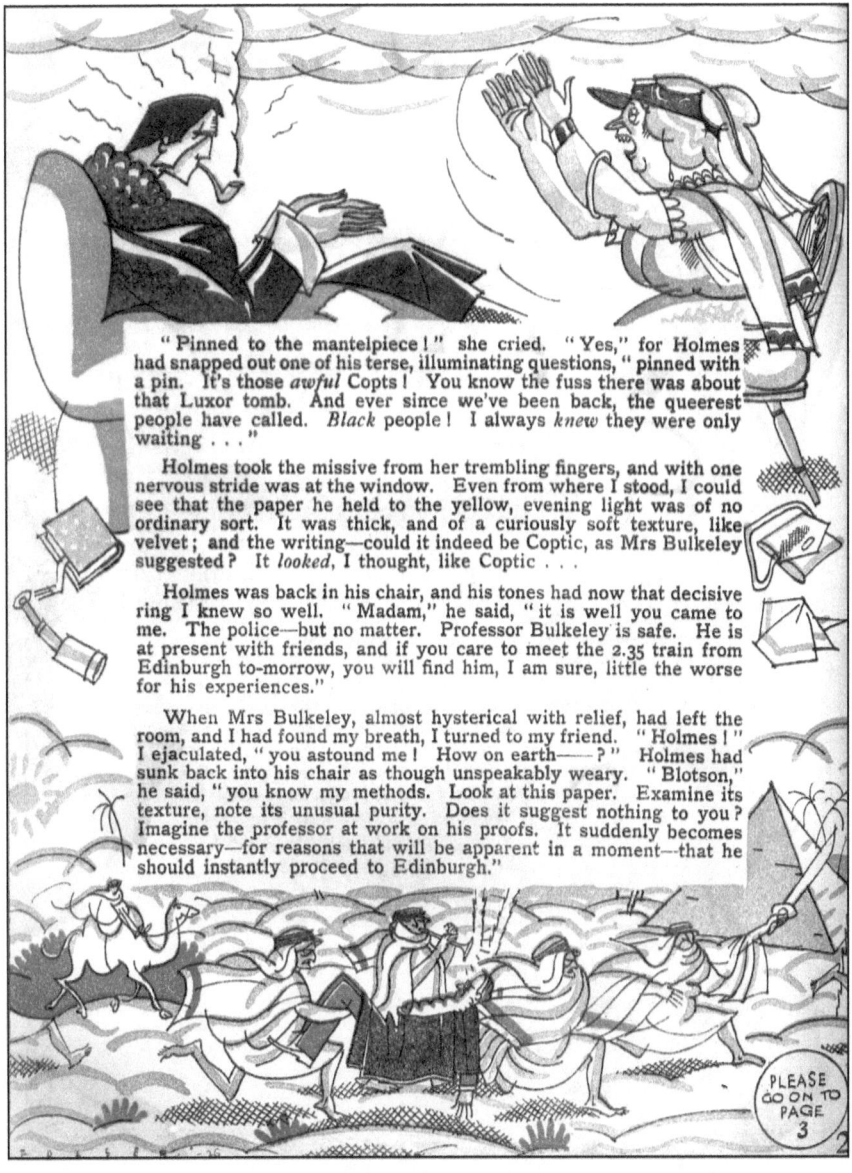

"Pinned to the mantelpiece!" she cried. "Yes," for Holmes had snapped out one of his terse, illuminating questions, "pinned with a pin. It's those *awful* Copts! You know the fuss there was about that Luxor tomb. And ever since we've been back, the queerest people have called. *Black* people! I always *knew* they were only waiting . . ."

Holmes took the missive from her trembling fingers, and with one nervous stride was at the window. Even from where I stood, I could see that the paper he held to the yellow, evening light was of no ordinary sort. It was thick, and of a curiously soft texture, like velvet; and the writing—could it indeed be Coptic, as Mrs Bulkeley suggested? It *looked*, I thought, like Coptic . . .

Holmes was back in his chair, and his tones had now that decisive ring I knew so well. "Madam," he said, "it is well you came to me. The police—but no matter. Professor Bulkeley is safe. He is at present with friends, and if you care to meet the 2.35 train from Edinburgh to-morrow, you will find him, I am sure, little the worse for his experiences."

When Mrs Bulkeley, almost hysterical with relief, had left the room, and I had found my breath, I turned to my friend. "Holmes!" I ejaculated, "you astound me! How on earth——?" Holmes had sunk back into his chair as though unspeakably weary. "Blotson," he said, "you know my methods. Look at this paper. Examine its texture, note its unusual purity. Does it suggest nothing to you? Imagine the professor at work on his proofs. It suddenly becomes necessary—for reasons that will be apparent in a moment—that he should instantly proceed to Edinburgh."

PLEASE GO ON TO PAGE 3

one o'clock she had returned; had vainly searched the house for her husband. The servants knew nothing. No one had called, or been heard to go out. There was not the smallest trace of the husband she had left apparently happy and in perfect health — nothing —except the sinister message she was now waving in the imperturbable Sherlock's face.

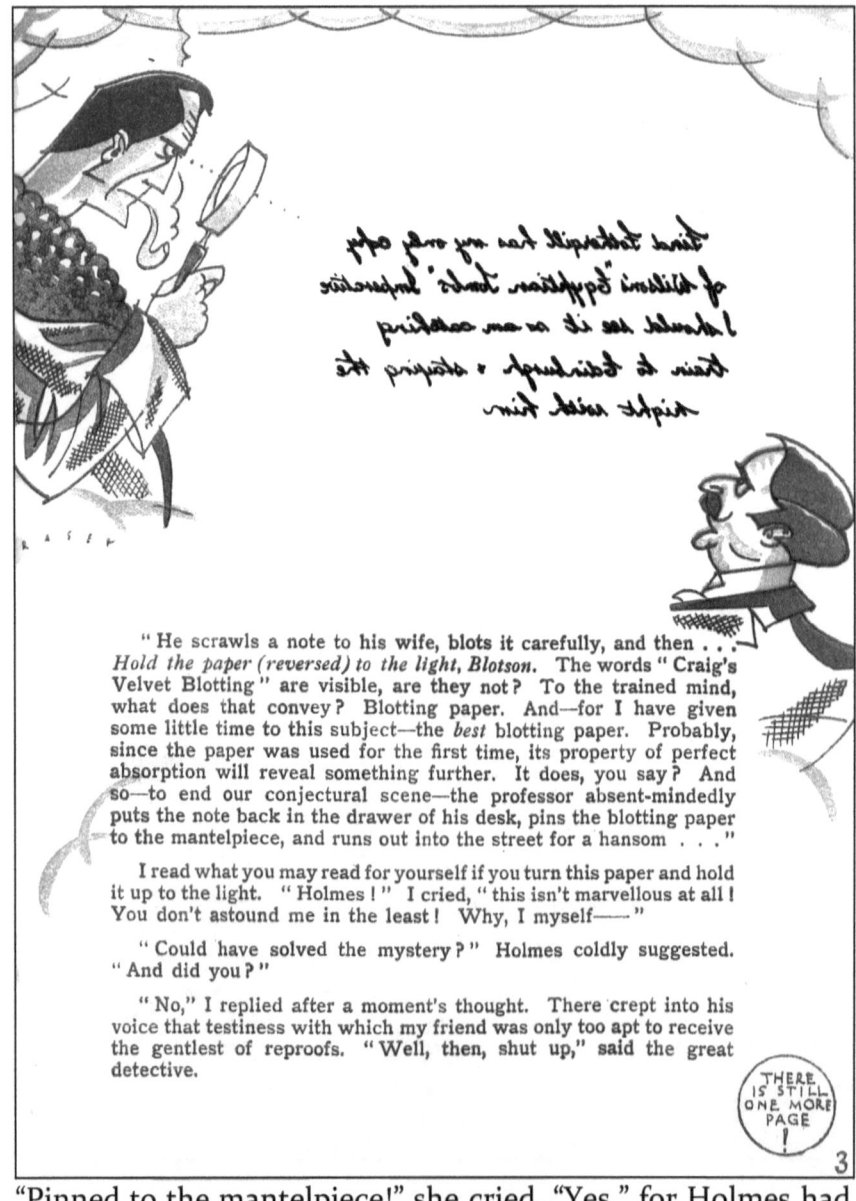

"He scrawls a note to his wife, blots it carefully, and then . . . *Hold the paper (reversed) to the light, Blotson.* The words "Craig's Velvet Blotting" are visible, are they not? To the trained mind, what does that convey? Blotting paper. And—for I have given some little time to this subject—the *best* blotting paper. Probably, since the paper was used for the first time, its property of perfect absorption will reveal something further. It does, you say? And so—to end our conjectural scene—the professor absent-mindedly puts the note back in the drawer of his desk, pins the blotting paper to the mantelpiece, and runs out into the street for a hansom . . ."

I read what you may read for yourself if you turn this paper and hold it up to the light. "Holmes!" I cried, "this isn't marvellous at all! You don't astound me in the least! Why, I myself——"

"Could have solved the mystery?" Holmes coldly suggested. "And did you?"

"No," I replied after a moment's thought. There crept into his voice that testiness with which my friend was only too apt to receive the gentlest of reproofs. "Well, then, shut up," said the great detective.

"Pinned to the mantelpiece!" she cried. "Yes," for Holmes had snapped out one of his terse, illuminating questions, "pinned with a pin. It's those *awful* Copts![1] You know the fuss there

---

[1] An ethnic Christian group indigenous to northeast Africa, including Egypt, Sudan, and Libya.

was about that Luxor tomb.[1] And ever since we've been back, the queerest people have called. *Black* people! I always *knew* they were only waiting ..."

Holmes took the missive from her trembling fingers, and with one nervous stride was at the window. Even from where I stood, I could see that the paper he held to the yellow, evening light was of no ordinary sort. It was thick, and of a curiously soft texture, like velvet; and the writing—could it indeed be Coptic, as Mrs Bulkeley suggested? It *looked*, I thought, like Coptic ...

Holmes was back in his chair, and his tones had now that decisive ring I knew so well. "Madam," he said, "it is well you came to me. The police — but no matter. Professor Bulkeley is safe. He is at present with friends, and if you care to meet the 2.35 train from Edinburgh to-morrow, you will find him, I am sure, little the worse for his experiences."

When Mrs Bulkeley, almost hysterical with relief, had left the room, and I had found my breath, I turned to my friend.

---

[1] Luxor is a city of a half-million people in southern Egypt. It is the site of numerous temple complexes. Near the city is the Valley of the Kings, the home of many tombs from the 16th to the 11th century B.C.. One of the most famous discoveries was in 1922 when the tomb of Tutankhamen (c.1341-c.1323 B.C.) was opened.

"Holmes!" I ejaculated, "you astound me! How on earth—?"

Holmes had sunk back into his chair as though unspeakably weary.

"Blotson," he said, "you know my methods. Look at this paper. Examine its texture, note its unusual purity. Does it suggest nothing to you? Imagine the professor at work on his proofs. It suddenly becomes necessary — for reasons that will be apparent in a moment — that he should instantly proceed to Edinburgh."

"He scrawls a note to his wife, blots it carefully, and then . . . *Hold the paper (reversed) to the light, Blotson*. The words "Craig's Velvet Blotting" are visible, are they not? To the trained mind, what does that convey? Blotting paper. And — for I have given some little time to this subject — the best blotting paper. Probably, since the paper was used for the first time, its property of perfect absorption will reveal something further. It does, you say? And so — to end our conjectural scene — the professor absent-mindedly puts the note back in the drawer of his desk, pins the blotting paper to the mantelpiece, and runs out into the street for a hansom ..."

> Find Fothergill has my only copy of Wilson's "Egyptian Tombs" Imperative I should see it so am catching train to Edinburgh + staying the night with him

I read what you may read for yourself if you turn this paper and hold it up to the light.

"Holmes!" I cried, "this isn't marvellous at all! You don't

astound me in the least! Why, I myself—"

"Could have solved the mystery?" Holmes coldly suggested. "And did you?"

"No," I replied after a moment's thought.

There crept into his voice that testiness with which my friend was only too apt to receive the gentlest of reproofs. "Well, then, shut up," said the great detective.

Hold this paper up to the light again. Did you notice the watermark — CRAIG'S VELVET BLOTTING? Make a note of it in your memory. After all, you would rather use good blotting paper than bad. Anyone would. If the blotting paper you buy is sometimes poor in quality — seems to be sold as blotting paper only because it does blot paper, instead of drinking ink — that is because you have never been given this very simple piece of advice. When you are buying blotting paper, hold a sheet of it up to the light —exactly as, just now, you were holding this. Either you see the words ROB. CRAIG & SONS' VELVET BLOTTING — and all is well; or you don't — and the stuff may prove to be good, indifferent or downright bad. Don't be content to pay your money and take your chance — with the odds against you. That's not good enough. Look for the water-mark that distinguishes perfect blotting paper from every other kind.

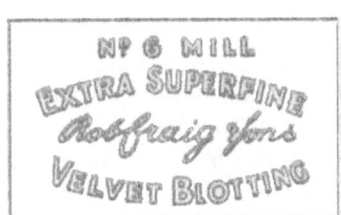

The Commencement Mystery

"G.S."

This story from June 1 issue of the Yale Record *humor magazine pokes fun at several local New Haven institutions, including the campus laundrywoman and a notable professor of literature.*

"Watson, my dear fellow," said Holmes, "send down to P. Rings[1] for some more cocaine; I am terribly bored with New Haven — Ah, good morning, Lestrade. Will you kindly explain your cablegram which has brought Watson and myself all the way from London to this wretched hole?"

"Why the fact is, Mr. Holmes," replied the Inspector, "there's been a bad business in these parts. Professor Phillips has disappeared on the eve of Commencement exercises, and we and the New Haven police can make nothing out of it. The President of the University himself requested that you be set upon the case immediately. The ladies of the Browning Club are on the verge of hysteria."[2]

"Are there no clues, Lestrade?"

"One only, Mr. Holmes. The janitor of the building in which Mr. Phillips holds his classes, an elderly person who introduced himself as the Lampson Professor of Light and Heat,[3] states he saw the unfortunate professor on the day of

---

[1] A jab involving a local store of some kind, mostly likely a druggist. An examination of city directories and Yale publications turned up only one hit: A comic poem in the *Yale Daily News* of 1929 about the drunk at dawn walking the streets of New Haven, "stops to hear the clocks a-tinkling / And the soapy Steam and sings, / Stops to see the faces twinkling / Into Smoke Shops and P. Rings".

[2] The poet Robert Browning (1812-1889) inspired cult-like devotion among readers, with clubs forming in the U.S. and Great Britain. The Boston club could count on the cream of literary society to attend. One meeting in 1891 was attended by Julia Ward Howe, Sarah Orne Jewett, William Howells, and Thomas Wentworth Higginson.

[3] The building's janitor would be responsible for heating and lighting the building. He also shares a similar name to William Lyon Phelps (1865-

his disappearance. Mr. Phillips, he reports, seemed slightly perturbed and was muttering to himself, 'God's in his heaven, all's right with the world', as though by way of self-assurance.[1] Beyond this we know nothing."

"Well, well," chuckled Holmes, rubbing his hands, "this is indeed a mystery worthy of our attention. Let us hasten forth, Watson."

As we were proceeding across the campus, an aged crone came limping up to us, propelling a large cart filled with laundry. Holmes nodded amiably to her, and she responded.

"Ah, God's blessin' on ye, sonny! Where do yer send yer laundry?"

"Don't mind her, Holmes," said Lestrade. "That's only God Bless You Mary."[2]

1943), who at the time was Lampson Professor of English Literature at Yale. Yale established the Lampson Professorship after bank president William Lampson (d. 1897) left his estate of $750,000 to his alma mater. Lampson inherited a fortune in real estate from his father, kept largely to himself, and spent nearly his entire life in Troy, N.Y. The bequest made national news, not only for its size, but because his aunt tried to break the will in court, claiming Lampson wasn't in his right mind when he made the will a few months before his death.

William Lyon Phelps was a popular advocate for literature. He was a literary scholar who championed Jane Austen, Mark Twain, and William Thackeray. He wrote a daily newspaper column, spoke on the radio, traveled the lecture circuit and wrote many books. But not everyone appreciated his wisdom. Reviewing his book *Happiness* (1927), in which he postulated that "The happiest people are those who think the most interesting thoughts," critic Dorothy Parker commented, "Promptly one starts recalling such Happiness Boys as Nietzsche, Socrates, de Maupassant, Jean-Jacques Rousseau, William Blake, and Poe."

[1] An oft-quoted line from Robert Browning's verse drama *Pippa Passes* (1841). Despite the sweetness of the passage — "The year's at the spring, / And day's at the morn; / Morning's at seven; / The hill-side's dew-pearled; / The lark's on the wing; / The snail's on the thorn; / God's in his heaven— / All's right with the world!" — the poem's intimations of regicide and frankness in sexual matters drew criticism and demands that he remove the offending passages. The poem is also amusingly notorious for misusing the vulgar word "twat," which Browning thought was part of a nun's habit.

[2] A campus character, "God Bless You Mary" was Mary Garrison, a laun-

Holmes, however, did not seem convinced.

"Watson," he whispered, his voice vibrating with excitement, "don't you recognize the steely glint of those eyes? — you don't? Well, never mind. We'll follow the old dame."

Our quest took us through some of the dingiest slums of New Haven. Finally we came out upon the harbour and observed our quarry making for the end of the docks, as though intending to wash her laundry there.

"Quick, Watson!" shouted Holmes. "There is no time to lose!" And with that he hastened up to the laundress and confronted her with his revolver.

"Lestrade," said he, "allow me to present to you Colonel Sebastian Moran, one of the most dangerous criminals in the world. And now, Watson, examine the laundry basket."

I did as he directed. What was my amazement to find beneath a pile of B.V.D.'s[1] the unconscious form of Professor Phillips, with a chloroform sponge attached to his face. With the aid of Holmes' brandy flask we quickly revived him.

"We arrived not a moment too soon, Mr. Phillips," Holmes said. "In another minute, you would have been at the bottom of the harbour. As it is, however, you have just time to get to your lecture at the Baptist Ladies' Union. Watson, I think I'll trouble you to get me that cocaine at P. Ring's."

---

dress who spent 45 years traveling the campus with a baby carriage, collecting and washing the undergraduates' clothes. She retired in 1929 and returned to her native England, where she died less than a month later.

[1] A brand of men's underwear, named for Bradley, Voorhees and Day, who founded the company in 1876. BVD began making bustles for women, then expanded in men's union suits. In 1908, the company introduced a loose-fitting underwear which became known as BVDs.

The End of Sherlock Holmes

"A.E.P."

It's rare to see Holmes bested at his own game, much less by someone who shares his genes! But this is not the only instance of writers who created progeny for Holmes. John Kendrick Bangs created Raffles Holmes, the product of a marriage between the great detective and the daughter of the great cat burglar. The 1910-1914 volume contains an example of Sidney Smith's Sherlock Holmes Jr.

This brief story appeared in the July 7 issue of the Manchester Guardian, *and a month later in* The Living Age *in America. The identity of "A.E.P." is unknown.*

[The following account of the real reason for Holmes's retirement was found among Dr. Watson's private papers after his death. It is not dated, but from internal evidence (noticeably the mention of ladies' hat pins) it may be placed about 1903-1905.]

It was my intention to close these memoirs with the remarkable chain of circumstances resulting in the marriage of my friend Sherlock Holmes with Miss Falkland. For some time after that event my friend gave up professional work and went abroad with his wife. Our rooms in Baker Street were of course destroyed, and my practice occupied my full time, and certainly prospered all the better for receiving my undivided attention. From time to time, however, he would be recalled to my memory by some startling and unexplained case claiming my attention in the morning's paper; and in the "unforeseen circumstances" and "unexpected turn of events" or remarkable instances of fresh light being thrown on some obscure point would recognize my friend's unparalleled genius, though, with characteristic modesty, his name never appeared.

For instance, there was the remarkable case of the Hereditary Princess of Sthoit-Leinengen,[1] which culminated in a

---

[1] The first question is: Does Sthoit-Leinengen exist? Indeed it does, although the correct spelling is Leiningen. "Sthoit" doesn't mean anything and was probably chosen because it sounds amusing.

royal divorce; and the still more recent affair of the Grand-Nurse-in-Waiting's tame monkey, which made such a stir and resulted in the suicide of a Russian Consul. It was when public excitement was at its height over the great Bribery Case in connection with the Pope's birthday celebrations, and suspicion had settled on a well-known workhouse official, that I again received intimation that Holmes was in England.

I had just come in from a long round when the maidservant brought in a note whose appearance struck me at once as familiar. As I tore it open I mechanically noticed that it was written on cream-laid paper, with a printed address, and that the stamp was in the right-hand top corner of the envelope. This lapse into long-forgotten habit made me think of Holmes, and I was not surprised to recognize his signature at the foot of the sheet.

"Dear Watson," it ran: "Can you come round to the old place at 3 P.M. to-morrow? Yours, S. H."

I hastily scribbled an acceptance, and the following day, having turned over my practice to my assistant and locked the dispensary door[1] for fear of accidents, I hailed a "City Atlas"[2] and soon found myself en route for Baker Street. (Holmes had taken rooms just above our former locality.)

The presence of a Leiningen in this story might be a nod to the royal family. In 1803, the seventeen-year-old Princess Victoria of Saxe-Coburg-Saalfeld was married off to Emich Carl, the Hereditary Prince of Leiningen (1763-1814). It was an unhappy marriage. Emich was 28 years older and was possessed of a bad temper. But she bore him two children and after his death in 1814, married the son of King George III, Prince Edward (1767-1820). They had one child, a daughter who they named after mom. This child, Princess Alexandrina Victoria of Kent, would grow up to become Queen Victoria (1819-1901).

[1] The dispensary is where prescription drugs and medical supplies are kept.

[2] The name of dark-green horse-drawn omnibuses, one of 200 lines that crisscrossed the city. An 1875 *London Guide* noted that one ran between St. John's Wood and London Bridge every 20 minutes from 8:15 a.m. to 11:25 p.m., with a stop at Baker Street. It was named for the Titan—a member of a race of deities—in Greek mythology who was condemned to support the celestial heavens for eternity.

The door was opened by a tired-looking maid. I entered, and encountered the gaze of a child about three years of age. He was wearing a miniature dressing gown, and had just been taking an impression of the cat's foot in a piece of dough.

Before I had time to speak he had crawled rapidly and noiselessly up the stairs and announced me: "Pa, there's a man to see you."

"Who is it?" answered Holmes's voice, and I was struck by the weariness of his tone.

"He's a doctor, poor, and he's got a wife, but she is away. He came up in the omnibus, it was very full, a lady got in too, but he didn't get up to let her have his seat, same as he ought to," said this remarkable child.

I entered in response to Holmes's invitation. The apartment was thick with tobacco smoke and Holmes was listlessly repairing a string in his violin. He held out his hand with something of his old heartiness, but there was a tired look in his eyes I did not like.

"Ah, Watson, I'm glad to see you again." Then, following the direction of my glance, "This is my son — Sherlock, come and say 'How do you do?' to the gentleman."

"He's quite well, he did have a cold, but that is quite well too, and he didn't put nothin' in the bag las' Sunday," finished this remarkable infant. I turned to Holmes in amazement. "But how on earth —"

"Oh, *he* knows," said my friend rather bitterly; "there isn't much he can't see. But it is your professional assistance I want you for now." Holmes was not the man to take such a step lightly, and my gravest fears were aroused. I glanced keenly at him. His eyes were closed, his temperature was normal, but the pulse was beating in quick irregular jerks, and symptoms pointed to a slight cerebral congestion; an application of the stethoscope showed me at a glance his nerves were all to pieces. He languidly turned up his sleeve.

"No," I said firmly, laying my hand upon a small hypodermic syringe he had taken from a pocket of his dressing gown, "I cannot allow any more morphia; you only need rest and a complete change."

"Heaven knows you're right, Watson, my dear fellow, but how the deuce am I to get it? Can you tell me that?"

I felt that here was something more than appeared on the surface.

"What is it that prevents you — not Moriarty again?"

Holmes looked at me in something of his old manner. "Watson, Watson, when shall I teach you to eliminate the obviously impossible? We have already twice disposed of Moriarty — once in the *Strand*, and again at the Lyceum;[1] you will remember the circumstances very well." He sighed. "No, it is not Moriarty."

His eyes wandered to his son, who was scraping the sole of a shoe and examining the matter so obtained by the aid of a powerful lens. "It *was* Martha that meddled with my specimens, and she said it was the cat," the infant announced conclusively. His face darkened, and he crawled off after the offending Martha.

Holmes turned to me. "What do you make of it, Watson?"

I hesitated. "It is evident he has your talents; it must be very gratifying."

"Watson, it is killing me. All day long and every hour of the day he is at it. My wife has broken down — nervous system entirely shattered; no one will visit us; we can't keep a servant — they won't put up with it."

"Surely," I said, "it is not so bad as that; he is only a baby —"

Holmes smiled bitterly. "He contrives to do a good deal in his way. He told the Dean's wife her husband had been married before, and that her diamonds were not real. He took the opportunity of announcing at an At Home[2] that Sir Ronald's

---

[1] The London theatre founded in 1834 where the play *Sherlock Holmes* was running. A lyceum is the Latin word for the Greek *lykeion*, a training facility dedicated to the god Apollo.

[2] A social occasion in which a hostess opens her home to visitors. Depending on the year and the neighborhood, the frequency could range from

grandfather was a tailor in Stepney,[1] that he made his money in patent pills,[2] and that he was afraid of his valet. He took an impression in wax of the vicar's thumb and subsequently told him that his sermons were not his own, that he had some money on Daystar at the St. Leger,[3] that his niece was a sempstress,[4] and that his brother-in-law was doing time for forgery. He tracked the area policeman for over three weeks to find out where he went when he was off duty — and he told the tax collector his back teeth were false. You have seen for yourself he is after Martha now. She'll give notice next."

"Why don't you keep him in the nursery?"

"They can't. He outwits them in every possible way. No, there is only one thing to be done: I must take on the job myself. Watson, Watson, if you are a truthful person you will faithfully recount this in the memoirs you are giving to the public. I who have baffled Moriarty, I who have had a hand in unravelling most of the mysteries that have perplexed Europe, with knowledge enough of the seamy side of courts and the back doors of politics to bring about a European war — I am now compelled to turn all my energies to circumventing my own son; and, Watson, it is killing me."

He plunged his hands deep in his dressing-gown pockets, and his chin fell on his breast.

I crept out softly and closed the door.

---

several times during the season to one afternoon every week. Lunch or tea may be served. In any event, strict rules of etiquette must be followed.

[1] An impoverished district in London, home to immigrants and poor people.

[2] Medicines sold over the counter and heavily marketed for their effectiveness against a wide variety of ills. Because the claims of many of these drugs were unproven, patent medicines were heavily criticized and led to the creation of government agencies to regulate them.

[3] The St. Leger Stakes is a horse race run at Doncaster in South Yorkshire. Open to three-year-old horses, it is one of five races that make up the Classics, the British equivalent of the Triple Crown.

[4] An alternative word for seamstress, a woman who earns her living through sewing.

The Strange Case of the Three Revolvers

Anthony Grey

This story is significant for not only starring Holmes, but another major figure in British detective fiction, Sexton Blake, and Nelson Lee, whose popularity once rivaled Blake's. It appeared in the Oct. 1 issue of The Passing Show, *a weekly tabloid newspaper that ran from 1915 to 1932 and emphasized humorous fiction and cartoons. Of its author, Anthony Grey, nothing is known except that he wrote a number of short stories during the 1920s and '30s.*

Sherlock Holmes snapped on his hat and took the Chief of New Scotland Yard by the hand.

"I'll not return till I find those pearls," he hissed. "Information which I have received leads me to believe they were taken from Liverpool to New York. I will look there first. Tomorrow I sail for New York. Goodbye."

"Goodbye," said the Chief of New Scotland Yard;[1] and the great detective evaporated from the room.

"Now," said Sherlock Holmes as he ran up Whitehall,[2] "we shall see something!" He dashed into the Underground at Trafalgar Square.

"Single to New York," he said.

"Change at Euston,"[3] said the booking-clerk.

A week went by. A fortnight. A month. At last the Chief of New Scotland Yard began to wear a worried look. Five weeks

---

[1] The home of London's Metropolitan Police Service acquired the "New" when it moved from Great Scotland Yard to a new building on the Victoria Embankment in 1890. As noted in the Edgar Wallace story, the original Scotland Yard was the site of a medieval palace that housed Scottish royalty when they visited London.

[2] A road in the City of Westminster where the center of Britain's government resides.

[3] A village in the county of Suffolk northeast of London. Of course, there is no subway to New York, nor is there any reason to change trains in a place that's farther away from the destination than London.

passed and still no word from the great detective. The Chief of New Scotland Yard began to get busy. He called his staff together.

"Holmes must be found!" he barked. "What can we do?"

"Send for Sexton Blake,"[1] was the best suggestion; and so the Chief sent for Sexton Blake.

"This is the position," he explained. "Sherlock Holmes went out on the trail of the Duke of Blankstare's pearls five weeks ago. He went to New York. Since then he has not been heard of. Can you find him for me?"

Sexton Blake snapped on his hat, and took the Chief of New Scotland Yard by the hand.

"I'll not return till I have found him," he hissed. "From what you say, I am of the opinion that Holmes must have gone to New York. I will look there first. Goodbye."

"Goodbye," said the Chief of New Scotland Yard; and the great detective went out sideways.

"This," said he, as he ran up Whitehall, "is easy."

He dashed into the Underground at Trafalgar Square.

"New York," he said to the booking-clerk

"Oh, yes, I know your brother," said the booking-clerk. "Change at Euston."

A week went by. A month. Two months. Not a word from anybody. The Chief of New Scotland Yard was aging rapidly. One day he realised that something had to be done, so he called his staff together.

"Sexton Blake is completely missing," he informed then. "What can we do?"

"Send for Nelson Lee,"[2] was the best suggestion and so the

---

[1] A fictional detective described as "the poor man's Sherlock Holmes." Since his debut in 1893, more than 4,000 Sexton Blake stories have appeared, along with many movie, TV, and radio tie-ins.

[2] A fictional detective created by Dr. John Staniforth (1863-1927), a doctor who, like Conan Doyle, wrote stories to supplement his income. When Amalgamated Press went searching for a detective to rival Holmes, they considered both Blake and Lee. Staniforth refused to sell the copyright to Lee, so A.P. turned to Blake. Later, Staniforth changed his mind and sold

Chief of New Scotland Yard sent for Nelson Lee.

"It's this way," he said. "Two months ago Sexton Blake went to New York on business for me. Since then he has at been heard of. What can you do about it?"

Nelson Lee snapped on his hat and took the Chief of New Scotland Yard by the hand.

"I'll not return till I've found him," he hissed. "It is pretty obvious that Blake went to New York. I will look there first. Goodbye."

"Goodbye," said the Chief of New Scotland Yard, and the great detective spirited himself away.

"Child's play!" he said as he spirited himself up Whitehall and into the Underground at Trafalgar Square.

"Change at Euston," said the booking-clerk.

"Where for?" said Nelson Lee.

"New York," said the booking-clerk.

"Ah!" said Nelson Lee. "One day, if you keep on like that, you will be a great detective."

A month went by. Two months. Three months. The Chief of New Scotland Yard was threatened with baldness. He was just about to call his staff together and seek their advice in the matter of Nelson Lee, when one bright morning, the door of his office opened, and in came Sherlock Holmes.

"I have got the pearls," he said.

"No doubt," grunted the Chief. "But we have lost something far more valuable than pearls. We have lost Nelson Lee."

"Tell me," said Sherlock Holmes. "I have lost touch with affairs. I have just come in through Asia and Europe. What has become of Nelson Lee?"

Lee to A.P., but by then Blake was entrenched.

Lee began his career as a detective, the "hero of Lhasa and Limehouse, confidant of Lloyd George and Kitchener," who traveled the world solving mysteries. He was virile and good-looking, but also preferred to lounge around his apartment in Gray's Inn Road and, like Nero Wolfe, solve crimes from there. His Watson was, first, a street urchin named Nipper, known for his acrobatics and knowledge of the great poets. Later, he added Eileen Dare, a young woman, as well as a bloodhound, Rajah.

The Chief told him.

"Then," said Sherlock Holmes, "I'll not return till I've found him. I am of the opinion that Nelson Lee went to New York, I will look there first."

He went out. Months passed. One day the door of the office opened and in came Sexton Blake.

"I have been all over Asia and Europe," he explained, "but I am afraid I have failed. I have no news of Holmes."

"Holmes sailed for New York six months ago," said the Chief of New Scotland Yard. "He went to find Nelson Lee for me, but since then I have not had a word from him."

"Leave this to me," said Sexton Blake. "I'll not return till I've found him. New York, eh? I'll look there first."

A year later the office door opened again and in staggered Nelson Lee. He had come by way of Asia and Europe.

"Have I failed?" he gaped.

"Can't say," said the Chief. "Sexton Blake was in here just a year ago today. He sailed for New York that very afternoon. We've heard nothing of him since."

"Don't lose heart," said Nelson Lee. "New York, you say? I'll look there first. Goodbye."

Two months later, by way of Asia and Europe, came Sherlock Holmes. "Well?" he said.

"He passed through here two months ago," said the Chief. "Bound for New York."

"I'll look there first. Goodbye."

All this was many years ago. The last time Sherlock Holmes passed through London, on the trail of Nelson Lee, who was on the trail of Sexton Blake, who was on the trail of Sherlock Holmes, he was eighty-five and grey, but bearing up well. It was as recently as last Wednesday afternoon. He sailed for New York on Thursday morning.

"I will not give in," he is reported to have said, "till I find him."

Nor will he, the stout old soul.

Boys, be a detective, and see the world.

Mary of the Prairie or, Should She Have Let Him?

Anonymous

In the 1890 census, the population density in the West rose above two people per square mile. The frontier was declared closed, and ever after it was fiction that defined how the West was explored, conquered, exploited, and "won." The Western became a popular genre, and conquered silent movies as well. It was only by the late 1920s that interest began to fade, when Dorothy Parker skewered stories about "golden-hearted cow-punchers with slow drawls." In short, the genre was ripe for lampooning.

This story in Carnival *magazine's October issue teases the popular tropes in movies starring cowboy stars such as Tom Mix, Bronco Billy, and William S. Hart. It even takes a side trip into the Arabian romance stories popularized by* The Sheik *(1919).*

Steve Roughneck was known throughout the long lone prairie where men are men as the toughest cowpuncher[1] yet. His features were striking rather than handsome, having in them something of the rugged simplicity of a worn brick-end. His steely blue eyes were penetrating and powerful. One glance from them would stop a fight; two would stop a clock.

Yet with all this, Steve had a heart of gold. Little children smiled at him. Little boys laughed at him. And he had never been known to punch a cow below the belt.

Mary (of the prairie) lived at Dead Dog Ranch. Except for her parents and five small sisters she was all alone in the world. All day long she would do useful tasks about the house, in spite of her mother's earnest requests that she should not; while in the evenings she would sit by the fire knitting bedsocks for the

---

[1] A reference to cowboys, seen in print as early as 1874. Although even then it was a general term to refer to workers who tended cattle, it might be derived from those who loaded cattle onto rail cars using a long iron pole with a spike on the end. They should more properly be called cowpokers.

cowboys, and gazing at her father with an expression of gentle wistfulness that nearly drove the old man frantic.

This was the innocent girl who had tied up Steve's rugged heart in a manner awful to think about. Often when he was scouring the long lone prairie where men are men, steering the cows (or cowing the steers), he would find a flower she had dropped, and would place it reverently next to his heart, under his pillow or in one of his boots. And, as he took it out to gaze on what was left of it, "She sure is the cat's pyjamas,"[1] he would murmur with emotion.

Thus it went on for years, till both his boots were half full of vegetation, and his pillow like an allotment.[2] And then, one fateful day, Mary disappeared. Rumour had it that Pedro the hunchback half-caste had abducted her, and Steve thought so, too. She had gone, and he had had no chance of telling her all. To her, Steve was merely a bone-headed cowboy, with the manners of a mule and the intelligence of a rock-rabbit.[3] And she was quite right.

Gabriel Syme, investigator, lay folded neatly in an armchair. He was smoking a hookah given him by the Rajah of Dambad, and a half-bottle of cocaine stood convenient to his elbow. Yet he was not unhappy.

"Blotson," he murmured, "this ennui is killing me. Hand me my violin." Blotson turned pale.

"No, Syme, no," he shrieked. "You promised me not to. I thought I had cured you of the dreadful habit. I beg you — not the violin. Try the cocaine," he added, pushing it over.

But fortunately at that moment the bell rang, and a mo-

---

[1] A popular slang phrase coined during the 1920s meaning excellent or highly sought after.
[2] In Britain, it is a piece of rented land used for growing vegetables or flowers.
[3] Another name for a rock hyrax, a small mammal that lives in Africa and the Middle East.

ment later a visitor entered. He was a country-looking man, worn and deadly pale. He had ridden two hundred miles since breakfast, which was enough to make any rider haggard.

"Mary, the pride of the prairie, is lost," he gasped.

"Is it a dog?" asked Syme.

"No, it's my daughter," replied the man.

Mary's father ran briefly through her babyhood, childhood, and girlhood. (Note to producer:[1] Here insert 500 feet of of girlhood, etc.)

"Right," said Syme. "I'll find her. Run away."

The old man dumbly brushed a tear from his eye, left the room dumbly, and fell dumbly down the stairs.

Syme dared into his bedroom, returning a moment later disguised as an Aberdeen terrier.

"If I'm not in early I shall be late," he said.

Sliding silently down the banisters, he disappeared.

The desert.

Vast, immutable, unspeakable, it stretched to the horizon — all the way. There was something indescribable about it which could not be described, almost baffling description.

Steve Roughneck sat looking at it. Coming as he did from the long lone prairie where men are men, to the desert, also long and lone, where the men again seemed apparently to be men, he felt at home. His horse seemed restive; it was a djibbah.[2] Steve got off.

Sitting down on a convenient Arab, he buried his face in the sand, and mused on the past year. He had roamed everywhere — Sunny Havana, Breezy Blackpool, Santiago, Shanghai, Selly Oak[3] — everywhere.

(Note to producer: Insert 1,000 feet of travel film, showing

---

[1] A note for a movie producer interested in turning this story into a film.
[2] A long loose outer garment with long sleeves worn by Muslims.
[3] An industrial and residential district in Birmingham, England.

Sunny Havana, etc., etc.)

Something stirred within Steve. It was his conscience. While he sat there Mary might be suffering worse than Death.¹ And something deeper beneath him stirred. It was the Arab.

"Bismillah," ² said the latter, chattily.

"I want to find Mary," said Steve.

"Can the streamlet find its source, effendi?" murmured the Arab.³

"I don't know," said Steve.

"Follow me. I will lead you to her," the Arab continued, whistling his camel.

And thus they went, into the long lone desert where men are men, eastwards towards the setting sun.

And Mary?

She awoke to consciousness in the hold of the *Saint Vitus*.⁴ She was bound hand and foot, her nose was bleeding, some one had gagged and blindfolded her, and a rat was thoughtfully chewing her ear.

She felt instinctively that something had happened. Then she remembered the villainy of Pedro (the hunchback half-caste). Half angrily she began to gnaw her bonds. In a few minutes she was free.

---

¹ More commonly described as "a fate worse than death," implying that Mary is being raped.
² An Arabic phrase meaning "In the name of God." It is the first phrase in the Qur'an.
³ *Source:* Although not contemporary with the story, Bernardine Evaristo (born 1959) quotes a proverb from the Yoruba tribe of west Africa in her novel *Lara* (2009): "However far the stream flows, it never forgets its source." *Effendi:* An Arabian courtesy title meaning lord or master.
⁴ A Christian saint (c.290-c.303) who was martyred by Rome. During the Middle Ages, his feast day was celebrated in some countries by dancing before his statue. The neurological disorder Sydenham's chorea, which causes seizures, poor coordination and muscle weakness, was given the name "Saint Vitus Dance."

But at that moment a terrible thing happened. The great bows of the liner *H.M.S. Emetic*[1] crashed into the *Saint Vitus*, and all was lost. Mary found herself in the water. Something was clinging to her leg; it was the captain.

"Manners, manners!" she exclaimed, kicking him firmly in the face, and striking out vigorously into the waste of waters.

For three days she swam steadily on. Around her the gulls swooped, the catfish mewed. On the fourth day she felt herself growing weaker. On the fifth her hair began to come down. On the sixth she spied land on her port bow, and on the seventh a wave landed her half dead, half not dead, on a reef of rocks. Her plight was terrible. Her wrist-watch had stopped, her shoes had let the water in, and she was completely on the rocks. And at that instant a file of cannibals appeared on the horizon.

Mary swooned.

On reaching the coast Steve, his faithful Arab and the patient camel stopped.

"I shall charter an aeroplane," muttered Steve. And he did. For the next few hundred feet of film he feverishly visited island after island, according to the Arab's instructions; but no Mary.

Steve's spirits sank. He was longing to find her again — to hold her in his arms. But she was in a more horrible situation than that, even. She was to be sacrificed.

Bound to a stake, with the pyre around her beginning to burn up nicely, Mary felt her position acutely. The cannibals were laying covers[2] for fifteen guests. They felt Mary would scarcely go any further.

Steve, approaching his seventy-fifth island, felt himself getting warmer. So did Mary.

---

[1] A British-registered ship; the initials stand for "His Majesty's Ship" (for the monarch George V). An emetic is an ingested substance that causes vomiting.

[2] A complete place setting, including the plate, silverware, and glasses.

(To producer: You ought to be able to finish this yourself now; rescue in the nick of time; long embrace; close up of chaste salute; then)¹

The Arab, wiping away a manly tear, removed his make-up; it was Gabriel Syme. The camel took off its head; it was Blotson.

---

¹ A kiss anywhere other than the lips. A New York newspaper from 1897 recounted a court case in which a peck on the cheek cost a man $37.50.

According to the *New York Journal and Advertiser*, Mrs. Viola Dias had bought on credit a pair of curtains for a doorway (called chenille portieres) from a furniture house where Marshall McDaniells was employed. The purchase might have been influenced by the friendship between McDaniells and Mr. Dias. In the interest of completeness, the newspaper reported that the curtains were purple with a border of yellow pansies.

Every week, after her husband left for work, McDaniells called upon Mrs. Dias to collect the weekly installment of fifty cents. We don't know the age of Mrs. Dias beyond the headline calling her "a buxom matron."

The newspaper does describe the incident in the Dias' apartment:

"Mrs. Dias gave him a two-dollar bill, and he handed her $1.60.

" 'You have given me ten cents too much,' said she.

" 'Oh, that is all right,' he replied, with a languishing sigh.

"Mrs. Dias marvelled. To this day she does not know whether her elderly [*Editor's note:* He was 55.] admirer meant to tender the odd ten cents as payment for the kiss to which he meant to help himself. Possibly it was partly indignation at his presumption in assessing her favors at such a low figure that prompted her to prosecute him so bitterly.

"At all events Mrs. Dias told the jury yesterday that McDaniells continued to chat for a few minutes after giving her a receipt and that when he rose to go he offered her his hand.

" 'It seemed a little unusual,' she said, in telling her story, 'but I thought he meant no harm and gave him my hand. He grasped it tightly and pulled me toward him, and before I could stop him he had kissed me.' "

The newspaper quoted with admirable accuracy how McDaniells' lawyer tried to pass it off as "nothing more dreadful than a chivalrous tribute to a charming woman. You know, gentlemen, and I know — ha! ha! — how hard it is to resist such a temptation. He! He!"

McDaniells didn't help himself by taking the stand. He stammered a compliment to Mrs. Dias, "but his wit had deserted him, and he was dumb."

The prosecutor, too, wasn't having any of this "boys will be boys" defense. He told the jury McDaniells was "a villain of the deepest dye, who would insinuate himself into a happy home, ostensibly on business, and try to wreck it." The jury found McDaniells guilty.

1928

The crusade for Spiritualism marched on. Through his lecturing and writing, Conan Doyle became news anchor at Spook Central. Newspapers worldwide breathlessly relayed and mocked his encounters with the spirit world, and the news he received of psychic phenomena.

In mid-March, airman Raymond Hinchliffe attempted to repeat Charles Lindbergh's Atlantic crossing from the year before, only flying from Britain to the U.S. Hinchliffe was an experienced pilot. He was an air ace in World War I, shooting down 7 German planes, and losing his left eye. He was accompanied by shipping heiress Elsie Mackay, who paid for the flight and wanted to be the first woman to make the crossing. They took off in terrible weather and were never heard from again.

Later that month, during a meeting of the London Spiritualist Alliance, medium Eileen Garrett made contact with Hinchliffe. An elderly lady in the audience, Beatrice Earl, got out her Ouija board and soon received messages from him as well. Earl wrote to Hinchliffe's widow asking for a meeting, but was turned down. As president of the alliance, Conan Doyle arranged an introduction between the mediums and the widow. The meetings were a major success. Through the mediums, Mrs. Hinchliffe heard details only she and her husband would know, including the location of a document hidden in her house. Emilie Hinchliffe converted to Spiritualism and lectured about her experiences.

Not all such encounters with the spirit world turned out as well. In May, Conan Doyle saw the work of Australian artist Will Longstaff and invited him to a séance. Longstaff was inspired to paint "The Rearguard," a Turneresque seascape showing the ghosts of Australian soldiers moving off the beaches of Gallipoli and into the next life. Conan Doyle bought it for his Psychic Museum, adding that "Longstaff painted the remarkable composition after a séance in which he received indubitable proofs of spiritualism, he worked nine hours, under strong psychic inspiration, and in that period completed the greater part of this wonderful composition."

Informed of this, Longstaff countered that, yes, he did attend a séance and was impressed by what he experienced. But he painted "The Rearguard" at Conan Doyle's request. "I regard the picture," he told the newspapers, "as an excellent composition ... Sir Conan Doyle, *nothing more."*

Nettled, Conan Doyle defended his conclusion, telling the Daily Express: *"He had been to a séance; he had got into touch with a vanished friend who was an artist, he was full of that spiritual elation, which comes with conviction, and then within a few days he painted, working at great speed, a picture which depicts the whole fate of man as Spiritualists conceive it. Surely, you cannot disconnect these events."*

Meanwhile, the messages from beyond kept flowing in. In September, at the International Federation of Spiritualists, Conan Doyle revealed that Earl Haig, who had commanded the British Expeditionary Force during the latter part of the war, contacted him three days after he died. Author Joseph Conrad (died 1924) also stopped to ask Conan Doyle for a favor. Conan Doyle didn't say what they wanted, only that he passed Haig's message on to the family.

He also continued to pump for the authenticity of the Cottingley Fairy photos. He claimed that the existence of a side curl on one of them, years before it became fashionable, was proof that the photos were real. *"These fairy creatures,"* he said, *"are separated only by a small vibration from ourselves. Quite a number of people can see them, but are ashamed to admit it."*

October saw both the publication of The Complete Sherlock Holmes Short Stories, *and Conan Doyle's trip with his family to Africa. For five months, they visited South Africa, Rhodesia, and Kenya. In between lectures, he visited landmarks from the Boer War. The only rough moment during the visit occurred in Bloemfontein, where he misread the Dutch words on a memorial to women and children who died in the war. Believing it to be a slur on the British, he called it* "a lie and a blot." *In reality, the plaque said no such thing, and after several hundred protestors marched outside his hotel, he sent an apology to the newspapers.*

While little was happening in the writing field, November saw a new edition of British Campaigns in France and Flanders *that was published in 1920, revised to include the Italian and Salonika campaigns.*

This year was also notable for the publication of Ronald Knox's Essays in Satire, *which contained his essay on Holmes that he had delivered in Oxford in 1912. Treating Holmes like a real person inspired S.C. Roberts (1887-1966), who had reviewed Knox's book, to respond with a pamphlet of his own,* "A Note on the Watson Problem." With this back-and-forth discussion, the seeds of future fandom were sown.

At least this time Conan Doyle was bemused by the energy spent on his fictional creation. "That anyone should spend such pains on such material was what surprised me," he wrote Knox. "Certainly you know a great deal more about it than I do, for the stories have been written in a disconnected (and careless) way without referring back to what had gone before. I am only pleased that you have not found more discrepancies."

Publications: *What Does Spiritualism Actually Teach and Stand For? (pamphlet, Feb.); A Word of Warning (pamphlet, Feb.);* The Complete Sherlock Holmes Short Stories *(Oct.);* The British Campaigns in Europe 1914-1918 *(Nov.).*

Conan Doyle with Will Longstaff before "The Rearguard."

An Adventure of Shylock Bones

"Goanna Jack"

Even today, there's not much going on in Goomalling. The small town of 500 in southwestern Australia is noted for its fields of wheat and cereal crops, and to us for this parody which appeared in the May 11 edition of the Goomalling Weekly Gazette. *The identity of "Goanna Jack," the newspaper's columnist, could not be learned. A goanna, by the way, is a general name for a monitor lizard, of which Australia boasts at least 25 species, some of which can grow to more than eight feet in length.*

Shylock Bones sat in his morris chair[1] in his rooms in Shaker Street, wrapt in thought and a patch-work dressing gown and blowing forth clouds of smoke from his antiquated briar, when Dr. Jotson entered on a recently eventful morning. That the great detective was concentrating on a knotty problem was evident from the puckering of his intellectual brow.

"You must be thinking of something," was Dr. Jotson's greeting.

"Sit down Jotson," said Bones. "I am in the act of elucidating a dark and dirty deed. Someone has stolen 83 aristotles[2] of

---

[1] An early version of a reclining chair, developed by a firm owned by William Morris (1834-1896) and introduced in 1866. The hinged back allowed it to be repositioned with the help of a row of pegs in each arm. Think of it as a primitive La-Z-Boy.

[2] Australian rhyming slang for bottles. Its origins are lost to history, but it was first recorded in London in the 1840s. The dialect emigrated to Australia when transportation became a punishment, and there it has taken on its own unique style.

An article in the Sydney *Truth* in 1900 noted the popularity of Cockney slang and gave this example. The slang is in *italics* and its translation in [square brackets]):

I 'ad a brown *I'm afloat* [coat], a green *Jacky Lancashire* [handkerchief] in me left 'andsky and tan *daisy roots* [boots]. When I meets the *cheese and kisses* [missus, his wife] and pratted orf down the *frog and toad* [road with her], I tell you I was a bit orl right. (Meaning he looked impressive.)

Other examples of Australian rhyming slang include *steak and kidney*

amber ale from Stan Heavens." [1]

"Good Heavens!" ejaculated Jotson.[2]

"I have gone carefully over the facts of the case," continued the great man, "and from my deductions have eliminated a number of suspects including the Band of Hope, Salvation Army and members of the Grand United Order of Free Teetotallers."[3]

"Marvellous," exclaimed the doctor. "Do you think the booty was carried away in hip pockets?"

"No! In bottles," was the reply, leaving the good medico amazed at his friend's powers of deduction.

At that moment, Mrs. Gasbag, Bones' good landlady, appeared with the evening paper which the great detective immediately seized and commenced to peruse.

"Ah ha!" he cried as staring headlines struck his eye and he commenced to read:— "Town of Goomalling Deserted. All Residents Take to the Bush."[4]

"What is the cause of that?" queried Dr. Jotson impatiently.

[Sydney], *trouble and strife* [wife], *rubbadedub* [pub], *Joe Blakes* [snakes], and *bag of coke* [bloke].

[1] Stan Evans (not Heavens) owned the Goomalling Hotel, which also sold alcohol. The hotel opened in 1904 and offered 12 rooms to guests. Renamed the Goomalling Tavern, it is still in business.

[2] A common dialog tag of the time, used to indicate an impetuous response. Now that the meaning of the word has shifted, it has become a source of merriment, especially if used in a romance (e.g., "'I love you!' he ejaculated cockily.").

[3] *Band of Hope*: A temperance society founded in Leeds in 1847. Members met once a week and participated in activities such as choral competitions and daytrips to coastal resorts; *Salvation Army*: A charitable group founded in 1865 by English Methodist preacher William Booth (1829-1912). An Australian branch was formed in 1880, where they focused on helping released prisoners find a home and a job. *Grand United Order of Free Teetotallers*: Unidentified.

[4] In general, the countryside. Today, with a population of 25 million, Australia's population density of 3.3 persons per square kilometer places it near the bottom of the list. It was even lower in 1925, when the population was 6 million. That's a lot of bush to wander about in, and it acquired a romantic veneer and became a source of folklore.

"My good friend," said Bones calmly as he laid his paper down with a sigh. "Observe the love of that peaceful community for law and order. Had it been 83 bottles of pickles stolen, the town would no more have gone in search of it than a butcher would attempt to sell pork sausages in Jerusalem.[1] But But Jotson, the solution of the community taking to the bush is — 83 aristotles of amber ale."

(To be continued—perhaps)

Goomalling Tavern in 1904.

---

[1] Both Jews and Muslims have religious objections to eating pork.

Help! Help! Sherlock!

Edmund L. Pearson

Edmund L. Pearson (1880-1937), librarian, true-crime aficionado, and Sherlockian, has appeared before in this collection. His "Adventure of the Lost Manuscripts" and "Sherlock Holmes Solves the Drood Mystery" appeared in the 1910-1914 book. Here we supply his last parody, which appeared in July 12 issue of the old Life humor magazine.

This one is noticeable for its inclusion of a newcomer to the mystery scene, Philo Vance, the brainchild of S.S. Van Dine (1888-1939). His debut in The Benson Murder Case *(1926) showed him to be an American version of Dorothy L. Sayers' Lord Peter Wimsey, only without the latter's humor. At the time, the true creator of Vance was unknown, and many suspected it was Pearson. This drove him crazy. While he told a friend that he might be envious of Van Dine's success, he still thought the man was "the writer of a not-too-good novel (my opinion, of course) who is simply hauling in fat profits from big sales. ... I cannot bear his ass of a detective, anyhow, since he lets pretty nearly the whole family be slaughtered, while he is making his awful epigrams and comments."*

It was in the summer of 1929 that I ran down to his home in Sussex to see my old friend, Sherlock Holmes.

I found Holmes seated in the garden near his beehives. His eyes were closed, and he sat without moving, a rug over his knees. Mrs. Hudson, his housekeeper, told me that he had been sorely afflicted with rheumatism, and could only hobble from his bed to his chair in the garden.

"Ah, Watson!" said he, without looking up, or even opening his eyes. "You bring the usual whiff of iodoform[1] with you."

"Holmes," I replied, "I have been talking by telephone with Creedon of the New York police. There has been a murder in the Browne family; in the old family mansion in 54th Street."

"Wonderful people, the Americans," murmured Holmes.

---

[1] A compound with a sweetish smell that was used as a disinfectant and antiseptic dressing in hospitals.

"Their motto is: A murder a day keeps the boredom away."

"Creedon says the situation is serious. It is now the custom in New York, it appears, for a murderer to establish himself in a household, and work right through, from the second housemaid up to the head of the family." [1]

Holmes opened one eye.

"One of the Browne family has been killed — or so I understood Creedon's phrase. 'Bumped off' was what he said. An amateur detective has been retained. He is the leading consultant in the States; the greatest criminal expert ever produced in America. His name, I understand, is Philo Vance."

Holmes sprang up, his eyes blazing.

"My God, Watson! Vance! Do you realize what happened when he handled the Greene murder case?[2] And now the Browne family! They're all doomed, I tell you; every man jack of them!"

In a second the aged detective, his rheumatism cured as by a miracle, was dashing toward the house, shouting for Mrs. Hudson to pack our bags. He rushed to the telephone, and put through a call to the Government aerodrome. Two hours later, Holmes and I, seated in the cockpit of one of the swiftest planes, were far out over the Atlantic, bound for New York on our errand of rescue.

Holmes, with his old fore-and-aft cap pulled down over

---

[1] A reference to the plot of Van Dine's best-selling *The Greene Murder Case* (1928).

[2] Perhaps one source of envy regarding *The Greene Murder Case* (1928) came from the positive reviews it garnered. The Washington D.C. *Evening Star* ran not one but two raves (and serialized the novel as well). One by book columnist Charles E. Tracewell (1889-1960) is typical of the raves: "We began this story in a very critical mood. We were tired of detective stories, for the time being, and resolutely told ourself that, we couldn't be entertained in that way at that time. We sat down in the middle of the afternoon with the book, telling ourself that we would read only a few chapters and before we knew it we were busily constructing just such mental pictures as the clever author had intended that we should construct. It is as if an author says, 'Stick along with me, and do as I tell you, and I will show you some excitement.'"

his hawk-like face, gazed straight ahead. He spoke only once during the next twenty hours. This was to mutter:

"Philo Vance retained! Poor devils!"

Next day, at noon, we stood in the library of the Browne mansion. There were present the District Attorney of New York, three detectives, and a large delegation of journalists. We had already viewed the body of young Jethro Browne. As we were talking with the officials, the policemen separated, and one of them announced, in tones of very deep respect:

"Mr. Philo Vance, sir!"

It was plain that they considered this a great moment: the meeting of the two famous detectives. We looked toward the door, where there appeared a young man, hastily fitting a monocle into his eye. It gave him much trouble, but at last he got it to stay in place, when he came forward and saluted Holmes.

"Mr. Holmes! Ah, most extraordin'ry! Simply rippin', I'm sure. Charmed to have you here."

Holmes bowed.

"Mr. Vance," said he, "perhaps if you will outline your plans, we need not work at cross-purposes."

"Right-o!" said the American detective. "Awf'ly toppin' of you, old bean. This is the way of it, d'ye see? This afternoon I shall take all these police johnnies up to the Metropolitan Museum[1] an' show 'em the old weapons in the Armor Room. Deliver a little talk, myself, what, what? All about the petronels, and arquebuses,[2] an' so on. While we are there I expect Grandpa and Grandma Browne to be assassinated.

Tomorrow, a little conference on modern music; I'll have the whole police force there, and describe how Gershwin de-

---

[1] The largest art museum in the U.S., "The Met" holds more than two million works. Its Arms and Armor gallery alone contains more than 14,000 objects covering nearly every era and culture.

[2] A *petronel* is a long-barrelled pistol with a matchlock or wheellock mechanism from the 16th and 17th centuries. An *arquebus* was an heavy long gun that appeared in the 15th century. It was so heavy and awkward a piece that it needed a fork rest so it could be aimed and fired.

rives from Bildad,[1] the Assyrian composer. Aunt Minnie, and the twins will prob'ly be murdered while we are absent.

At noon, my friend the District Attorney and I will lunch at the Club, and settle the question of the difference between Eggs Benedict and Eggs Benedictine.[2] Directly after lunch I expect to hear that Sister Susie, the butler, little Ned, and old Uncle Peter have been slain.

That evening I'll compile a bibliography of crime, while our friend the murderer is at work on Browne pére, the cook, and the rest of the girls. I may find a moment to enlighten old Markham on the work of the Viennese psychiatrists.

Thursday I'm going down to the Grosvenor[3] to see a chap who has a collection of Japanese sword-guards, and when I come back I expect to hear that, except for little Eloise, they're all jolly well mopped up. What, what?

Then I'll bring my powers to bear, and maybe drag dear, dear Eloise off to the dungeon. If they're all dead but Eloise it will be clear she's the murderess. Clever, what? *N'est-ce pas? Nicht wahr? Hoi polloi? Lambda, mu, nu?* You are a linguist, Mr. Holmes?" [4]

---

[1] George *Gershwin* (1898-1937) was a composer and pianist. Coincidentally, he died of a brain tumor on July 11, the day before this issue of *Life* appeared. There is no *Bildad* the composer, but he does appear in the Book of Job as one of Job's three friends.

[2] According to M.F.K. Fisher's *Masters of American Cookery*, eggs Benedict is poached eggs laid on top of ham or bacon, and an English muffin or toast and topped with hollandaise sauce. Eggs Benedictine is a richer version in which, instead of ham and toast or muffins, the nest consists of pureed codfish, garlic, oil, and a cream called *Brandade de Morue*. An Egg McMuffin is the fast-food version of eggs Benedict.

[3] Possibly the Grosvenor Hotel on 35 Fifth Avenue. An upscale hotel in an area reserved for millionaires, the Grosvenor rented to wealthy guests who wanted to live in the neighborhood but did not want the expense and upkeep of a mansion. The first six-story Grosvenor lasted from 1876 to 1926, when it was torn down and replaced with a new 15-story edition that kept the name. The building was sold to New York University in 1964 for use as a residence hall.

[4] *N'est-ce pas?* French for "don't you agree?" *Nicht wahr?* German for "not

"Not precisely," said Holmes. "It is very satisfactory to know your program, Mr. Vance, and I am sure we shall not conflict in any way. Also, to use your racy American phrase, it is quite clear to me now where the Browne family get off. I will meet you here, Thursday afternoon — in time for the arrest."

Holmes went to work with his usual energy, and on Thursday we were again in the library of Mr. Browne. In addition to the others, there were present a group of eight or nine ladies and gentlemen who were not at the other interview. Vance had not yet arrived; it was understood he had taken the traffic police up to see the paintings in the Hispanic Museum.[1]

Finally he came in, polishing his monocle.

"Ah!" said he. "Simply top-hole,[2] eh, what? Quite ready for the arrest? Where's little Eloise?"

"My daughter," said Mr. Browne, coming forward, "is here. But I do not think she will be arrested. You see, Mr. Vance, my family and I myself have an aversion to being murdered. We wouldn't for worlds interrupt your delightful causeries[3] on art, but we observed how our neighbors, the Greenes, were slaughtered one by one, while you enlightened the American public on Venetian glass and German criminology. As a detective, if I may say so, you are a charming professor of aesthetics.

"Mr. Holmes, here, pursuing those methods which have made him celebrated, arrested my chauffeur two days ago. The chauffeur has confessed to killing my son, and planning to kill the rest of us. He is now in the Tombs,[4] and I take pleasure in

---

true." *Hoi polloi?* Greek for "the many." To complete the procession of nonsense phrases, *Lambda, mu, nu?* are three letters from the Greek alphabet.

[1] The Hispanic Society of America has a museum and reference library at 155th Street and Broadway.

[2] A variation of "top notch" that was favored by the British upper class during the Edwardian era.

[3] Informal talks or lectures.

[4] The colloquial name for the prison in Lower Manhattan, now called the Manhattan Detention Complex. Starting as the Hall of Justice, built in 1838, it was replaced in 1902 by the City Prison, in 1941 by the Manhattan House of Detention, and the present complex in 1983.

proffering Mr. Holmes this check."

"Oh, I say, y'know!" exclaimed the American detective.

"Mr. Vance," said Holmes, "had you any relatives in Scotland Yard?"

"I studied under Inspector Gregson,"[1] said Vance.

"Ah, I thought as much. I seemed to recognize the old Gregson touch. It has grown lighter, with the years. Dear old Gregson! How I loved him! How the murderers relied on him! Do let me present Dr. Watson—you have so much in common!"

The dapper S.S. Van Dine, with cigarette, posing with actress Jean Arthur to promote *The Canary Murder Case*. (1929).

---

[1] The cool and occasionally callous Scotland Yard inspector who worked with Holmes in *A Study in Scarlet*, "The Adventure of the Greek Interpreter," "The Adventure of Wisteria Lodge," and "The Adventure of the Red Circle." Holmes called him "the smartest of the Scotland Yarders."

The Seven Corpse Case

F.M.J. Wood

Every month, from 1893 to 1975, the St. Bartholomew's Hospital Journal *published articles of interest to the medical community. It was an eclectic mix of advances in treating disease and injuries, feature articles about doctors' experiences around the world, lists of examination results, changes of address, marriages, births and deaths, and other notices of interest. And between 1928 and 1930, the magazine published four pastiches by F.M.J. Wood, about whom nothing is known.*

I come now to one of the most notable of all our cases, inasmuch as it showed me a hitherto unsuspected aspect of the kaleidoscopic character of the great criminologist.

He had invited me to supper and we sat in his old familiar rooms at Baker Street waiting for the meal. I knew he had something on hand, but as usual waited for him to announce it at his leisure. He was sitting in his customary attitude in his armchair, attired in dressing-gown and slippers and watching the clouds of his tobacco smoke through half-closed eyes. He shot a keen glance at me from beneath his shaggy eyebrows.

"Are you busy at present, Watson?" he asked.

"As a matter of fact, I have nothing very urgent at present," I replied, "although I have a patient in my nursing home who is suffering from eclampsia.[1] I am as yet undecided how to treat her; there are two alternatives — the method of Stroganoff and the Dublin method. The former means active measures which will necessitate my presence there to-night; the latter consists of sedatives, rest in bed, and light fluid diet, all of which can be applied without my aid. But I am afraid I am talking Greek to you."

---

[1] Eclampsia is a serious complication during pregnancy in which high blood pressure causes violent shaking. Women can develop preeclampsia, but only 1 in 200 with the condition suffer from eclampsia. Despite the amusing names, the Dublin and Stroganoff methods for treating eclampsia are real, if outdated treatments.

"Not at all, my dear fellow," said Holmes, smiling faintly, "on the contrary, eclampsia is a condition with which I am perfectly familiar. You may be unaware that I published a small monograph on the subject some ten years ago. I had at that time a large and powerful bulldog named Herbert who suffered from recurrent fits. A glance through the literature satisfied me that the animal was an eclamptic, and I at once embarked upon an active course of treatment as recommended by Stroganoff, who, I may add, is a personal friend of mine. The fits, however, increased in frequency and violence. One afternoon, during a particularly violent fit, when I was endeavouring to examine the optic discs I was severely bitten"; he tenderly felt his lean calf with his long, sensitive fingers — "I was alone and had to walk to the top of the house in order to get the necessary instruments, and it was only at the end of two hours and thirty-seven minutes, after extracting eighteen of the animal's teeth and sawing through the lower jaw that I was free. I returned the beast to his kennel and dealt him a heavy blow on the head with a spanner[1] in order to restrain his movements.

"On my next visit a week later I was aston— gratified to find him amenable and free from any suggestion of a fit. I published the results of my researches, which were particularly well received in Ireland, with the result that what you facetiously term the Dublin method is really—"

"—the Holmes method," I put in.

"Exactly. But to turn to business, Watson, I have some work to-night, dangerous work, in which I shall need your assistance, so if you can leave your patient I shall be grateful for your company."

"Splendid," I replied. "I have just engaged a new night superintendent — an excellent woman. I will telephone at once and order the Dub— the Holmes treatment" — he bowed

---

[1] A tool that is also called in the U.S. a wrench. Both words share a phrase in common — "throw a [spanner / monkey wrench] in the works" which any workman who has experienced what happens when a tool interferes with machinery would understand.

slightly and smiled — "for my patient."

When I returned I found Mrs. Hudson had just placed on the table an appetizing meal of gin and kippers.[1] We ate for an an hour in silence, the only sounds being the crunching of fish-bones and the melodious gurgle of gin. We finished our meal, lit our pipes, and Holmes introduced me to the night's work.

"I have for some days," he began, "been interested in a large and gloomy-looking house on the outskirts of London. I will not describe its situation more fully for reasons which I will give you later. I was walking past it four days ago when I saw the front door open; a coffin was carried to a waiting vehicle which drove off down the street. As is my custom, I searched the obituary columns of all the daily papers the same night, but found no death mentioned under that address, and decided to watch the house next day.

"Accordingly I spent the whole day before the house playing a barrel-organ,[2] and was fortunate enough to see another coffin brought out and carried away. I followed it, pulling my organ after me, but unfortunately ran over a dog, and in the confusion which followed the coffin disappeared. Yesterday I spent the day in the same street hawking onions, and at 5 p.m. a vehicle arrived; a coffin was carried out as before, and the driver made off at a rapid pace. I followed at a run, pushing my barrow before me. Unfortunately, in negotiating the corner my near wheel struck the kerb and the barrow overturned, scattering some four hundredweights of onions in the road; a crowd rapidly collected, and before I could gather the vegetables and

---

[1] A whole herring which has been split from head to tail, gutted, and preserved by salting or pickling, and cold-smoked over woodchips. It is small and greasy, and often served for breakfast. Expert kipper eaters learn how to pull the flesh off and leave the bones behind, but some insist on eating the small bones as part of the culinary experience, as well as a source of calcium.

[2] An instrument for making music, typically a stand on wheels which is operated by turning a crank. A tune is played when a metal drum with perforations or spikes inside the box rotates against tines. Organ grinders were a common sight on city streets.

continue the pursuit the coffin was again lost to sight.

"But even to you, my dear Watson, it must appear odd that three deaths in as many days, occurring in the same house, should escape comment in the press, and yet even in the obituary columns the address of the house has not been mentioned. As far as I know there is no epidemic in that part. I am convinced that no less a person than our friend Professor Larkin, the notorious and elusive blackmailer, thief and murderer, is at the bottom of this; delay may cost more lives, and I propose to-night to enter the house from the back and bring the mystery to light. Larkin has been a thorn in my flesh for many years, and I expect to find abundant evidence to bring him to the gallows."

We smoked on and Holmes played his violin and talked brilliantly of relativity and vaccine therapy[1] until midnight sounded from a neighbouring clock. We then arose, put out the lights and descended to the street.

The night was cold and there was no moon. Gusts of wind made us button our coats around our throats and pull our hats over our eyes. Holmes walked in silence and took his way by a devious road, threading his path as only he knew how with unfaltering step through dark alleys, low-browed slums and winding lanes with lights neither in the streets nor in the mean houses which bordered them until I was hopelessly lost.

At last we emerged at one end of a long wide street, apparently more prosperous than we had hitherto passed. It was lit by a wearying length of street-lamps, and as far as could be seen we were at the back of a row of houses.

We walked rapidly on until he came to the forty-fifth

---

[1] We think of *relativity* as something Albert Einstein came up with, but the term is used to describe any relationship between two bodies. Galileo Galilei (1564-1642) postulated the first relativity theory when he attempted to prove that the Earth rotated. Of course, Holmes would be discussing the theory of special relativity postulated in 1905 by Albert Einstein (1879-1955) and generally accepted by this time in the scientific community. *Vaccine therapy* is when a drug is used to spur the body's immune system into action against a tumor or infection.

lamp-post, where he stopped. A wall four feet high surmounted by a row of iron spikes confronted us, and some fifty feet on the other side was the back of a house five stories high, with but one light glimmering fitfully in a window at the very top.

"This is the one," whispered Holmes; "we shall proceed in single file, and on no account must you attempt to draw abreast of me. Now for it!"

He vaulted lightly over the wall after a quick glance up and down the road. But he failed to clear the top completely, and his trousers, which were made for him in his stouter days, and were now rather baggy at the back, caught on a spike. He hung there for about five minutes, kicking and lunging like a child learning to swim at the end of a rod and line. At last I went to his assistance; one snip with my scissors was sufficient to divide the suspending band of trousers, and Holmes dropped with a loud crash into a cucumber frame[1] just beneath him.

I found a gate near by through which I entered just in time to see him emerging from the cucumbers. There was a large tear in the back of his trousers through which a considerable area of his white shirt protruded. This served me as a beacon in the dark.

He again encountered some difficulty a few yards further on by walking with his head down into a clump of gooseberry bushes. He extracted as many thorns as he could in the dark, but time was pressing and he started at a run to cover the remaining twenty feet to the house. I followed hard on his heels when suddenly he rebounded on me and we fell in a heap on the ground.

After we had disentangled ourselves we found the reason, for Holmes had run into a wall of wire-netting provided as an encouragement for the sweet peas, and had been shot back like a stone from a catapult. After that we had no more diffi-

---

[1] Cucumbers grow on vines, and need a frame to support the plants. A typical frame at the time would built in the shape of an A so that two rows could be planted.

culty. He prised open a small window through which we climbed, and we found ourselves in the basement.

Holmes flashed his torch around and revealed a grim sight — four long tables covered with white sheets. He raised the first to discover the face of a newborn child. The left ear was missing, the jaw broken and the face badly mangled.

He replaced the sheet and I saw at once that he was deeply moved; his face was as pale as the sheets themselves, and his jaw protruded like a battering ram.

"I have seen enough," he whispered; "someone shall hang for this," and he crept stealthily but swiftly through the open door.

But a vague suspicion had entered my mind, and I lifted the sheet again. Somehow the face had appeared familiar, and feeling in my pocket I produced a tiny ear, which I applied to the left side of the child's face. It fitted exactly. My heart stood still as the truth flashed upon me — WE WERE IN MY OWN NURSING HOME!

Here was an unsuccessful forceps delivery[1] I had attempted the previous day. Next was a man on whom I had performed a radical mastoid operation — my osteotome[2] had penetrated a trifle too deeply. Next was the infant's mother who had succumbed to an intractable P.P.H.[3] in spite of continuous blood-transfusion. It was not my fault, I explained to the husband; "I cannot give a transfusion and compress the uterus at the same time — I am a human being, not an octo-

---

[1] A medical procedure in which a hinged instrument shaped like a pair of large spoons is applied to the baby's head to help guide it out of the birth canal.

[2] The mastoid is the part of your skull located behind the ear. It is filled with air cells, so if an ear infection spreads to the mastoid, it must be removed through a radical mastoidectomy. In the operation, depending on the spread of the infection, the eardrum, middle ear structures, and even the ear canal may need to be removed. The *osteotome* is a medical tool that looks like a small chisel and is used to cut bone.

[3] Postpartum hemorrhage, in which a woman has heavy bleeding after giving birth.

pus." Last of all was the blood-donor — a nice lad, I was sorry to lose him; he was a universal donor and his blood was always reliable.[1]

But Holmes must be stopped at all costs. I ran out of the basement and upstairs into the hall, and standing in the well of the staircase looked up. Far ahead, half-way up the fourth flight, I saw Holmes's shirt-tail gleaming in the gloom and oscillating rhythmically as he went up on all fours with incredible speed, his nose on the ground like a hungry bloodhound after a lamb chop.

Hastily removing my boots I ran up the stairs and arrived panting at the top just as he disappeared round the corner. He was now lying flat on his stomach and worming his way along the corridor. I pursued him silently and was about to grasp his ankle when a door opened in front of us. We both lay flat close against the wall as a figure approached, clad in white, carrying a shaded green light, and apparently engrossed in a paper.

It drew nearer, and at last was level with Holmes. I was about to heave a sigh of relief, when in passing him it planted a large and heavy foot on his long, sensitive fingers. He squealed and sat up. Instantly there followed a crack like a cricket bat meeting the ball; Holmes gave a yell and lay down.

The corridor was flooded with light and revealed my recently appointed night superintendent — an excellent woman — brandishing a large stone hot-water bottle,[2] Holmes

---

[1] There are four blood types — A, B, AB, and O — with different compatibilities when it comes to blood transfusions. Each type is also listed with a positive (+) or negative (-) symbol indicating the presence or absence of Rh antigens. This combination of blood type and Rh antigens determines which blood types can be used during a transfusion. Type AB+, for example, cannot be mixed with any blood type except AB+. At the other end of the scale, a donor with type O- blood can be used with every blood type. It's also worth noting that when patient and donor are switched, the opposite occurs. A patient with type AB+ can received blood from any donor, while the type O- patient can only accept blood from a type O-.

[2] This precursor to the rubber hot-water bottle was a ceramic "loaf" shape

crouching by the wall with the fingers of one hand in his mouth, his other hand clasping his jaw, which was no longer protruded like a battering ram, and myself a short distance behind in stockinged feet.

"Good evening, Dr. Watson," she began in icy tones; "this is an unexpected visit."

I have always been afraid of "night supers," as we affectionately called them in my hospital days, but the gin stood me in good stead.

"I was worried about my patient," I replied, "and came up to see her with my friend Dr. Holmes. He found the stairs rather tiring, so we were just — er — resting," and I looked her in the eye with an unblinking stare.

"Indeed," and she sniffed suspiciously, but the kippers fortunately predominated; "well, here is the patient's chart," and she pointed out its features with her forefinger. The temperature was typical of the condition known as rat-bite fever.[1]

"Well, Sister,"[2] said I, and started as the front door slammed violently below, "this is indeed not typical of eclampsia, but we are fortunate in having my colleague Dr. Holmes here is an authori—" I broke off as I realized we were alone.

"One moment," I cried, and rushing downstairs I tore open the front door and ran out onto the pavement. The sound of flying footsteps came to my ears and I saw far away down the road a white spot, for all the world like the tail of a white shirt, which flashed light and dim alternately as it passed the street-lamps with the speed of a greyhound.

It was Holmes going home.

---

with a flat bottom and a knob-handle on the side. A screw on top allowed hot water to be poured in. The flat bottom allowed it to be placed in bed, a coach or a railway car so it can't roll away.

[1] An infectious disease (streptobacillary RBF) caused by a bacteria transmitted through contact with rodents. Symptoms include fever, swollen lymph nodes and a rash near the bite wound or all over the body. Left untreated, the fever could be fatal in one in ten cases.

[2] A senior nurse. The name survives from the early Christian era, when nuns took care of the sick and injured.

1929

The last full year of Conan Doyle's life saw the continuation of his spiritualism crusade, the successful conclusion of a crusade for justice, and an intimation of the future for Sherlock Holmes.

Movies were learning how to talk, and among the first of them was a Sherlock film. British actor Clive Brook (1887-1974) starred in The Return of Sherlock Holmes (1929), based on "His Last Bow" and "The Adventure of the Dying Detective." Brook would go on to play Sherlock twice more, in the anthology film Paramount on Parade (1930), and Return's sequel, Sherlock Holmes (1932).

In May, Conan Doyle celebrated his 70th birthday, and in July, his last collection of fiction was published. In August, fire struck Bignell House, the family's home in New Forest. Sparks from the kitchen chimney set the thatched roof afire. Neighbors rushed over to help, although Conan Doyle admitted that "one or two, I regret to say, showed a disposition to remove the goods even further." He thought the fire might have been started by psychic phenomenon, and his wife, Jean, agreed. She had seen a "bad psychic cloud" over the house, and as repairs were being made, the property was also "cleansed."

Meanwhile, Conan Doyle contemplated his own mortality. His heart was clearly giving him trouble, he wrote a friend, and "I may talk it all over with Houdini himself before very long. I view the prospect with perfect equanimity. That is one thing that psychic knowledge does. It removes all fear of the future."

In October, he took his Spiritualism crusade to Holland and Scandinavia. He was well-received, and he made plans to continue southward; to Rome, Athens, and even Constantinople.

But in Copenhagen, during his lecture, disaster struck. Conan Doyle felt sharp chest pains that forced him to grip the podium for support. He powered through his talk and prepared to move on. The pain in his chest continued. They reached Oslo, but Conan Doyle grew so weak that he couldn't take off his overcoat. Alarmed, his family took him back to England.

"You say that I left my mark upon Sweden," he said. "That may be so, but Sweden has left its mark on me. My last exertions were too great — they have left me a wreck."

His doctors did their best, and ordered him to rest. Despite their advice, he visited London on Armistice Day to speak before a spiritualist gathering. In the cab, he suffered another heart attack. With the help of his sons, Denis and Adrian, he spoke at the meeting in a weak, faltering voice, then gave a second speech later that day.

Back at Windlesham, he was confined to his bed, where he continued to work with the help of his secretary. The end was near.

Publications: "The Disintegration Machine" (Challenger novella, Jan., The Strand); The Maracot Deep (collection, July); Our African Winter (Sept.); The Roman Catholic Church — A Rejoinder (Oct.).

Movie poster for *The Return of Sherlock Holmes* (1929) starring Clive Brook.

Expert Assistance

James J. Montague

James J. Montague (1873-1941) was a newspaper reporter, humorist, and poet whose verse was published in papers nationwide. After a stint at a Portland, Oregon, newspaper, he was recruited by William Randolph Hearst in 1902 to go to New York City. Reluctant to go, Montague asked for double his salary — to $60 a week — and was shocked when he got it. He stayed with Hearst's New York American *and* New York Evening Journal *until 1919, when he jumped to Joseph Pulitzer's* World. *Over his 25-year career, he produced more than 7,500 poems. Many of them were tied to the news of the day, including this one, which was discovered in the Jan. 29th* Seattle Post-Intelligencer, *about Holmes and his creator.*

> In Conan Doyle's creative youth
> He gave the world an able sleuth
> Who brought to light the hidden truth
> Concerning craft and crime.
> No mystery was too profound
> For this lean-visaged human hound,
> By mental synthesis, to sound
> In half a fortnight's time.
>
> When gems were lost, or men were slain.
> Sometimes for spite, sometimes for gain,
> In good King Edward Seventh's reign,[1]
> And dread spread far and near,
> The baffled coppers scratched their domes,
> And called in Mr. Sherlock Holmes,
> Who read a few old tattered tomes
> And made the whole thing clear.

---

[1] Holmes' career spanned the reign of Queen Victoria (1819-1901) as well as that of her son "Bertie" (1841-1910), and with "His Last Bow," the reign of George V as well. But poetry makes its own demands and attention to it must be paid.

But now, when spooks and spirits foil
The wit of even Dr. Doyle;
When, as he burns his midnight oil,
He sees them near and far;
When through his country home they stray,
Half-formless shapes of foggy gray,
He owns he really cannot say
Just who and what they are.

I wish the doc would resurrect
That keen deducing intellect,
And have those spirits tagged and checked,
And either jailed or shot.
For I am sure that in three shakes,
And with no guesswork or mistakes,
He would turn them up as fakes,
If Dr. Doyle cannot!

James J. Montague

The Adventure of the Missing Tenants

August Derleth

In 1928, a young August Derleth (1909-1971) wrote Conan Doyle a letter with a request only a passionate fan and amateur writer could ask. Since no more Holmes stories were going to come from his pen, could he take over the business? A good-humored Conan Doyle said no. Instead of accepting his decision, Derleth created Solar Pons of Praed Street, whose career ran to 70 stories in the post-World War I era, such as this story which appeared in the June issue of Dragnet *magazine.*

While Pons never achieved the Holmes' level of fame, he has his fans, including Vincent Starrett, who called the stories "as sparkling a galaxy of Sherlockian pastiches as we have had since the canonical entertainments came to an end." In addition to his own novels and stories, Derleth is also known for his friendship with H.P. Lovecraft (1890-1937), with whom he corresponded. After Lovecraft's death, Derleth co-founded Arkham House to republish Lovecraft's letters and stories. His efforts shaping and popularizing the Cthluhu Mythos helped introduce Lovecraft's imaginative worldbuilding to popular culture.

In the early hours of a winter night within the first decade I shared with my friend, Solar Pons, I was awakened by his hand on my shoulder and his voice at my ear, "We are about to have a visitor who will not be put off. You may care to sit in, Parker."

"What time is it?" I asked, struggling awake.

"Two o'clock."

"Two o'clock!" I cried. "What is it, then?"

"Some little crisis at the Foreign Office," replied Pons. "Bancroft is on his way."

I was just emerging into our sitting-room, tying the cord of my dressing-gown, when Pons' brother, Bancroft, having come noiselessly up the stairs of 7B, opened the door and stepped into our quarters. He was an impressively tall, formidable man, with a mind far keener than my companion's, for which I had had Pons's word on several occasions.

He nodded in my direction and said to Pons without preamble. "Ercole d'Oro, the Italian consul, has disappeared. The Italian government has begun to make some inquiries, and the situation is delicate."

"You ought to have called in the Pinkertons," said Pons. "*They* never sleep." [1]

"They can afford not to; the Foreign Office cannot," said Bancroft. "You are needlessly waspish. We have not seen fit to apply to the Yard.[2] There is good reason here for the utmost discretion in this inquiry."

"I fancy there is a woman other than the Countess involved," observed Pons.

"Elementary. Spare me these trifling exercises of yours," said Bancroft testily. "But, of course, there *may* be some involvement with a woman, since d'Oro was last seen entering the house in Orrington Crescent which he had been using for some months as a rendezvous for his amatory exploits."

"Ah, these Italians," mused Pons. "I fancy their Foreign Office could be demoralized by an attractive woman."

"You know of Count d'Oro?"

"I met him socially some years ago. Since 1921, he has been the Italian consul. Born in 1882. Now forty-four. Privately tutored, some study at the University of Genoa. At one time rumored to have some connection with the Mafiosa. His hobby: entomology. One of his monographs is used as a standard reference in the field. Married in 1900 to Harriet Jackson, niece of the Earl of Ellenbroke. No children."

"Yes, yes," interrupted Bancroft, "I know these details."

"Of the house in Orrington Crescent, however, I know

---

[1] The Pinkerton National Detective Agency was founded in 1850 by Allan Pinkerton (1819-1884). Its logo consisted of a large unblinking eye and the motto "We never sleep."

[2] The nickname for Scotland Yard, London's Metropolitan Police. Although its original location was at 4 Whitehall Place, its rear entrance opened onto a courtyard called Scotland Yard. It was originally the site of a medieval palace that housed Scottish royalty when they visited London.

nothing," said Pons. "Presumably you do." Suddenly a light broke upon Pons's face. "Unless, that is, it is number 27."

"It is."

"Ah, that puts a different light on the matter. A house notorious in the annals of London's unsolved mysteries. Let us now have the details."

"D'Oro left home three days ago, early in the evening, bound for the house in Orrington Crescent. His wife was told his destination, of course — she had been given to understand when d'Oro leased the house a month ago, that it was to be used for clandestine meetings concerned with the affairs of government — bluntly, espionage. I rather think the woman is convinced that some foreign agent is at the bottom of d'Oro's disappearance. It is not impossible."

"Which means that someone at the Foreign Office — characteristically — -entertains the same suspicion."

Bancroft brushed this impatiently away. "D'Oro was reported missing two days ago, after a full day during which he had not appeared either at his home or at his official quarters. No doubt the facts of his vanishing had also been transmitted to his government, for since yesterday we have had representations made to His Majesty's Government about d'Oro's safety.

"We have naturally examined the house. He had certainly reached it, and he was alone there — one does not customarily engage in this kind of dalliance in the company of a third person — and he had made some preparations to receive the lady — a Miss Violet Carson of Upper Hampstead, a secretary by profession. The hour of their rendezvous had been set for ten o'clock, and the lady — in accordance with the usual arrangements — arrived by cab at that hour, and let herself into the house.

"All evidence plainly indicated that her arrival was expected — the house was lit with subdued lights, d'Oro had bathed and was clad only in dressing-robe and slippers. All was as usual, except that he himself was not there.

"This was Miss Carson's seventh rendezvous with d'Oro.

She said, on interrogation, that she had 'got ready' — by which I take it she had undressed and got into bed, which had been turned back, and lay there waiting for d'Oro to make his appearance. She thought that perhaps he had gone below stairs for champagne or something other to serve her, as was his custom, but presently, hearing no sound in the house beyond the ticking of a clock, she got out of bed, slipped into the robe d'Oro kept for the use of such women as shared his nights there, and went to look for him. She searched the house. There was no sign of him. His car — a small Fiat — was in the adjoining garage, and the garage locked; it is still there.

"Some of our people have been through the house. Nothing untoward has been found. No sign of forced entry. Nothing. It is as if d'Oro simply vanished all in an instant. Miss Carson waited for an hour, then she dressed again, called a cab, and went back to her flat.

"A significant factor — if we can rely on Miss Carson — is that d'Oro telephoned her at a quarter to nine to let her know he had reached the Carrington house. Between that hour and her arrival a light snow fell. Miss Carson says that there were no footprints in the snow on the walk leading to the house, which suggests that d'Oro either left soon after he had telephoned — which is unlikely in view of his having bathed and shaved after he had telephoned — presumptively — or went by another door. Of course, by the time his absence had been reported, the snow had thawed away.

"But you shall see for yourself. I am going home. The car will return for you within the hour. That will give you ample time to dress and take breakfast, if you need it. Here are the keys."

He threw them to the table, and took his leave as noiselessly and unceremoniously as he had come.

"We are all presumed to be at the instant services of His Majesty's Government, Parker," said Pons, smiling. "Come, let us get dressed."

"You said it was a house notorious in the annals of London's unsolved mysteries," I said.

"So it is. A writer in the *Chronicle* — one of those devotees of that vein of fantasy known as science-fiction — scarcely three months ago wrote a sensational article about it under the heading, 'Orringron Crescent House Hole in Space?', speculating about a favorite gambit of investigators of curious, unexplained facts — like Charles Fort[1] — that strange, motiveless disappearances — of, for instance, persons seen walking in at one end of a street and never seen to emerge at the other, vanishing utterly — as having stepped into 'holes in space' or into other dimensions, or some such phenomenal 'openings' in time or space. Number 27 lends itself very well to such an article for the press. D'Oro is the fourth resident of it to disappear in the course of less than five years. All, if memory serves me, vanished in very much the same fashion, without motive, without trace."

He crossed the room and took down one of the files in which he kept cuttings about crimes and criminals. As I dressed in my room, I could hear his going through clippings that were never in the best of order, though Pons maintained a loosely alphabetical arrangement frequently disorganized by the hasty addition of new data. From time to time I caught muttered references to crimes he passed over — the case of Williams, the owl burglar, the Van Houtain murder, the multiple murders on Illington Moor.

---

[1] An American writer (1874-1932) who specialized in collecting information that might be charitably called pseudoscience, if not outright fakery. For 30 years, Fort visited libraries and read widely in newspapers and magazines to record stories about unexplained phenomena on note cards and scraps of paper. Out of this mish-mash of dubious information, he wrote four books, *The Book of the Damned*, *New Lands*, *Lo!*, and *Wild Talents*, in which he postulated the existence of teleportation, spontaneous human combustion, levitation, unidentified flying objects, and artifacts found in unlikely locations. This spawned an interest in "Fortean phenomena" that influenced authors such as Stephen King, Robert Anton Wilson, Philip K. Dick, and Robert Heinlein.

"Ah, here we are!" he cried as I came back into the sitting-room, his keen eyes rapidly scanning the clippings before him. "The house appears to have been built in 1920, by Dr. Roland Borstad, son of the one-time ambassador to Germany, Henry C. Borstad. The younger Borstad was a surgeon with an interest in psychoanalysis. Author of three published papers on psychoanalysis, and one monograph on Dr. Sigmund Freud. He appears also to have had some ability in architecture and undertook part of the building of his home. Overwork brought on a nervous breakdown, after recovery from which he went to live in the Orrington Crescent house, from which he vanished on December 17th, 1921. The papers made much of the fact that Borstad had evidently been planning a journey, for he had withdrawn a large sum of money, and his bags, already packed, were standing in the vestibule in preparation for his departure."

"I know the Borstad papers," I put in. "A brilliant young man. His death was a decided loss to psychoanalysis. As I recall it, he had some very advanced, unorthodox theories, and there was conflict with his peers. They fell out about his radical theories and experiments in the domain of pain and pain therapy, and this ultimately brought about a break in their relations, endangering his position in the hospital where he was briefly the resident, and ultimately brought on a nervous breakdown."

"The house stood empty for over a year. Then it was turned over to be let, though its ownership remained in the Borstad family where it presumably still is. The second disappearance was on February 24th, 1923; it was that of Clyde Lee, son of the Duke of Dunwich.[1] After Lee, Mr. and Mrs. John Tomlins and their family took the house. They remained for

---

[1] While Dunwich is a village in Suffolk, England, it is also part of the title of a seminal work in H.P. Lovecraft's Cthluhu mythology. "The Dunwich Horror" was published in the April 1929 issue of *Weird Tales*, a few months before this story appeared. Since Derleth and Lovecraft (1890-1937) were correspondents, the possibility that Derleth inserted this name as a shout-out to his friend is a possibility.

only five months, complaining that now and then distant sounds disturbed them. They made no charge against the house as 'haunted.' Tomlins, an engineer, said that the house obviously lay in a place that echoed sounds from far away — chiefly mechanical. The third disappearance was that of Howard Eliot, a writer of short stories and sensational newspaper pieces on occult subjects; he had taken the house because of its reputation and meant to 'lay its ghost,' as he put it, since there had been occasional reports of ghostly figures in the grounds. He vanished on May 17th, 1925. As in this fourth disappearance, investigation disclosed no motive for any one of the disappearances. Dunwich waited on the arrival of ransom notes; none was received."

"That is certainly a curious record!"

"Is it not!" He stood for a few moments tugging at an earlobe. "It has, however, some parallels. None of the missing tenants at the Orrington Crescent house was married. Except for Lee, who had a man-servant and had the house done by an occasional cleaning woman, each of the missing tenants lived alone; and Lee disappeared on his man's night free. What does that suggest to you, Parker?"

"A necessary condition," I said.

"Which in turn implies a related plan."

"What connection, if any, was there among the men who disappeared?"

"Other than the common tenancy of the house in Orrington Crescent, none has been turned up. They were not known to one another." He shrugged. "But it is idle to speculate with so little knowledge available. Bancroft will have a dossier on d'Oro in my hands by the time we return. Let us just have a look at the house."

He crossed to his chamber to dress.

The house in Orrington Crescent was, for lack of any classification, modern Victorian. It was without the ornateness of many Victorian houses, but its lines — what could be seen of them through the massed foliage of many bushes — though suggesting the Georgian, were a far remove from the classical, it struck me, in the wan light of a post set in the street outside the bordering hedge, as very much an expression of the undisciplined architectural preferences of its builder. Perhaps the late Dr. Borstad had designed it himself.

Its interior, however, was essentially simple. The front door opened upon a vestibule; this in turn opened directly upon a sitting-room, adequately but not richly furnished, dominated by a fireplace which bore no signs of recent use. A table lamp was lit on a reading table next to a stuffed chair; on the table a book lay face down, as if someone had been interrupted at reading. It was, I saw, not surprisingly, a collection of Leopardi's poems, in Italian[1] — clearly the book the Count d'Oro had been reading while he waited upon the arrival of Miss Violet Carson.

This room, in turn, led to two bed-chambers, a bath, a kitchen and adjacent pantry, a study or library, and a compact little room that might have served at one time as a laboratory

---

[1] Certainly an odd book for a man to read while awaiting his lover. Giacomo Leopardi (1798-1837) is considered the greatest Italian poet of the 19th century. He also had a depressing worldview that makes Cormac McCarthy look like Will Ferrell. During his short life, ended as the result of a cholera epidemic in Naples, Leopardi poured his pain into his poetry. He was born with scoliosis, but brilliant and hard-working enough to master Greek, Latin, and several modern languages by age 16. He worked so hard he went blind in one eye and damaged his health. His father was so overprotective he refused to let Leopardi leave the house without a tutor until he was 20. His mother was a religious fanatic who seemed to desire death as much as Leopardi. He was unable to form any romantic relationships. His worldview was best summed up in his notebook, "Everything is evil. I mean, everything that is, is wicked; every existing thing is an evil; everything exists for a wicked end. Existence is a wickedness and is ordained for wickedness. Evil is the end, the final purpose, of the universe. . . . The only good is nonbeing; the only really good thing is the thing that is *not*, things that are *not* things; all things are bad."

— something which the original owner of the house might well have put to use, though of all its original contents only a small microscope, a retort,[1] and some of the lesser paraphernalia of the surgeon stood on shelves in a small glass case on one wall. The furnishings in the house were sturdy, useful pieces, all for the most part ordinary, severe, and entirely unornamented.

There was no basement beneath the building, though there was a rear entrance to the house, and an enclosed stairway led to the top floor. This floor consisted of one large room, just above the study, a bath, and two other rooms of almost equal size, opposite the larger room. None of the rooms bore any evidence of ever having been furnished, though all were scrupulously clean, even to the obvious scrubbing of the variegated width oak flooring. The chimney leading up from the fireplace below stood apart from the wall, which was set back from it, and was windowless, with some shelving boards piled beside the uncommonly massive chimney, as if Borstad had meant to line this wall, too, as the wall below had been lined, with books.

Pons examined each room cursorily, then returned to the head of the stairs and stood in deep thought, caressing the lobe of his left ear.

"Does not this cleanliness surprise you, Parker?" he asked presently.

"I can't say that it does."

"Curious. Most curious. Are we to believe that Count d'Oro scrubbed down the floors of rooms for which he had no use before taking his mistress to bed?"

"Hardly. It strikes me it is you who are now doing what you so frequently accuse me of doing — overlooking the ob-

---

[1] A device used to distill a substance. Think of a glass ball with a neck at the top that acts as a spout, which is bent over and down. The substance is placed inside and heated. The neck acts as a condenser that collects the liquid and lets it flow down the spout. Frequently seen in mad scientists' labs in the movies.

vious. He had some charwoman¹ in to do it."

"Possible, if improbable," said Pons.

He led the way back downstairs and once more made a tour of the rooms, pausing to examine each room more closely. Everything was in order, save in the bedroom, where the bed still stood as Miss Carson had left it — turned carelessly back and disarranged as it would be had someone lain in it for a while, as Miss Carson had testified she had done while waiting on the appearance of her lover. Only one pillow showed any indentation, and that slight.

"I never cease to marvel at the sexual habits of my fellow men," said Pons, as he gazed at the bed. "To go to so much trouble and expense for a little casual dalliance!"

"Spoken like a true abstainer," I said. "We are not all so abstemious."

"Why not install her here permanently?" mused Pons, though it seemed to me that he was not really concerned with this question.

"Elementary!" I replied instantly. "Because d'Oro did not always meet the same woman here."

"Ah, Parker — you are wiser in this aspect of the world," said Pons, his eyes dancing.

"I will not deny it," I said.

"But let us look into the scene with more care" said Pons, then, leading the way back to the sitting-room. "It is evidently from this room that d'Oro took his departure, either voluntarily or involuntarily. Now it is patent that d'Oro was interrupted at his reading, for the Leopardi is turned face down. He could have risen to go into another room — to go outside; he could have simply lain back to rest; he could have grown tired

---

¹ An old term for a paid worker who came in to clean a house or office. This distinguishes them from a maid, who lived in the household. The word, along with chargirl, charlady, or even plain char, is derived from "chore woman." The charwoman was a popular character in fiction, and survived long enough for comedian Carol Burnett (born 1933) to create a character around her.

— the possibilities, while not endless, are varied. On the other hand, he may even have become aware of some unusual sound — or smell."

At this, Pons flashed a curious glance at me. "Is there not an uncommon odor in this room? Perhaps my use of the weed has troubled my sense of smell."

"I noticed how clean the room smells," I said.

"Antiseptic?" ventured Pons.

I agreed that the room had an antiseptic odor, as if it had been thoroughly cleaned. But there was nothing to meet the eye that gave evidence of anything more than ordinary cleaning.

Pons now began to walk around the room. He made a circuit of the walls, paused at the fireplace, and came back to the chair d'Oro had left. He dropped to his knees, took his magnifying glass from the inner pocket of his coat, and began to examine the floor around the chair, crawling about in an ever-widening circle. His glance darted here and there; from time to time he bore down upon a chosen spot, putting his glass to use, his keen eyes missing nothing, his face, feral in appearance when he was engaged in such intense an examination, betraying nothing.

When he came to his feet again, his face was a study in perplexity. "This room is a marvel of cleanliness," he said reflectively. "I submit that that is extraordinary indeed."

"Why should it be? D'Oro—," I said, gesturing toward the Leopardi poems, and the books on the shelves crowding the fireplace wall, "is obviously a man of taste. Such a man would hardly want to receive his mistress in a setting lacking for cleanliness."

"That is surely well put, Parker," agreed Pons. "However, I submit you have forgotten something — this house was surely examined with some care by men from the Foreign Office; Bancroft inferred as much. There is everything to show that this room was thoroughly cleaned since then. I have not found so much as a grain of sand in the carpet."

"Incredible!"

"You may well say so," said Pons.

"On second thought," I put in — "wouldn't it be likely that investigators from the Foreign Office may have vacuumed the carpet in search of some clue in the dust?"

"Such matters are usually too mundane for the Foreign Office."

"Even under pressure from the Italian government?"

Pons was lost in thought; he did not answer. Having completed his examination of the floor, he was now gazing at the walls of the room. He crossed to the street side of the house and scrutinized the window sills and frames; he did the same with the opposite wall. Neither the fireplace wall nor that opposite, which was a partition dividing the house, contained windows. Then he gave his attention to the hearth; this gave him pause.

"What do you make of this fireplace, Parker?" he said, from his position on his knees.

I crossed and bent. "It is as clean as everything else in the room," I said.

"Nothing more?"

"It must have been scrubbed with the same antiseptic thoroughness we've already noticed," I said. "The smell of it is even stronger here. And it doesn't have the look of having had much use. D'Oro apparently goes to no more than minimal trouble to satisfy the appearances."

"Other than scrupulous cleanliness," said Pons. "I put it to you that the romantic setting ought to have more than subdued lights — a fire on the hearth, music, flowers or some pleasant scent — which, I submit, ought not to be antiseptic in essence."

I laughed, I fear, with some cynicism. "For the purpose of seduction, perhaps, Pons. But once an arrangement has been made, I assure you that most ladies are as interested in getting to the heart of the matter as the men."

"Ah, I must defer to your greater experience in these matters, Parker. I am naive enough to have believed that the ladies are invariably partial to the romantic accoutrements."

He came to his feet once more. He stood for a moment examining the bookshelves. Then he began to remove the books from the shelves. "Lend me a hand, Parker," he said. "These shelves at least do not appear to have been cleaned recently."

I followed his lead in piling the books on the floor, seeing as I did so that the shelves behind the books were covered with dust and lint.

"These can hardly be d'Oro's books," I said, looking at some of the titles.

"Capital, Parker! I am always delighted at evidence of your growing inductive skill," answered Pons.

"Surely some of these books must have been the original owner's," I went on. "Medical books and case histories. And they've not been disturbed for years."

"I fancy d'Oro had no need to maintain a library here," said Pons. "Half a dozen books should have served him. These D'Annunzios and a set of Proust[1] are probably d'Oro's; there is is some disturbance of the almost uniform dust here."

"And here," I said. "Behind two textbooks used at Guy's[2] — which certainly cannot be of much pertinence any more, considering their date."

Pons came to my side. He stood looking thoughtfully at the shelving from which I had removed the books. I saw for the first time a neat round hole in the wall behind, as if a knot had fallen from the wood, though the knot was not in evidence. Pons gazed in silence at the dust that had so manifest-

---

[1] Gabrielle D'Annunzio (1863-1938) was an Italian writer, poet, and journalist who dominated his country's literature and political life. Marcel Proust (1871-1922) is best known for *In Search of Lost Time*, published in seven books between 1913 and 1927.
[2] A London hospital built by Thomas Guy (1644/45-1724) from the proceeds of his investment in the South Sea Bubble, a notorious financial scandal that beggared thousands but from which he profited. It is one of the two oldest teaching hospitals in the country.

ly been disturbed behind the books from Guy's; then he stepped back from the shelving and surveyed the wall in its entirety, after which he returned to a spot at a point on his side of the chimney approximately uniform with my position.

He removed books from the shelves, and stood with a small sound of satisfaction to contemplate the empty shelf.

Joining him, I saw that here, too, the dust had been disturbed — he still held in his hands the compact little German books he had removed from the shelf — and here, too, another knot had come loose.

"It was folly on the part of the builder to put in knotty pine so close to a chimney," I said, as he bent to examine the shelving there.

"Was it not!" agreed Pons. "Let us return the books to their proper place."

His demeanor baffled me. He said not a word as we restored the books to the shelves. After we had finished, he returned to the enclosed stairway and went up the stairs on his hands and knees, scrutinizing the steps and the adjacent walls with the aid of his glass, making almost inaudible muttering sounds as he went along. Now and then he took from the stairs or the rough plaster walls something invisible to me, inserted it into one of the glassine envelopes he invariably carried, and went on. From the top of the stairs be backed down, still examining every stair.

Once more down the stairs he said, "The stairs have also been carefully cleaned." He shrugged. "But I fancy we are all but finished here. It is growing light outside, and I want to have a look at the exterior of the house."

So saying, he made his way to the front entrance.

Outside, he stood back from the stoop and viewed the facade looking out upon the street, where I saw the Foreign Office car in which we had come still waited, though the driver appeared to have fallen asleep. Pons stood but a few moments so; then he made his way rapidly around the house, myself at his heels.

On the fireplace wall of the house, he gestured in passing, "The chimney is completely inset. That is somewhat of an architectural novelty apart from our country houses, I daresay." He paused at the rear entrance and subjected it to a brief examination that had to be cursory in the absence of any but the dawn's light. Then he went on around the house, and, without pausing again, made straight for the car at the kerb.

Pons maintained a thoughtful silence all the way home.

At No. 7, he asked our driver to follow us up to our quarters, and that young man, accustomed no doubt to orders, obediently trailed us up the steps to 7B, and stood just over the threshold waiting while Pons scribbled hastily on a sheet of notepaper. He folded this presently, slipped it into an envelope, which he sealed, and handed the envelope to the driver.

"Deliver this to Mr. Pons at once. He must be awakened if he is sleeping — though I fancy he is waiting to hear from us."

"Yes, sir," said the driver, and slipped out of the room.

"There is just time for a spot of tea," said Pons then, rubbing his hands together in that annoyingly self-congratulatory way of his, quite as if he had solved the puzzle of Count d'Oro's disappearance. "What do you make of it, Parker?"

"There are several possible explanations," I ventured cautiously.

"I am glad to hear it," he said. "Pray enlighten me."

"Consider first, the woman." I said.

"A classic consideration," interrupted Pons, nodding and smiling.

"A jealous lover may have preceded her to Orrington Crescent, summoned d'Oro to the door, struck him down, and carried him away."

"Leaving no footprints in the snow. A remarkable accomplishment, indeed!"

I ignored his thrust. "D'Oro may have rushed from the house for some powerful motive unknown to us."

"Powerful, certainly, to take him into the snowy night clad only in bathrobe and slippers."

I abandoned my effort and sought to divert him by pointing to a sealed manila envelope on the table. "Surely that was not here when we left."

"I saw it," said Pons. "It is the dossier on d'Oro, sent over by Bancroft. I fancy we have no need of it."

"Ah, you know where he went?"

"Say, rather, I have a grave suspicion."

More than this he would not say. Instead, he turned to his microscope. There he emptied the glassine envelopes and put what I saw now were strands of some substance on glass panes for examination. There were three such strands, and two of them did not long occupy Pons's attention. He studied the third for some time before he turned from the microscope.

"Well, what have you found?" I asked.

"Fragments of cloth. Two are almost certainly from the kind of cloth commonly found on bathrobes, and the third from a cloth with cleaning oil on it. The first two came from the wall, the last from one of the steps."

"Then d'Oro must have been on the stairs at some time that night."

"He has occupied the house for months," replied Pons, "but he or his bathrobe was certainly present on the stairway at some time during his tenancy."

We were interrupted at tea and the crumpets[1] our good Mrs. Johnson had brought up to us by a ponderous step on the stair and an equally ponderous knock that followed.

"Inspector Jamison," said Pons, and opened the door to him.

"A fine thing, Pons," he grumbled, walking in: "To be routed from bed at this hour of the morning and sent over here by the Foreign Office!"

---

[1] A crumpet is a cake made from an unsweetened batter of water or milk, flour and yeast. It is cooked on one side and can be toasted. English muffins, on the other hand, are made from dough instead of batter and are cooked on both sides.

"I sent for you," said Pons. "I have decided to reward your invariable courtesy and graciousness by presenting you with what I hope is the solution to a remarkable mystery."

Lowering his portly body into a chair, Jamison settled his bowler on his knee, touched his dark moustache with an index finger, and viewed Pons through eyes narrowed in suspicion. "I will listen," he said in a voice that dripped cautious doubt.

"Though it has been kept strictly under wraps — you know the Foreign Office, Inspector — Count Ercole d'Oro, the Italian consul — has vanished from a house in which he had an assignation."

"When?"

"Three days ago."

"And now the trail's cold, they call on the Yard!" Jamison said bitterly.

"They've not called on you, Inspector. I have."

"Where's the house?"

"In Orrington Crescent."

Jamison's eyes widened with sudden interest. "Not Number 27?"

"Number 27," said Pons.

"So. Another one. That makes the fourth disappearance from those premises. So we are to be troubled by such matter again!"

"Not for long, I trust," said Pons, as a car scraped to the kerb outside. "But here, if I am not mistaken, is the car from the Foreign Office." He crossed to the windows, and drew aside a curtain. "Are you prepared, Inspector?"

"I was ordered to come armed."

"Good. Let us go down."

He snatched up his deerstalker and ulster[1] as he spoke, and made for the door.

---

[1] A long overcoat worn during the daytime. Until the 1890s, it was worn with a cape attached. Named for the Irish town where it was originally sold.

❖   ❖   ❖   ❖

The house in Orrington Crescent was to all appearances exactly as we had left it. The subdued lights were still burning, and so far as it was possible to ascertain at a casual examination, nothing and no one had disturbed the setting.

"Moore, follow us with the materials," said Pons as he left the car.

"Yes, sir."

Glancing behind us as Pons stood unlocking the door to the house, I saw that the driver was coming up the walk carrying two wrapped objects; a rubber hose dangled from one of them.

Once inside, Pons moved with dispatch. "Help me clear this shelf, Parker," he asked.

We dumped the books unceremoniously on the floor, and in but a few moments we had cleared the chosen shelf — that which we had last cleared. Over his shoulder, Pons said, "Now, Moore, if you please."

The driver now came forward. He had uncovered "the materials" and disclosed two metal canisters, hoses dangling from their nozzles, canisters much like oxygen tanks, with which I was, of course, familiar. They were marked in large letters, "HM War Mag W."

Pons grasped one of them, laid it on the shelf before him, pushed the hose into what I had taken for the open knothole behind the shelf, and turned the nozzle. Then he applied the second canister to the hole on the other side of the chimney and turned the nozzle. I could hear their contents hissing into open space behind the bookshelves.

Pons took a revolver from the pocket of his ulster and pressed it upon the driver. "If by any miscalculation of mine, a stranger to you should appear in this room, hold him at bay. And do not hesitate to shoot, if you value your life, young man." With a sweep of his arm as he turned, Pons said,

"Come," and hurried over to the stairs leading to the floor above.

He bounded up the steps and into the room directly above the sitting-room where Moore waited upon the canisters to empty themselves. He took his stand facing the wall behind the chimney.

"To arms, inspector," he said crisply.

The three of us stood there in silence, waiting upon events which Pons showed by his confident expression that he expected to take place. Two minutes, three — five — while below us the canisters were emptying into the wall.

Then there rose from within the wall an urgent, scrabbling sound. And suddenly the entire wall behind the chimney began to slide noiselessly downward to recess behind the wall of the story below, disclosing a passage leading down.

But we had only a moment in which to become aware of this before a disheveled figure in a white surgeon's gown came struggling up the steps of the passage and stumbled gasping into the empty room.

"Watch your nostrils," said Pons sharply, covering his face with his handkerchief.

"Stand where you are!" shouted Jamison.

But his admonition was needless, for the man who had come up out of the wall collapsed upon the floor, senseless.

"Inspector," said Pons, "let me introduce you to Dr. Roland Borstad, the author, if I am not mistaken, of the Orrington Crescent disappearances — and, I fancy, of others that have gone unrecorded and equally unsolved. Handcuff him hands and feet, Jamison, and drag him to the car as unceremoniously as he dragged his victims up the stairs after drugging them with gas through those same holes in the wall that served to turn the tables on him." He flashed a glance at me. "Not, Parker, with antiseptic, but with some form of anesthetic very probably of his own devising.

"Now, then, that gas we've sent below is a harmless but effective soporific developed by the scientists in the War Office.¹ We'll give it time to settle, and then go down to learn what diabolical matters have engaged Borstad all these years. Pray that we find d'Oro still alive. Moore will give you a hand with Borstad, Jamison."

And in half an hour we descended — to find below the house fully equipped living quarters and an elaborate laboratory, on an operating table in which lay Count Ercole d'Oro, strapped down, unconscious, showing marks of torture, but alive and not in critical condition, despite Borstad's experiments.

On a desk not far away lay a thick manuscript in Borstad's hand — sickeningly annotated, detailing accounts of his experiments, not only on Clyde Lee and Howard Eliot, but on others — the hapless victim Borstad had lured out of the London night into his devilish laboratory, some of those whose names set down by Borstad Jamison recognized as among London's undiscovered missing persons. His manuscript bore the revealing title of *Beyond the Threshold of Pain*.

As we rode back to 7B, with the still unconscious Dr. Borstad slumped in the front seat beside Moore, and d'Oro on his way to the nearest hospital by ambulance, Pons answered Jamison's impatient questions.

"Quite apart from the fact that there was no manifest motive for d'Oro's disappearance — the Foreign Office's almost paranoid view of espionage as the inevitable explanation of all such events involving any diplomat, even one of the minor status of Count d'Oro, could be discounted at once — the matter devolved basically upon one of two alternatives: d'Oro — and his predecessors, whose bones have long since been

---

¹ *Soporific:* A sleep-inducing agent. Sometimes also used to describe something other than drugs, such as a politician's speech, an author's earnest essay, or a minister's sermon. The government department that oversees administration of the British Army.

buried when Borstad had finished exploring their reactions to pain — disappeared either from the house or within it. I chose to act upon the latter alternative, and made such examination as I could on that assumption.

"Your remembering, Parker, that Borstad's difference with his superiors was rooted in his audacious experiments with the response of the human body to pain suggested a tenable, if horrible motive for Borstad's disappearance, which was obviously carefully planned, as the house he built at No. 27 was planned in its entirety to serve as a trap for his victims, such as he did not take off the streets by night — the derelicts and drunkards to be found in any city during the hours of darkness. 'Nervous breakdown' is one of those ambiguous diagnoses which covers everything from fatigue to madness.

"Once the assumption of the victim's disappearance within the house was acted upon, certain corroborative evidence was readily found. It was not the Foreign Office that cleaned the house in Orrington Crescent — it was Borstad himself, making sure that every trace of his work was eliminated. Save, of course, the threads from the bathrobe that caught on the plaster when he dragged d'Oro, unconscious from the anesthetic seeping into the room from the openings in the bookcase wall, up the stairs to the cleverly concealed entrance to his sub-surface quarters. You ought to have noticed, Parker, that the difference in the disturbance of the dust on the bookshelves was marked — where books were withdrawn and put back, the marks of withdrawal were in the dust; in the vicinity of the openings the dust was disturbed as by air, not by the withdrawal of books."

He shook his head grimly. "The dedicated scientist is constantly in danger of losing his humanity, and forgetting that he too is as integral to nature as the ant or the tree. Borstad's work in progress might better and more pointedly have been titled *Beyond the Threshold of Sanity*."

Connie

Frank Godwin

Running from 1927 to 1944, Connie *was the first adventure strip in which its hero was a woman. Not a woman-as-sex-symbol such as* Sheena, Queen of the Jungle *or* Wonder Woman, *but a woman who also happens to undergo a lot of adventures. Also unusual for the time,* Connie *is wonderfully illustrated, as realistic in places as later strips by Milton Caniff* (Terry and the Pirates, Steve Canyon) *and Alex Raymond* (Flash Gordon).

In this sequence, Connie learns that she was named in a rich relative's will. But in order to inherit a fortune, she must make the front page of the newspapers four times within 30 days (I didn't say these were realistic adventures). She decides to become an aviator, following the example of Amelia Earhart, who became the first woman to fly across the Atlantic in June 1928. Her relative, Foanie, tries to stop her, and enlists Padlock Jones to help.

Frank Godwin (1889-1959) was a prolific magazine and comic book illustrator who drew art for editions of Treasure Island, Kidnapped, Robinson Crusoe *and* Robin Hood.

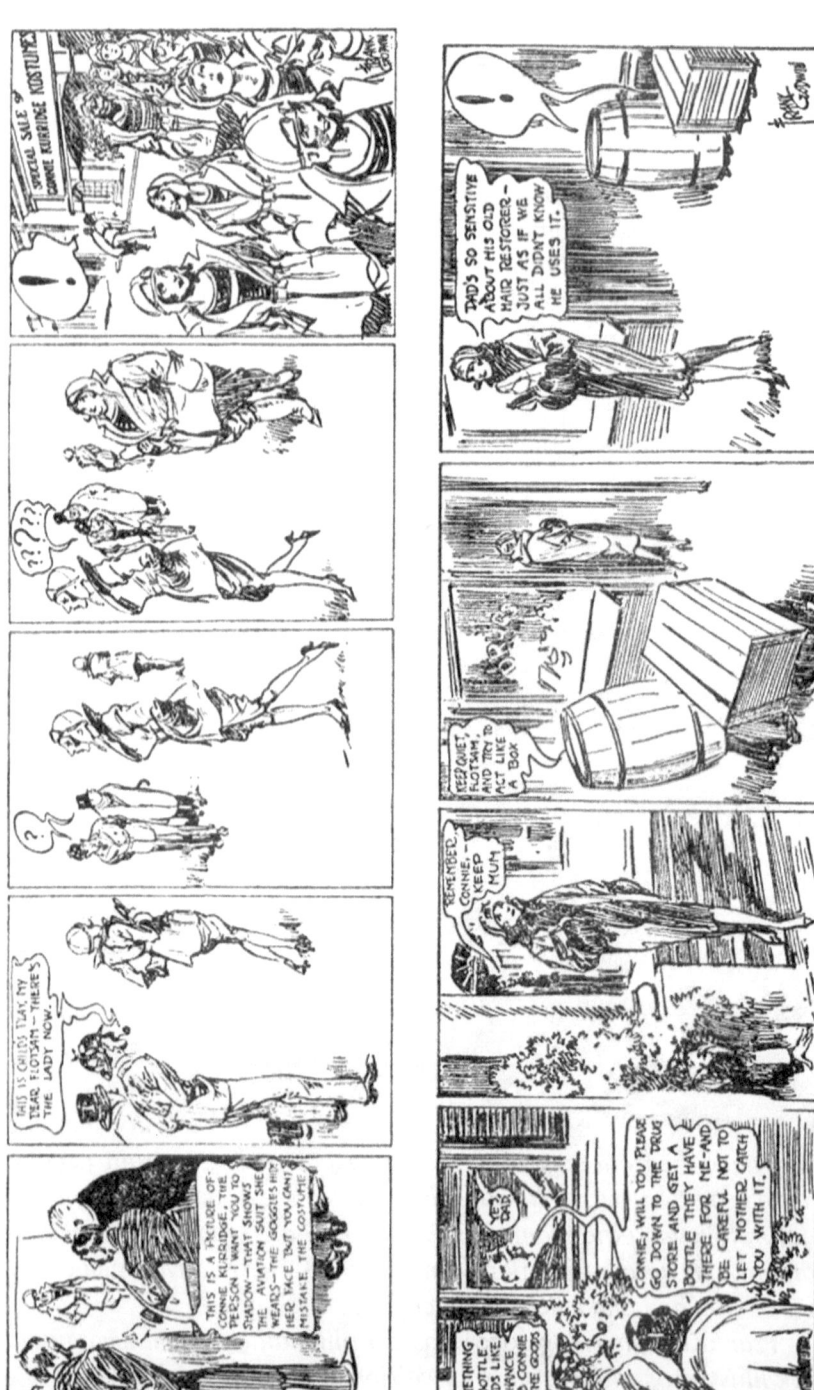

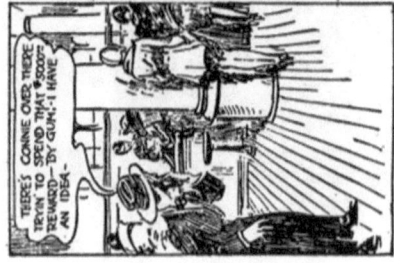

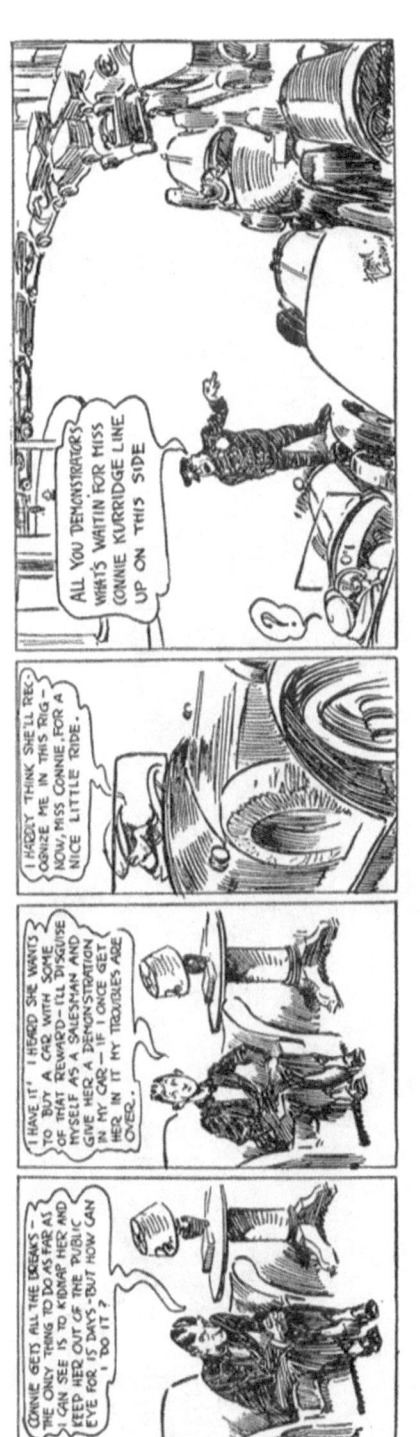

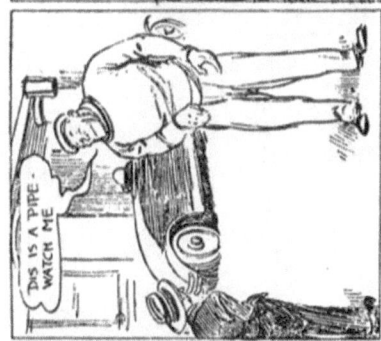
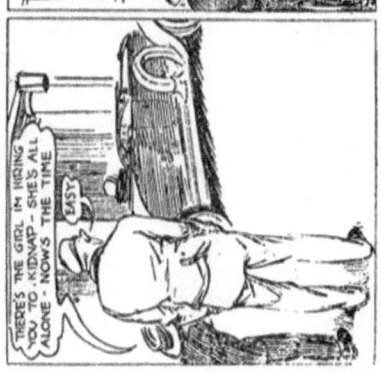

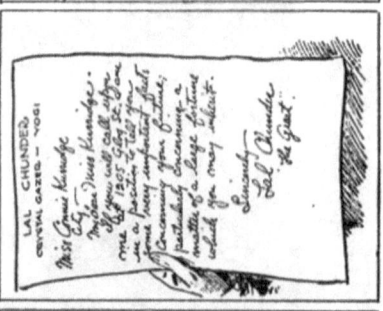

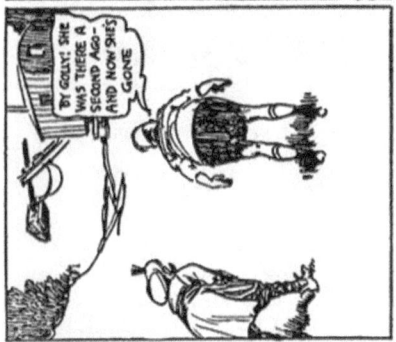

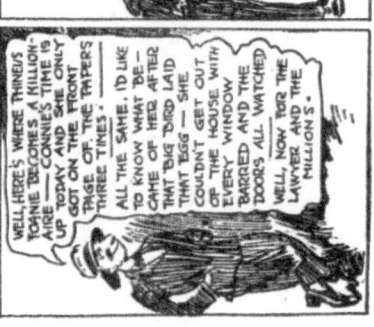

The Omnibus Murder

R.E. Swartwout

As a source of Sherlockian parodies, The Granta *undergraduate magazine of the University of Cambridge, stands out as a witty supplier of material. It was co-founded by R.C. Lehmann, who wrote the Picklock Holes stories collected in* The Complete Punch Parodies of Sherlock Holmes. *Two other* Granta *stories have appeared in the 223B Casebook series: "The Episode of the Bold Bad Undergraduate and the Postage Stamps" in the 1910-1914 volume, and "The Bounder of Camberville" in the 1920-1924 book.*

Published in the Oct. 18 issue, "The Omnibus Murder" satirizes many of the era's most notable authors. It's written in the form of a round-robin story, in which one author begins the tale, stops at a cliffhanger, then passes it along to the next writer. Perhaps not surprisingly, when many of Britain's great authors formed the Detection Club in 1930, they raised money to support it by publishing round-robin novels such as The Floating Admiral *(1931-32). Three of the authors parodied below contributed to that volume!*

The author of "The Omnibus Murder," Robert E. Swartwout (1905-1951), was an American-born author who made a mark for himself at Cambridge not only as a satirist but as the first American coxswain to lead the university rowing team to victory over rival Oxford. He constructed crossword puzzles for The Spectator, *wrote humorous pieces for* Punch, *and used his rowing background to write* The Boat Race Murder *(1933) and* Rhymes of the River and Other Verses *(1927).*

I.
DIRTY WORK AT THE CROSSROADS
by Sir A. Conan Doyle

It was, as I remember, a rainy afternoon in the Strand of October, 1892—

Editor: *The Strand?*

Sir A.C.D.: Tut, tut. I mean the autumn of 1892.

Editor: Very well. Proceed.

—that I called upon Holmes. "Ah, Watson!" he cried,

through the fog of Empire tobacco.¹ "Come in. I am writing a monograph upon the symphonic symphonies of Corregio. Don't sit on the blood-stained sofa, it is a valuable clue in the extraordinary case of Major McMurdo Bilson and the sinister activities of the Red-Nosed League. The opium's in the coal-scuttle. I have here a pair of braces,² carelessly left behind by a visitor who called this morning when I was out. I deduce that he is a bald-headed, left-handed Liberal,³ with a second cousin in the Indian Civil Service.⁴ And, if I mistake not, that is his ring."

II.
THE ADJOURNED INQUEST
By Edgar Wallace[5]

---

¹ A type of shag tobacco for pipe smokers. It typically combined tobacco from several nations in the British Empire. One particular blend, Player's, used leaf from Rhodesia, Nyasaland, India, or Canada. Another advantage of Empire blends were their lower prices, since tobacco from within the Commonwealth was taxed at a lower rate than imports.

² The British word for suspenders, those strips of wide elastic that hold up trousers. So what are suspenders in that country? Those are the small bits of elastic women use to attach their stockings to garter belts (if they wear stockings) and men use to keep their socks up (ditto).

³ The Liberal Party was one of two major parties in Great Britain during the 19th and early 20th centuries. During the Edwardian era, the party introduced reforms that laid the foundation for the welfare state in Britain. They instituted restrictions on drinking alcohol, instituted free school meals for children, increased scholarship availability for working-class students, introduced pensions for the elderly, and set up labor exchanges to help the unemployed find work. Infighting and the rising popularity of the Labour Party caused the Liberal Party to fall into a decline, and by 1988 it merged with the Social Democratic Party to form the Liberal Democrats.

⁴ The permanent bureaucracy of the government in India, which in 1929 was under the control of the British. The organization and culture of the civil service was carried over after the partition of India in 1947 and the end of British control.

⁵ Wallace (1875-1932) was a prolific English writer and journalist. He wrote so quickly that it was joked that a friend of his called the house and was told that Wallace was writing a new novel. "That's okay," he said, "I'll wait." Despite his success, few of his books are in print today. His story "The Little Dragon of Jade" appears in this volume.

I picked it up. It was a plain gold circlet, inscribed with the mystic letters—

Sir A.C.D.: Idiot! I meant a ring at the door-bell.

E.W.: Sorry.

A furtive, foxy-eyed creature shambled in.

"Evenin' gents," it said. "I'm Sid Blibers, alias Sid the Soaker. I don't mind sayin' as I'm a lag.[1] I just done a ten-stretch on the moor,[2] and while I was incarcerated in that melancholy locality, I fell in with a bloke called Bert the Biffer."

"Ah!" said Inspector Holmes, his kindly grey eyes twinkling. "Go on."

"Bert conked out two years ago. But he gives me a message ter pass on ter you: BEWARE OF THE CRIMSON ARRER!"

III.
SUPERINTENDENT WATTS IS PUZZLED
By Agatha Christie[3]

"Duck ze 'ead!" cried Poirolmes sharply. I did so. There was a shattering of glass, and, as I looked round, I saw the body of Sid the Soaker stretched upon the carpet. Protruding from his breast was — *a crimson arrow!*

"Haha!" said my friend. "Zat was a narrow squeal, as you say in your English idiom."

"Narrow squeak, you mean," I said.

A.E.W. Mason:[4] Look here! That sort of thing is my copy-

---

[1] Criminal slang for a convict who has finished his sentence.
[2] Wallace frequently flavored his stories with criminal slang. A "ten-stretch" is a 10-year sentence, and "moor" meant Dartmoor prison in Devon.
[3] Probably the world's best-selling mystery writer, Christie (1890-1976) created Hercule Poirot, the retired Belgian police detective, for her first novel *The Mysterious Affair at Styles* (1920). She would go on to write 33 novels and more than 50 stories about the detective, who has been portrayed by actors such as Kenneth Branagh, David Suchet, Albert Finney, Peter Ustinov, Tony Randall, and Orson Welles.
[4] Mason (1865-1948) was a politician and popular author. His *The Four Feathers* (1902) has been filmed several times, the latest in 2002 with

right. That's Monsieur Hanaud.

A.C.: Sorry.

"But zey cannot fool Poirolmes," he continued. "Ze little grey cells—!"

IV.
THE VERDICT
By R. Austin Freeman[1]

I took the crimson arrow to my friend Thorndyke. He beamed at me from behind a zareba[2] of learned tomes. I glanced at the titles of a few of them. *Science for the Million, The Boy's Guide to Elementary Chemistry, The Young Electrobiologist, in Words of One Syllable*. What a brainy man Thorndyke was!

"My dear disciple!" he cried. "I am feeling very scientific this morning. Let me tell you something. Iodine," he said impressively, "was discovered in 1812 by Courtois, in the ashes of certain sea-plants. Its presence was revealed by its beautiful violet vapour. *You* didn't know that."[3]

I did not and confessed as much. I then gave him the crimson arrow. He seemed very pleased. "We must put Polton on to this!" he chuckled, as he rang the bell. As he did so, I could not help noticing that it was a diving bell of the latest Admiralty pattern.

"A singular case," said Thorndyke, smiling. "I found a

Heath Ledger and Kate Hudson. His Inspector *Hanaud* was a French detective considered to be a model for Agatha Christie's Hercule Poirot.

[1] The British writer (1862-1943) created forensic investigator Dr. John Thorndyke, who was helped by his lab assistant Nathaniel Polton. Beginning with *The Red Thumb Mark* (1907), the solution to his cases hinged in various branches of scientific knowledge. Among his admirers were Raymond Chandler, who called Freeman "a wonderful performer. He has no equal in his genre, and he is also a much better writer than you might think."

[2] An Arabic word meaning a cattle corral. In northeastern Africa, a zareba is built by interlacing thorn bushes and stakes.

[3] That is correct. The Thorndyke stories turn on arcane points of knowledge such as toxicology, metallurgy and tropical medicine.

corpse the other day — but here is Polton. Polton," he went on, "I want you to photograph this arrow in forty-nine different positions. And, Polton! Lunch for two."

Polton's face crinkled. It always does. Thorndyke once explained to me that his sales would be nowhere if it didn't.

V.
THE INSPECTOR MAKES A DISCOVERY
By Ronald Knox[1]

As soon as Polton had left the room, Father Thorndyke—

R.A. Freeman: What do you mean, Father Thorndyke?

R.A. Knox: Father Brown, if you prefer it. But that's Mr. Chesterton's patent.[2]

Father Thorndyke turned to me excitedly. "Watson! We have been a pack of silly fools!" He flourished a Bradshaw[3] in my face. "Do you realize that the 10.34 from King's Cross stops at Hitchin at 11.12 and not at 11.13, as we had imagined? And that the Flying Scotsman does not go to Leicester at all?"

"Yes, but why?" I said.

"Why!" he shouted. "Did you see the *Telegraph* crossword

---

[1] Ronald Arbuthnott Knox (1888-1957) was a Catholic priest and author of detective stories featuring insurance investigator Miles Bredon. Knox is also notable for writing "Studies in the Literature of Sherlock Holmes" (1928), one of the first papers that is part of "the game" played by fans as a way of explaining Conan Doyle's role in a world where Sherlock and Watson are real.

[2] Gilbert Keith Chesterton (1874-1936) was a notable public figure in his time. He was a writer, poet, playwright, philosopher and Christian apologist. His priest-detective Father Brown gave him a way to use popular fiction to also expound on religious questions. A dramatic figure who stood 6 feet 4 inches and weighed 280 pounds, he was such a public figure that P.G. Wodehouse described a loud crash as "a sound like G. K. Chesterton falling onto a sheet of tin."

[3] A guide to Britain's railways, including their timetables. It was first published in 1839 by George Bradshaw (1801-1853) as *Bradshaw's Railway Timetables*, later *Bradshaw's Railway Companion*. In the Golden Age of mystery fiction, railroad timetables were a trope, used to create or break a suspect's alibi (see for example *The Five Red Herrings* by Dorothy L. Sayers).

last Saturday? *These little people apparently dislike woolly hats.* Bantams, of course! What fools we have been! Do you mean to say you didn't get Polychrytudination in Torquemada[1] on Sunday? My good man, the person who shot Sid Blibbers was the acrostic editor of the *Cambridge Review!*[2] What could be more obvious?"

VI.
THE BEGINNING OF THE END
By J.S. Fletcher[3]

Meanwhile, Inspector Sims sat twiddling his thumbs in the Silchester police station. Nothing had happened for chapters and chapters, and he was becoming sleepy. So were the readers. Suddenly there was a knock at the door, and a figure entered. It was Bert the Biffer, heavily disguised as the Provost of Oriel.[4]

"I have information for you," said the figure.

"When will you give it?" cried the Inspector hoarsely.

"In another thrilling installment next week," said the figure, and vanished the way he came.

VII.
MURDER MOST FOUL!
By Freeman Wills Crofts[5]

Hastily summoning a dirigible,[6] the Inspector dashed af-

---

[1] The pseudonym for Edward Powys Mathers (1892-1939) who created crossword puzzles for *The Observer* from 1926 until his death. He adopted the name of the notorious Spanish cardinal Tomas de Torquemada (1420-1498) who led the Spanish Inquisition.

[2] An intellectual journal that was founded at the university in 1879.

[3] Joseph Smith Fletcher (1863-1935) was a prolific writer who was a contemporary of Conan Doyle. He wrote more than 230 books on a variety of subjects, including several featuring private investigator Ronald Camberwell.

[4] In Britain, a provost acts as the head of the college. Oriel is one of 38 colleges that make up the University of Oxford.

[5] Crofts (1879-1957) was a mystery author who is best remembered for Inspector Joseph French. His works were admired by Agatha Christie and Raymond Chandler.

[6] A lighter-than-air craft consisting of a gasbag filled with hydrogen or

ter him. "Paddington,[1] and double fare!" he cried to the driver. But he was held up at Tottenham Court Road, and had to sit fuming while the stream of traffic ebbed down Jesus Lane to Tilbury Docks. Finally he reached Euston. Too late! The Golden Arrow was just steaming out of Bletchley Junction. Was this then the end?

Yes.—Ed.

R.E. Swartwout wearing his cap as a Cambridge coxswain.

---

helium and pushed forward using an engine and propellers. Also known as airship, blimps (basically dirigibles that are not rigid and act more like balloons), or zeppelins (airships made in Germany by the German Zeppelin Co.). Dirigible the word is from the French *balloon dirigeable*, with the latter word from *diriger* for to steer or guide.
[1] Paddington Station, in the City of Westminster, is a major railway, bus and underground terminus. What follows is a series of real locations that cannot be reached in any kind of logical order. For example, Tilbury Docks is a port east of London, Euston is a railway station in central London, and Bletchley Junction is in the county of Buckinghamshire northwest of London.

The Return of the Native

"Cohan and Doyle" (Lester A. Blumner)

This story appeared in the Cornell Daily Sun *of Nov. 23. As with many collegiate parodies, it contains references humorous to fellow classmates. But sussing out the author uncovered a now-forgotten hoax that made national news at the time.*

First, we need to identify the author. Despite the byline of "Cohan and Doyle," the bottom of the story also contained at its end the notation "CD XVI." This clue, and a look at the newspaper's masthead, helped identify the author as Lester A. Blumner (1909-1989), the editor of the Sun's *humor section.*

Cornell alumni also know Blumner for his role in a 1930 hoax that snared President Hoover's vice president, Charles Curtis, and other high Republican Party officials. Blumner and another student created the fictional Hugo N. Frye and sent letters to GOP officials inviting them to Cornell for a dinner honoring the founder of New York's Republican Party. If they couldn't attend, they were asked to send a message. Trusting the word of Cornell men, several officials duly sent messages of praise, which were read at the celebratory dinner. The story was picked up by newspapers nationwide, including The New York Times.

Blumner went on to work in newspapers and then as a marketing consultant. During World War II, he served as special agent in the Counter Intelligent Corps., working on espionage cases in North Africa, Italy, and France. For his service he received the Croix de Guerre, the Croix de la Liberation, and the Bronze Star. To this I would add a medal for this Sherlockian parody, for gallantry in action.

I was sitting on my chest in my study when Sherlock came in and sat down beside me. I didn't move. I couldn't. He was sitting on my chest.

"Ah," growled the master mind. "When are you going to move, Watson?"

"Not until the first of the month," I grumbled, for I was exceedingly discomfited.

Two of his friends came in and sat down.

"Now, fellows," I said. "This chest may have strong ribs,

but it was never intended as a community chest." [1]

"Watson," said the great detective sternly, "I see that Ithaca is back in its normal state."

"New York," I asked.

"No, dolt," he replied. "Frigidity."

"Oh, Sherlock," I gasped, "You've been out with a co-ed again."

He accepted the reproof with a smile and bowed his head.

"To tell the truth, Watson, I really feel at home, now that the ground is once more covered with snow and ice." The great detective frowned. "So ho! young man! You've been eating at Willard Straight."[2]

"Marvelous, Sherlock, marvelous!" I exclaimed.

The great criminologist lit his foul-smelling pipe, and I was instantly reminded of the cheery, little blaze that is to be found every afternoon between South Baker Hall and the new World War Memorial.[3]

All of a sudden there was an unusual flapping noise overhead. I looked at Sherlock. He merely nodded and said, "Pay no attention. It is merely a pin-headed flapper." [4]

---

[1] More than just a card in Monopoly, Community Chests were a forerunner of the United Way, which raised money and distributed it to local groups. The first group was founded in 1913 in Cleveland, Ohio.

[2] In his short life, Cornell alumni Willard Straight (1880-1918) was a foreign correspondent, founder of *The New Republic* magazine, who courted W. Averell Harriman's sister and Theodore Roosevelt's daughter before marrying into the wealthy Whitney family, and fathered three children before dying in the Spanish influenza epidemic. Cornell named a building for Straight which contains a dining hall.

[3] *South Baker Hall* was built in 1915 and the *War Memorial* in 1920.

[4] A combination of innovations in fashion combined with the trauma caused by the war created an environment in which a rising generation of young women felt themselves liberated from the social and sexual norms of the past. These women bobbed their hair, listened to jazz, smoked, drank, and treated sex casually. The word "flapper" could have come from northern England, where it referred to a young girl whose pigtails "flapped" on her back. An alternative source might come from "flap," an old slang word for prostitute that by the 1890s morphed into "flapper." It first appeared in Desmond Coke's

"So it is," I said. "I had forgotten that this is the time of the year when they migrate to the South."

"The bitter cold of the region drives them all to Miami and Palm Beach," he observed.

There was a raucous sound, and again I looked questioningly at Holmes. "Merely a rough-necked captain," he said, "Calling to his mate."

There was another sound and another. Again Sherlock answered my silent inquiry, "Just one swallow after another — also on their way South. But you wouldn't think they'd make such a noise. Of course," he added, "The swallows in themselves don't make so much noise. It's the going south."[1]

"And are all these feathered friends making the southern trip?" I asked wonderingly.

"Yes, yes. And many more," smiled Holmes. "The high-hatted topper, the green-eyed catbird, and the whip-poor-william."

"They make quite a party, don't they?"

"O yes," Sherlock replied. "And now is the time for all good men to come to the aid of the party,[2] and crack a couple of good travelling salesmen jokes."

"Quick, Watson, the needle!"[3]

"Why?"

"I have a rent in my coat."

"The rent," I asked. He nodded, and I smiled because I knew he was as broke as I was.

"Sew," I said, "It would seam."

---

novel of Oxford life *Sandford of Merton* (1903), and for the next decade it was used to refer to young women on the London stage, dancers of the Charleston who flapped their arms like a bird, and in 1920 was used as the title of a silent film comedy starring Olive Thomas (1894-1920).

[1] Swallows doesn't refer to birds in this case, but to drinking.

[2] A phrase created by typing instructor Charles Weller that appeared as early as 1889.

[3] A phrase credited to Sherlock Holmes but which never appears in the canon. Its earliest appearance is difficult to track down, but it apparently appeared on stage in burlesque parodies of Holmes after the success of William Gillette's production.

The Modern Radio Sleuth

As Visualised by JAY COOTE

This amusing satire on a type of popular fiction will entertain you. And, in addition, it hides some helpful hints for knob turners and DX "fans." Read on.

Jay Coote

Illustrated by "K"

Holmes has been used to promote an astonishing array of products and services, including air travel, tobacco, laxatives, and even the British income tax system. Advertisers could rely on the icon to be instantly recognized, and copy writers could draw on his image, his idiosyncrasies, and his tics to create their ads. In this example, which appeared the Dec. 7 and 14 issues of Amateur Wireless, *he instructs radio owners on the right way to tune into and identify foreign radio stations. Nothing is known of the artist, nor of Jay Coote except that he reported on the development of radio stations across Europe.*

In the later stages of his brilliant career, Sheerluck Coames, sated with problems in criminology, had turned his activities to the study of radio, and in all leisure moments could be found seated in his chambers in Dacre Street, before a multi-valve receiving set. As was his wont, even in the case of a mere hobby, he was thorough in all his methods, and brought to play, in every instance where difficulties arose, those amazing qualities of deduction which had secured to him in other circles so great a name in the solving of problems.

It would be impossible to set down the innumerable puzzles which, in his characteristic graciousness, he was willing to elucidate for beginners in the new science, but such outstanding episodes as "The Tragedy of the Hoarse-voiced Announcer," "The Incident of the Straying Wave," "The Adventure of the Lost Transmitter," and other equally startling European sensations have been chronicled by me in their time.

Visualise, therefore, one foggy evening in November,

when no duties compelled Sheerluck Coames to leave the comfort of his bachelor flat. Picture again this great man, wrapped in a flowered dressing gown, the indispensable pipe stuck in his mouth, idly twirling with his delicate hands the condensers of his latest instrument. A peal at the front door bell, steps on the stairs, and Dr. Botson, bringing with him the full flavour of the "London particular"[1] outside, entered the room and carefully closed the door behind him.

"Sit down, Botson, and make yourself comfortable. The decanter, syphon,[2] and glasses are on the table to your right;

---

[1] A common phrase referring to the pea soup fog. While it looked charming in the movies, it was really industrial pollution containing equal parts of soot particles and poisonous sulfur dioxide. Caused by industrial processes and homes burning soft coal, the result was a gaseous vapor that hung in the streets and ruined the health of its inhabitants, particularly the elderly and the very young. Rollo Russell in *London Fogs* (1880) described it as "brown, reddish-yellow, or greenish, darkens more than a white fog, has a smoky, or sulphurous smell, is often somewhat dryer than a country fog, and produces, when thick, a choking sensation. Instead of diminishing while the sun rises higher, it often increases in density, and some of the most lowering London fogs occur about midday or late in the afternoon. Sometimes the brown masses rise and interpose a thick curtain at a considerable elevation between earth and sky. A white cloth spread out on the ground rapidly turns dirty, and particles of soot attach themselves to every exposed object." By the 1920s, when traffic lights and electric billboards were installed, the lights of Piccadilly Circus must have gleamed under a thick blanket of English industrial fog. It wasn't until the Clear Air Act of 1956 that an attempt was begun to clean up the problem. Conan Doyle vividly describe the fog in several canonical stories. In "The Adventure of the Bruce-Partington Plans" (1912), he describes "a dense yellow fog" that has settled down over London, and later notes "a greasy, heavy brown swirl still drifting past us and condensing in oily drops on the windowpane."

But where did "particular" come from? As far back as the 1790s, a "London particular" referred to a special brown Madeira wine that was imported solely to London. That it was exclusive to London might have encouraged adopting the phrase to refer to the soot particles that were difficult to remove from clothing.

[2] A glass device with a nozzle that combines water with a mix of tartaric acid and sodium bicarbonate. The combination infuses the water with carbon dioxide to create carbonated water. It was also called a gasogene. A

"But my dear Coames, how did you know it was I?" cigarettes to your left."

"But my dear Coames, how did you know it was I?"

"Botson, there are twenty stairs to this flat and I have noticed that you take exactly eighteen seconds to climb them."

Botson seated himself by Sheerluck Coames, lit a cigarette, and took from his breast pocket a small slip of paper, bearing a number of written notes:

"You are marvellous!"

"Perfectly simple, as you see. You look worried. Has your latest set given you any trouble, or have you brought with you

---

decanter is a bottle used to hold spirits or decanted wine. Not only did it look nicer on the sideboard than the labeled commercial bottles, it also helped the frugal-minded host hide his cheap spirits from his guests.

a number of these little problems which so often puzzle you?"

"A good guess, my dear Coames, and I should like your help."

Sheerluck Coames lay back in his chair and adopted his characteristic attitude.

"Life during the past few days has proved tiresome, the local programmes have contained but little of interest; any break in this monotony is welcome. I am listening."

"Well, last night I heard the song of the nightingale. Roughly speaking, it was—" said Dr Botson.

"Be more precise, my dear sir. The song of that bird, in November, is unusual. I have here a small paper I wrote—"

"Well, last night I heard the song
of the nightingale . . ."

"It was undoubtedly a nightingale. I was on the point of adding that the time was about 9 p.m., and that the wavelength of the transmission, although not registered at the time, was well below that of London. I may say that I also heard it again later in the evening."

"Here we have some data to work upon," replied Coames. "Let us consider two alternatives, namely, the relay of the bird's song, or a gramophone record. The first supposition we discard, for the reason already stated; the second is possible. On the other hand, as a means of entertainment the record would be a poor one, and as it was repeated, we must presume that it was not part of a programme, but used for a specific purpose."

"I have it. An interval signal!"[1]

"Exactly; it is that adopted by Turin.[2] Make a note of it, and also bear in mind that there are other bird calls, such as that of the canary used by Lille, and the cuckoo practised by Wilno, Ljubljana, Strasbourg, and Leningrad.[3] Any more questions?"

"Many more," replied Botson. "Later in the evening I caught a portion of a call, but the only word I picked up clearly was *Allah*. This would point to a Turkish station, perhaps?"

"No, for firstly, the word would not be used; secondly, you cannot believe that you heard the Muezzin[4] calling the Faithful to prayer; and, thirdly, the only Mohammedan station you might possibly tune in would be Stamboul.[5] You say yourself

---

[1] A sound or musical phrase used by broadcast stations. It was used to serve as a station identifier and to help a listener tune into the correct frequency. It would be played between programmes or during breaks in transmission.

[2] A city in northern Italy.

[3] To continue identifying the other cities: *Wilno* is the Polish word for Vilnius, the capital of Lithuania; *Ljubljana* is the largest city of Slovenia; *Strasburg* is a city in Germany; *Leningrad* was St. Petersburg until the Soviet Union changed it in 1924. It was changed back after the dissolution of the Soviet Union in 1991.

[4] A man who calls Muslims to prayer from the minaret of a mosque.

[5] An alternative name for Istanbul, a major port in Turkey that was earlier called Constantinople.

that you only registered a portion of the call. On about what wavelength was it?"

"Somewhere between Kalundborg and Warsaw." [1]

"In that case, the problem is solved. The words heard were Stockholm-*Motala*.[2] The latter name is not pronounced in the Italian fashion, with a long A, but sounds uncommonly like *Mott-allah*. Next please?"

Sheerluck Coames had dismissed the problem with a wave of the hand, as though it were beneath his dignity to bring his powers to bear on such an easy solution.

"Now here is where some concentration of thought will be necessary," said Botson, with a smile. "According to all wavelength lists — and the one given in *Amateur Wireless* 'Broadcast Telephony' is peculiarly complete — there exist no Spanish or Italian stations operating on more than 550 metres, yet an evening or so ago, just under the Hilversum[3] transmission, I listened to an announcement in a language which had a Latin flavour to it. I must definitely emphasise that it was not Russian, and, consequently, it could not have been Leningrad or Moscow Experimental.

"Why definitely?" replied Sheerluck Coames, with a pitying sort of smile. "The Russian language is a difficult one and seldom learnt by other nationalities; yet the Russian is anxious that his programmes should be heard by foreign and more distant listeners. For this reason news bulletins — "cooked,"[4]

---

[1] Kalundborg is a city in Denmark; *Warsaw* is the capital of Poland.

[2] Both *Stockholm* and *Motala* are cities in Sweden. In 1927, a telephone wire connected the two cities allowing both cities to transmit the same programs. As a result, announcers would declare the call sign "Stockholm-Motala."

[3] A city in the Netherlands.

[4] In the Soviet Union, every aspect of life was subjected to the control of the state. With the goal of exporting revolution in mind, news bulletins were designed not to convey the facts, but to filter them through Marxist philosophy to serve the state's goals. This could lead to suppressing and even denying the existence of events such as the widespread famine in the Soviet Union in the early 1930s.

maybe, for special consumption abroad — are given out in a language which is rapidly gaining numerous adherents, Esperanto,[1] my dear Botson; a tongue which possesses a decided Italian — but not a Spanish sound. Your station, if you were so close to Hilversum, was undoubtedly Leningrad. You can prove this at any time by comparing the condenser readings for that powerful transmitter. Besides, from that station you will also hear the cuckoo calling to his mate. These questions are childish and I am surprised you should put them."

"In no instance do you appear to encounter any difficulty. How is this?" replied the crestfallen Botson.

"It is merely a question of practice, some experience, and a good memory for data collected at a number of sittings. If you spend some time at your receiver, you must necessarily become familiar with both the calls and the peculiarities of the various studios. Although you may not know more than your own native language, after a few days you should experience no difficulty in differentiating between Teutonic or Latin tongues, and further experience will soon permit you to classify in your mind, as you hear them, the languages of Slavonic origin. The actual identification of transmissions heard is dependent on two important factors, language and position of the transmitter in the wave band."

"I don't quite follow you when you say that the actual identification of a transmitter depends upon language and its position in the waveband, Coames."

"Shall we put it this way? You have at your disposal in *Amateur Wireless* a full list of wavelengths adopted by the European transmitters. You may or may not memorise them — no matter — but the list should be within reach as you pick up the various transmissions. Surely, my dear Botson, you must have found by now that some method is necessary in any work undertaken by man? It is essential that you should

---

[1] A specially constructed language invented by a Polish ophthalmologist L.L. Zamenhof (1859-1917) in the belief that a universal language would reduce misunderstandings and foster peace.

know approximately to what wavelength or frequency your receiver is tuned. Unless you are actually told by a studio announcer in a language you understand, to what station you are listening, you cannot, except with considerable difficulty, identify the transmitter."

"But, then, how can I—"

"Some indispensable data is essential; it may be approximate wavelength, type of or actually recognised language."

"Surely, Coames, this is a very onerous way of securing the information."

"It is the last method to which I resort. Language and wavelength should give you all the clues required."

"I might agree with you but for the fact that to me, as well as to thousands of other equally unfortunate listeners, all languages but our own are merely classed as foreign. I might say that a talk sounded to me like French or Italian, or that an announcement was guttural, but I could not definitely state what language I had heard."

"Admittedly," replied Coames, "this is a difficulty which to the tyro appears insurmountable, but you will be surprised to find that after a short time, as I already said, you will have no hesitation in narrowing down the possibilities by stating that the words heard were, say, neither French, Italian, Spanish, nor German, in which case you are left to choose from a reduced number. By this time your search would be limited to the Scandinavian tongues or to those comprised by or akin to the Slavonic group. With this knowledge, and a rough idea of the wavelength, if the list be consulted, you will again limit your search to two or three transmitters. A little patience, a little knowledge, a methodical process of elimination, and you have attained your aim, that of correctly identifying the transmission picked up."

"It seems easy," said Botson pensively.

"My dear Botson, it is not so difficult as it appears at first sight, for the stations possess peculiarities apart from — in most instances — distinctive calls or interval signals, either of which must be picked up in the course of a broadcast. It is obvious that in the event of a doubtful case, some minutes may have to be sacrificed. Personally, where, in my mind, I am uncertain, and where, owing to the length of an item, I cannot immediately secure the information required, I make a note of my condenser readings, and return to this exact position at intervals. No time is actually lost, for in the meantime you may have found interesting items in other cities."

"This question of languages—" commenced Botson.

"Usually one can recognise them from the sounds picked up, even if actual words are not understood at the outset. The greater number of European transmissions you will hear at one sitting are German, Scandinavian, Dutch, French, or Spanish. Now, most of the German announcers precede their call by the word *Achtung-anglice:* Attention! Look out! It is a guttural language, with a big proportion of achs and words ending in *ung, ing, bt,* and so on. Bear in mind, though, that the Austrians and the Swiss stations of the German-speaking districts say *Hallo!*

"Dutch, Swedish, Danish, and Norwegian are not so guttural; they are a cross between English and German. A peculiarity to note in the Swedish studios is the inclination of the announcers and speakers to adopt a sing-song intonation, more usually associated with French stage artistes.

"The majority of Italian words end in vowels, such as O, A, and I; they have an open sound and every syllable is clearly pronounced. Spanish, on the other hand, is somewhat more guttural and contains many lisped words; also, as a rule, you will find that French, Italian, and Spanish speakers are more vehement than other nationalities, even in the ordinary educational talks.

"If you listen to Moscow or Leningrad, you cannot fail to observe that the language contains a large proportion of labial and dental sounds, such as b, p, v, f, d, t, rolling r's, and a slight tendency towards the Italian endings.

"Polish is softer, perhaps, and in announcements you will pick up a goodly number of —*ski*s, but Warsaw, Kattowitz, and Posen will considerably assist you, inasmuch as on many evenings the lady announcers in the studio will give you a French translation of statements previously given out in their native tongue."

"Well, I have made copious notes of all you have told me, but how should I recognised Czech or Magyar?" [1]

"There is, perhaps, no need to worry so much in those cases, for, fortunately for all of us, the studios using those languages invariably make announcements in others as well, such as French, Italian, or even English, and the calls are put out so frequently that it would be impossible to fail to identify them."

"But then, Coames, you appear to have made a study of these peculiarities."

"Only to a certain degree; I possess a retentive memory, and consequently should I, by chance, tune in a new transmission, after listening for a few minutes, during which period I am dissecting probabilities, a process of elimination will nearly always provide me with the solution. It is not in every case necessary to hear a call, for a number of stations have adopted distinctive interval signals which are repeated frequently in the course of a programme. It would be impossible to confound the chimes, say, of Budapest (B, A, B, G sharp, G sharp) with those of Munich (E, F, G, A, B, C, followed by a hoot), or those of Cologne, imitation church bells, or with the sounds G, D, E, B, D, B put out by Huizen." [2]

"As your chronicler, I have set these down; are there no other bells?"

"Yes," replied Coames. "For instance, the single stroke of Radio Toulouse, exactly thirty-four to the minute, or the silvery-toned C, E, G, G of Bratislava. Then, again, Copenhagen comes on the air with three sharp pongs on a gong; Radio Vitus,[3] Paris, emits a carillon on two notes (F sharp, A sharp);

---

[1] An ethnic group related to the Hungarian people. People in this region refer to themselves as Magyars, not Hungarians.
[2] A city in the Netherlands.
[3] A privately owned radio station in Paris that operated between 1926 and 1934.

and Radio Paris, Westminster chimes, imitative of Big Ben.[1] Next, we have flute-like tones produced by oscillating valves, such as the three notes C, D, G, adopted by Stuttgart, and the A flat and D flat of Koenigsberg, the three pizzicato notes, F, D, A flat, as from a violin, of Cracow, or the long dash — the Morse letter T — used by Milan."

"Are Morse signals also used?" asked Botson.

"Too many of them, as a matter of fact, to make your task easy, although, in some instances, they help, by the letter or combination of letters sent. Warsaw may be recognised by the W, Hamburg by its HA, Bremen, BMN, Graz, K, Hanover, HR, and Kiel, KL. Many studios have kept to the metronome, which was introduced some two or three years ago by Breslau,[2] and here again a small amount of observation may assist in identifying the transmitter, as the beats per minute vary greatly. Count those of Berlin through Koenigswusterhausen; you will register roughly two hundred and ten in one minute. I can give you a list of others which may prove useful."

"In those instances in which a call can be heard, I admit the task is facilitated, but on occasions I have not understood the name of the city mentioned by the announcer."

"For the sole reason, my dear Botson, that the native name was used, and did not necessarily correspond with that to which we are accustomed in the English language. You would hear Belgrade as Beograd, Bucharest as Boo-koo-recht, and Budapest as Bood a-pescht, Huizen as Hoyzen. The Italians call their stations Torino, Rona, Napoli, Genova; the Poles, when announcing, would mention Warsaw (Varschavva), Kat-o-wit-see, Posnan (Posen), and Cracooff (Cracow); Wilno retains its name, but the word Uwaga is substituted in the call for Hallo. As a matter of fact, many native names are used. I may mention

---

[1] The nickname for the bell in the Clock Tower (renamed in 2012 the Elizabeth Tower to mark the queen's Diamond Jubilee) at the Palace of Westminster. The bell, cast in 1856, is named for Sir Benjamin Hall (1802-1867), who oversaw the rebuilding of the Houses of Parliament after the fire of 1834.

[2] A city in western Poland, now called Wroclaw.

Moskva (Moscow), Wien (Vienna), and Kaunas (Koo), not forgetting Dublin and Cork calling under the disguise, Se Seo Radio ath Cliath agus Radio Corcaighe.[1] And now, my dear Botson—"

BROADCAST TELEPHONY

Broadcasting stations classified by country, and in order of wavelengths. For the purpose of better comparison, the power indicated is *aerial energy*.

Metres	Kilocycles	Station and Call Sign	Power (Kw.)	Metres	Kilocycles	Station and Call Sign	Power (Kw.)	Metres	Kilocycles	Station and Call Sign	Power (Kw.)
		GREAT BRITAIN		*283		Montpelier (PTT)	0.2	*441	680	Rome (Roma)	3.0
25.53	11,751	Chelmsford (5SW)	15.0	286	1,049	Petit Parisien...	0.5	453	662	Bolzano (IBZ)	0.3
*200	1,500	Leeds (2LS)	0.13	288.5	1,040	Mont de Marson	0.3	*501	599	Milan (Milano)	7.0
*242	1,238	Belfast (2BE)	1.0	291.4	1,0293	Radio Lyons	0.5			**YUGOSLAVIA**	
261	1,148	London (2) tests		*291	1,020	Limoges (PTT)	0.5	308	973	Zagreb (Agram)	0.7
*288.5	1,040	Newcastle (5NO)	1.0	304	986	Bordeaux (PTT)	1.0	420	668	Belgrade	2.5
288.5	1,040	Swansea (5SX)	0.13	305.5	981.7	Agen	0.25	583	507.2	Ljubljana	2.5
288.5	1,040	Stoke-on-Trent (6ST)	0.13	309	970	Radio Vitus	1.0			**LATVIA**	
288.5	1,040	Sheffield (6LP)	0.13	*316	950	Marseilles (PTT)	0.5	*525	572	Riga	3.0
288.5	1,040	Plymouth (5PY)	0.13	329	914	Grenoble (PTT)	0.5			**LITHUANIA**	
288.5	1,040	Liverpool (0LV)	0.13	364	824	Algiers	12.0	*1,935	155	Kovno	7.0
288.5	1,040	Hull (6KH)	0.13	368	815	Radio LL (Paris)	0.5			**NORWAY**	
288.5	1,040	Edinburgh (2EH)	0.35	*381	788	Radio Toulouse	8.0	240	1,250	Rjukan	0.18
288.5	1,040	Dundee (2DE)	0.13	411	729	Radio Maroc (Rabat)	2.0	*283	1,058	Notodden	.05
288.5	1,040	Bournemouth (6BM)	1.0	447	671	Paris (Ecole Sup. PTT)	3.0	345	869	Frederiksstad	0.7
288.5	1,040	Bradford (2LS)	0.13	468	640	Lyons (PTT)	5.0	364	824	Bergen	1.0
*301	995	Aberdeen (2BD)	1.0	1,444	207.5	Eiffel Tower	12.0	453	662	Tromsoe	0.1
*310	968	Cardiff (5WA)	1.0	*1,725	174	Radio Paris	12.0	453	662	Aalesund	0.3
356	843	Brookman's Park 30				**GERMANY**		453	662	Porsgrund	0.7
*377	797	Manchester (2ZY)	1.0	*218	1,373	Flensburg	0.5	*493	608	Oslo	1.5
*309	753	Glasgow (5SC)	1.0	*227	1,319	Cologne	4.0			**POLAND**	
*470	626	Daventry (5GB)	25.0	*234	1,283	Muenster	3.0	*318	959	Cracow	0.5
1,554	193	Daventry (5XX)	25.0	*239	1,256	Nurnberg	2.0	*335	896	Posen	1.2
		AUSTRIA		*246	1,220	Kiel	0.55	385	779	Wilno	0.5
*246	1,220	Linz	0.5	*246	1,220	Cassel	0.25	*408	734	Kattowitz	10.0
*283	1,058	Innsbruck	0.5	*253	1,184	Gleiwitz	2.0	*1,411	212.5	Warsaw	8.0
*352	851	Graz	7.0	*260	1,157	Leipzig	1.5			**ROUMANIA**	
*453	666	Klagenfurt	0.5	*270	1,112	Kaiserslautern	0.25	*304	751	Bucharest	12.0
*517	582	Vienna	15.0	*276	1,085	Koenigsberg	2.5			**RUSSIA**	
		CZECHO-SLOVAKIA		*283	1,058	Magdeburg	0.5	*825	364	Moscow (PTT)	20.0
*263	1,139	Morava-Ostrava	10.0	*283	1,058	Berlin (E.)	0.5	938	320	Moscow (C.C.S.P.)	75.0
*270	1,076	Bratislava	12.5	*283	1,058	Stettin	0.5	1,000	300	Leningrad	20.0
*293	1,022	Kosice	2.0	*319	941	Dresden	0.25	1,080	283	Tiflis	10.0
*342	878	Brunn (Brno)	2.4	*319	941	Bremen	0.35	1,100	272.7	Moscow Popoff	40.0
*487	617	Prague (Praha)	5.0	*325	923	Breslau	1.5	*1,304	230	Kharkov	4.0
		BELGIUM		*360	833	Stuttgart	1.5	1,481	222.5	Moscow (Kom)	40.0
208	1,440	Radio Conference, Brussels		*372	806	Hamburg	1.5			**SPAIN**	
235.5	1,273.5	Charleroi (LL)	0.25	*390	770	Frankfurt	1.5	251	1,193	Almeria (EAJ18)	1.0
246.1	1,218.8	Schaerbeek-Brussels	0.25	*418	716	Berlin	1.5	258	1,121	Barcelona (EAJ13)	
241	1,229	Ghent	0.5	*453	662	Danzig	0.25	311	956	Oviedo (EAJ9)	0.5
270	1,111	Radio-Binche		*456	657	Aachen	0.35	*343	860	Barcelona (EAJ1)	8.0
294	1,020	Liege	0.1	*473	635	Langenberg	13.0	*368	815	Seville (EAJ5)	1.5
312	961.4	Arlon	0.25	527.8	568	Herzogstand (Bavaria)	0.3	403	743	San Sebastian (EAJ8)	0.5
339	887	Louvain	8.0	*533	563	Munich	1.5	424	707	Madrid (EAJ7)	2.0
*509	590	Brussels	1.0	*560	536	Hanover	0.35	453	662	Salamanca (EAJ22)	1.0
		DENMARK		566	529.8	Augsburg	0.25			**SWEDEN**	
*281	1,067	Copenhagen (Kjobenhavn)	0.75	575	527.7	Freiburg	0.35	231	1,301	Malmo	0.6
1,153	260	Kalundborg	7.5	*1,635	183.5	Zeesen	30.0	*257	1,160	Hoerby	10.0
		ESTHONIA		2,100	142	Norddeich	10.0	270	1,112	Trollhattan	0.45
*297	1,010	Reval (Tallinn)	0.7	2,290	131			*322	933	Goeteborg	10.0
		FINLAND				**GRAND DUCHY**		332	905	Falun	0.5
*221	1,355	Helsingfors	0.9	223	1,346	Luxembourg	3.0	*435	689	Stockholm	1.5
*1,703	167	Lahti	40.0			**HOLLAND**		*542	554	Sundsvall	0.6
		FRANCE		31.4	9,554	Eindhoven (PCJ)	25.0	*770	389	Ostersund	0.6
31.85	9,479	Radio Experimental (Paris)		*208	1,004	Hilversum (until 5.40 p.m. G.M.T.)	6.5	1,200	250	Boden	0.6
175	1,714	S. Quentin	0.1	*1,071	280	Hilversum	6.5	*1,348	222.5	Motala	30.0
214	1,400	Fecamp (Radio Normanie)		*1,071	280	Scheveningen Haven	5.0			**SWITZERLAND**	
220	1,364	Beziers	0.5	*1,875	160	Huizen (from 10.30 a.m. to 5.40 p.m. B.S.T., after 5.40 p.m. G.M.T.)	0.5	*403	743	Berne	1.0
238	1,260	Bordeaux (Radio Sud-Ouest)	1.0			**HUNGARY**		*453	653	Zurich	0.63
231	1,256	Radio Nimes	0.25	550	545	Budapest	20.0	466	644	Zurich (during afternoon)	0.63
241	1,229	Juan-les-Pins	0.3			**ICELAND**		680	442	Lausanne	0.25
*255	1,175	Toulouse	1.5	*1,200	250	Reykjavik	1.0	760	395	Geneva	0.25
*205	1,130	Lille (PTT)	0.7			**IRISH FREE STATE**		1,010	297	Basle	0.25
208	1,121	Strasbourg	0.3	*225	1,337	Cork (1FS)	1.0			**TURKEY**	
*273	1,103	Rennes (PTT)	0.5	*413	725	Dublin (2RN)	1.0	*1,200	250	Stamboul	5.0
						ITALY					
				291	1,031	Turin (Torino)	7.0	All wavelengths marked with an asterisk have been allotted according to the *Plan de Prague*.			
				*330.3	908	Naples (Napoli)	1.5				
				*385	779	Genoa (IGE)	1.5				

Amateur Wireless' guide to help listeners locate stations.

---

[1] Irish for "This is Radio Dublin and Radio Corcach."

The Mystery Than Which

Rupert Hughes

Rupert Hughes (1872-1956) lived a life full of wide-ranging experiences. Before he became an Oscar-nominated screenwriter and director, he had been a globetrotting researcher for the Encyclopaedia Britannica, served as an officer in the Mexico border service and in the U.S. Army in World War I. In New York, he was a successful best-selling novelist, playwright, and biographer — his book on George Washington in 1926 revealed the man behind the mythology. Selling his novels to Hollywood studios lured him to the West Coast. His first marriage ended in a divorce trial in which his wife testified that she had "seen Mr. Hughes kiss nearly every woman who came into our house," and that he "boasted openly of his illicit relations with other women." But he is best known as the uncle of an 18-year-old boy whom he introduced to the movie business: future billionaire Howard Hughes.

This story appeared in Morrow's Almanack and Every-day Book *for 1930, with the following introduction.*

Whose novels have had millions of readers, who would have been burned to a crisp in Chicago, for his biography of George Washington, had the cow kicked over another lantern.

"Among the uniquer murders I have known, the Affaire Klaus was far and away — oh, farther and awayer — the uniquest."

The Master mystery-monger was speaking, and I, being merely his Quick-Watson,[1] asked:

"What made this Affaire so especially unique, Master?"

"Ah, that takes a bit of tellin'."

"So long as it takes no longer than that," I said, "I can still catch my train, which leaves in exactly three minutes." We were in the Grand Central Terminal[2] at the time and the Mas-

---

[1] Probably named for the phrase which appears in so many of the parodies: "Quick, Watson, the needle!"

[2] A commuter rail terminal at 42nd Street and Park Avenue in Manhattan. Opened in 1913, it was named for the New York Central railroad which built it. Still in use today, it is the largest train station still in operation in the U.S.

ter, sniffing snow in a backhanded manner[1] and giving himself a deft shot in the arm, to the amusement of the throngs, began:

"Old Johann Klaus — no relation to Santa of that ilk — was just the man you'd expect to be findin' murdered in his library. Fearin' such a fate at the hands of his dissipated and impatient nephew, he had had the library torn out of his house and what he quaintly called a 'set'n' rum'[2] substituted. Even that gave him little comfort because he had a feelin' that his nephew was ready to murder him in any room in the house or his property in order to acquire his property. The nephew was a hard drinker."

"Still," I put in, watching the train-gate anxiously, "many drinkers have soft hearts."

"And hard arteries," laughed the Master with that arch drollery of his, which he concealed except for a merry twinkle in his eye, and a habit of jabbing one in the ribs with his elbow while emitting loud guffaws.

"But jokin' aside," he resumed, "old Klaus was afraid of his nephew, and the last person he was known to speak to was the chief constable."

"My train is going. Good-by," I said.

"Don't interrupt!" he retorted, putting his foot on my suitcase and his elbow on my shoulder:

"As I was sayin', the old man was sayin' to the local Dogberry,[3] 'Chief, I'm goin' home tonight with a mort o' money.[4]

---

[1] A reference to sniffing cocaine off the back of the hand, like snuff. Snow was one of its many contemporary slang names alongside coke, happy dust, and candy.
[2] Sitting room.
[3] The comic night constable character from *Much Ado About Nothing*. Used as slang, it refers to a particularly stupid constable or magistrate.
[4] While more commonly known as death, derived from the Latin word *mors*, or *mort*, it appears most often as a root word related to death, such as mortuary, mortician, and mortality. In this instance, there is a second definition that seems to have come from another source as an English regional saying to mean "an abundance of." The phrase has been traced to

I'm buyin' a farm off a man who won't take a cheque. I want you should put a guard around my set'n' rum. Tell your men to saw off their shotguns and peel their eyes, for somethin' tells me I may never see another rosy-fingered dawn gently dror aside the misty curtains of jocund day.'[1]

"The constable did as he was told, but the old man never reached home. He was found foully murdered on the way, lying in a pool of blood. But you have a train to catch. I'll solve the mystery in the next installment."

"You'll solve it now," I answered with unsuspected vim. "You've lost me my train, and I have an hour to kill."

"Too bad it isn't a rich uncle," the Master roared. "But jokin' aside, old Klaus was dead and the mort o' money was conspicuously missin'. Rememberin' his words, the chief pursued and — to everybody's amazement — caught the nephew red-handed and red-nosed — gorgeously drunk.

"There was blood on his clothes. His fingernails were full of it. His shoes were caked with blood and mud which chemical analysis showed to be the same mud and blood in which the old man lay.

"He had in his possession the entire mort o' money except what he had spent acquiring his hot, cross bun.[2] His fingerprints conformed exactly to the numberless fingerprints sprinkled all over the scene of the crime. He was thrown into a cell. The grand jury indicted him without leaving the room.

---

many English counties, including Sussex, Kent, Lincolnshire, Devonshire, and Cornwall, so it's difficult to tell how it came into the language.

[1] There are two classical references combined in the same sentence. *Rosy-fingered dawn* comes from Homer's *Odyssey*, where the poet uses that phrase some twenty times to describe the new day. The second half is a Shakespearian reference drawn from *Romeo and Juliet* (1597). When Romeo prepares to leave Juliet after their wedding night, he says "night's candles are burnt out, and jocund day stands tiptoe on the misty mountain tops." *Jocund* means cheerful and lighthearted.

[2] While there are many euphemisms associated with bun, this one refers to an obscure one from the late 19th century for a state of drunkenness, as in "having a bun on."

Court bein' in session, for once, his trial began forthwith."

"Master," I gasped spellbound, "this is indeed a mystery. Then they called you in, of course, to solve it."

"No, they refused my services and went ahead."

"Who sprang to the defence?"

"Nobody. The defendant swore he was at a distance from the crime courtin' the young and innocent Miss Sarah Kringle."

"Aha, the woman in the case!"

"But not for long. Sarah swore she hadn't seen the Nephew for weeks and hoped he'd swing."

"This suspense is killing me," I panted. "Who saved him in the dramatic court-scene?"

"Nobody. The jury brought in a verdict of guilty."

"I can't bear it. Who confessed?"

"Nobody, except the Nephew, when he learned the Governor wouldn't commute, reprieve, or pardon."

"The poor man perished to shield another! Quick, Master, the answer. Who was it?"

"Nobody."

"Then whom do you suppose committed — pardon me! Who do you suppose committed the crime?"

"The Nephew indubitably."

"Hell's bells, Master! Where's the mystery in that?"

"This is America, my boy. The mysteries are many and all unique. They suspected the guilty man; they caught him at once; they gave him a prompt trial; he was not a foreigner, or a poor and homely defective; yet, it was not the jury but the murderer that hung. He was a red-blooded 100 percent typical American killer. And they killed him. Did you ever hear of anything like that?"

"Master, you are marvelous," I confessed. But I was sorry I had missed my train.

Shylock Bones

Joe Archibald

Joe Archibald (1898-1986) might stand as an exemplar of a man who produced much in his lifetime, but — to paraphrase Percy Bysshe Shelley — his works might well have been written on water. He started out as a comic strip artist for newspapers and moved up to illustrating pulp novels. He moved on to fiction, writing more than 900 stories that appeared in more than 70 pulp magazines, including Doc Savage, The Shadow, *and* Argosy, *as well as the "slick" magazines* Colliers, Liberty, Coronet, *and* The Saturday Evening Post. *Late in his career, he produced more than 50 books for young readers, many of them sports-related such as* Rebel Halfback *(1947) and* Three Point Hero *(1973).*

As for Shylock Bones, *one of his many strips, the best information found suggests it appeared in American newspapers during the 1920s, culminating with an appearance in* The Funnies No. 1 *in January 1, 1929. This publication was a 16-page color periodical similar to those found in Sunday newspapers. That it was sold on newsstands made it a precursor to the comic book. Only two examples of this strip were found.*

Joe Archibald

SHYLOCK BONES   *By Joe Archibald*

The Mary Queen of Scots Jewel

William O. Fuller

This is one of the best pastiches in the series, an easy call considering that both Ellery Queen and Otto Penzler published it in their collections. It mimics the style and pace of the original stories, in which a victim visits Holmes and Watson at Baker Street, giving Holmes a chance to rattle off a couple astonishing conclusions about the guest before getting to the matter at hand. The story even borrows elements from "The Reigate Puzzle."

William O. Fuller (1856-1941) was a newspaper editor and lifelong resident of Rockland, Maine, where he published the thrice-weekly Rockland Courier-Gazette. *Like Conan Doyle, he was a public figure but on a smaller scale and less-controversial subjects. Among his friends he counted Mark Twain, magazine editor and author Edward Bok, and English poet Alfred Noyes. His interests were many: Republican Party politics, the Maine Press Association, even writing two books, the comic novel* What Happened to Wigglesworth *(1901) and* An Old Town by the Sea *(1912) about the Thomas Bailey Aldrich Memorial House. He was even chosen Rockland's postmaster in 1910, succeeding his father at the post. But journalism was central to his life. A 1931* New York Evening Post *story about the Fossil Club, composed of old men who were amateur press publishers in their youth, described Fuller as someone who "pursued the vocation of printing continuously from the time of their amateur days until the present."*

It was one of those misty, rainy mornings in early summer when the streets of London contrive to render themselves particularly disagreeable, the pavements greasy with mud[1]

---

[1] This elegant phrase neatly avoids describing exactly what the streets of London were greasy with. Think of a city with 6.7 million people (in 1900) with an estimated 300,000 horses within its limits, not counting those who bring produce in from the farms nearby. Few of these horses were ridden. They hauled trams and wagons, moving people, mail, and goods about the city. Think of the urine and dung they dropped, an average of a thousand tons a day. The human sewage was even more frightful, but at least that was directed into the Thames to flow out to sea. Add to that mix the industrial fog that tinted the streets yellow and dropped soot everywhere, and you can

and the very buildings presenting their gloomy facades wreathed in a double melancholy.

Returning from a professional call and finding Baker Street in my way, I had dropped in on my friend Sherlock Holmes, whom I found amid the delightful disorder of his room, his chair drawn up to a fire of coals and himself stretched abroad in it, pulling at his favorite pipe.

"Glad to see you, Watson," he called heartily. "Sit down here, light a cigar and cheer me up. This infernal wet spell has got on my nerves. You're just the company I require."

I helped myself to a cigar, put a chair to one side of the grate and waited for Holmes to talk, for I understood that in this frame of mind he had first to relieve himself of its irritability before a naturally pleasant mood could assert itself.

"Do you know, Watson," he began, after some moments of silent smoking, "I don't at all like your treatment of my latest adventure. I told you at the time that the part played by that country detective threw my methods into a comparison with his such as tends to overrate my abilities."

Holmes's querulous allusion to the now famous Amber Necklace Case, to my mind one of his most brilliant exploits, I could afford to let pass in silence, and did so.

"Not," he added, with a suggestion of the apologetic in his voice, "not that, on the whole, you let your pen of a ready chronicler carry you too pliantly into the realm of romance — but you must be careful, Watson, not to ascribe to me the supernatural. You know yourself how ordinary my science is when the paths of its conclusions are traced after me. As, for instance, the fact that I am about to have a caller — how I know this may for a moment appear a mystery to you, but in the sequel most commonplace."

There came on the instant a rap at the street door, and to my surprised look of inquiry Holmes replied, with a laugh:

"My dear Watson, it is kindergarten. You failed to hear, as

---

see the difficulties facing reformers charged with cleaning up the streets.

I did an instant ago — for you were listening to my morose maunderings — the faint tooting of the horn of a motorcar, which it was easy to perceive was about to turn the upper corner of our street; nor did you observe, as I was able to do, that in the proper space of time the unmistakable silence caused by the stopping of a motor engine was apparent under my window. I am persuaded, Watson, that a look out of that window will plainly disclose a car standing by my curbstone."

I followed him across the room and peered over his shoulder as he put back the curtains. Sure enough, a motorcar had drawn up to the curb. Under its canopy top we perceived two gentlemen seated in the tonneau.[1] The chauffeur stood at the street door, evidently waiting. At this moment Holmes's housekeeper, after a warning rap walked into the room, bearing two cards on a tray,[2] which she passed to Holmes.

"MR. WILLIAM S. RICHARDSON[3] — MR. WILLIAM O. FULLER," he said, reading the cards aloud. "H'm. Evidently our friend the Conqueror has many admirers in America. You may ask the gentlemen to walk upstairs, Mrs. Hudson," he added.

"How do you know your callers are from America?" I was beginning, when following a knock at the door, and Holmes's brisk "Come in!" two gentlemen entered, stopped near the threshold and bowed. They were garbed in raincoats; one, of medium height, smooth-shaven, resembling in features the actor Irving;[4] the other, of smaller stature, distinguished by a

---

[1] An open-top rear passenger compartment on automobiles. Because the early models were shaped like barrels, they were called tonneaus, from the French word for cask or barrel.
[2] Known as calling cards, or, nowadays, business cards, these would be presented at a home or business as a way of introducing oneself to strangers belonging to the social class that employed servants.
[3] *Conqueror*: This is most likely an attempt at levity, coming from Holmes noting that both men were named William. Richardson could not be identified, but he is probably Fuller's friend.
[4] Henry Irving (1838-1905) was the dominant stage actor in the Victorian era. Over a career that spanned nearly a half-century, he performed many major roles, and as an actor-manager exercised a profound gatekeeping

pair of Mr. Pickwick spectacles.[1]

"Pray come in, gentlemen," said Sherlock Holmes, with the courtesy of manner that so well becomes him. "Throw off your raincoats, take a cigar, sit here in these chairs by the fire, and while you talk of the circumstances that have given me the honor of a visit so soon after your arrival in London, I will busy myself in mixing a cocktail,[2] one of the excellent devices

---

influence on what plays would appear, which late in his life would earn him the enmity of George Bernard Shaw, who wanted to inject more realistic plays (including those by Ibsen and himself) onto the British stage. He became the first actor to be knighted. He also inspired his loyal assistant and close friend Bram Stoker to use Irving as the model for Dracula.

[1] The hero of Charles Dickens' "The Pickwick Papers," wore small wire-rimmed glasses with round lenses that were a distinctive part of the character.

[2] Throughout history, spirits have been mixed with everything in order to be drunk, so what we're looking at here is how specific drinks became known as cocktails and why Britain would consider them a novelty in the 1920s.

The cocktail is considered to be of American origin, appearing in print in 1803, although there is a mention of a "cock-tail (vulgarly called ginger)" in a London newspaper from 1798. The word has two horse-related origins: one found in the practice of docking the tails of inferior horses to set them apart from thoroughbreds (cock-tailing); and the shady racing practice of inserting ginger in a horse's anus to make them run faster. In 1862, the first cocktail recipes appeared in bartenders' guides.

Most likely, it was Prohibition (1919-1933) that popularized cocktails. Beer and wine were harder to find. Gin could be produced quickly, and with the threat of raids drunk quickly. House parties were frequently held where "bathtub gin" was produced and consumed, and flavorings could be added to mask the terrible taste.

But there was also a class element involved. A scan of newspapers published soon after Prohibition was introduced in the U.S. lamented the loss of cocktails, but not beer nor wine.

Prohibition also raised the image of the cocktail as rebellious, naughty, and American. It even became a symbol of resistance. The *New York Tribune* published "In Memory of the Cocktail," a half-page story that credited the invention with helping to win the American Revolution. British author E. Phillps Oppenheim (1866-1946), during a visit to the U.S., complained that "the American cocktail used to be the passport to gayety. You have banished it. ... The kill-joy spirit exists in England, too, but I

which your American people have introduced to an appreciative British public."

The visitors responded readily to these overtures of cordiality; from a tray on the table selected with unerring discrimination what I knew to be Holmes's choicest cigars, and in a brief time the four chairs were drawn in a half-moon before the glowing grate. Introductions had quickly been got through with.

"Dr. Watson, as my somewhat o'erpartial biographer," said Holmes as he lighted his pipe, "was on the point of wondering, when interrupted by your entrance, at my having in advance pronounced upon the nationality of my callers."

The taller of the gentlemen — it was the one bearing the name Richardson — smiled.

"I was myself struck by that allusion," he responded, "no less than by your other somewhat astonishing reference to our being but newly come to the city. In point of fact we have been here a period of something less than twenty-four hours."

Sherlock Holmes laughed pleasantly. "It is the simplest of matters when explained," he said, "as I have often pointed out to Dr. Watson. In the line of research to which I occasionally turn my attention, as he has so abundantly set forth in his published narratives, acquaintance must be had, as you will know, with a great variety of subjects. The motorcar, for instance, that ubiquitous invader of the realm of locomotion, naturally falls within the periphery of these attentions; nor could I long study its various interesting phases without coming to recognize the cars of different makes and nationalities. There are, if my memory is not at fault, some one hundred

---

think we are slowly getting back to normal appreciation of the pleasant things of life." In 1922, the front page of the *New York Herald*'s travel section printed a full-page story on the night life in Havana. Although the story carries a strong moralistic tone ("Americans seek the night life, the false, unreal Havana, and find it, and become pallid and wan and broke under its spell — or tired and bored and resolveful that home is the sweeter after all.") the illustration with the caption tells another story: " 'The Cocktail Trail' at a typical Havana cabaret — at tea time, dinner time — midnight supper — it is always cocktails, banter and laughter."

and thirty varieties of patterns easily distinguishable to one adept in this direction. When Watson looked out of the window, at my shoulder a moment ago, his investigations, pursued in quite different channels, did not disclose to him what was evident to me at a glance, namely, an American machine frequently encountered in this country. It was easy to guess that its occupants were also from the States.

"As to the other matter — among the earliest things the American man or woman of taste does on reaching London is to give an order to the engraver for his name card in the latest London style. The card this season, as we know, is small, the type a shaded variety of Old English. The cards brought me by the hand of Mrs. Hudson were of medium size, engraved in last year's script. Plainly my American callers had at the longest but a short time come to the city. A trifle hazardous — yes — but in these matters one sometimes has to guess point-blank — or, to quote one of your American navigators, 'Stand boldly to the South'ard and trust to luck!'[1] You find this holds together, Watson?"

I confessed with a laugh that I was quite satisfied. The American gentlemen exchanged glances of gratification. Evidently, this exhibition of my friend's characteristic method of deduction afforded them the highest satisfaction.

"Which brings us," remarked Holmes, whose pipe was now drawing bravely, "to the real object of this visit, which I may say at once I am glad to be honored with, having a high appreciation of your country, and finding myself always indebted to one of your truly great writers, whose French detective I am pleased to consider a monumental character in a most difficult field of endeavor.[2] My friend Watson has made some bold es-

---

[1] The source of the quote cannot be found, although there are frequent references to navigators forced to "trust to luck" in difficult situations when visibility is poor or charts nonexistent.

[2] A reference to Edgar Allan Poe (1809-1849), who is credited with launching the mystery genre with C. Auguste Dupin, the detective in "The Murders in the Rue Morgue," "The Purloined Letter," and "The Mystery of Marie Roget."

says in that direction," added Holmes, with a deprecatory shake of the head, "but it is a moot question if he ever has risen to the exalted level of 'The Murders in the Rue Morgue.'"

As Sherlock Holmes ceased speaking, the visitors, who had turned grave, looked at each other questioningly.

"It is your story," said the one in spectacles.

The gentleman by the name of Richardson acknowledged the suggestion.

"Perhaps," he said, "I would best begin at the beginning. If I am too long, or obscure in my details, do me the honor to interrupt me."

"Let us have the whole story," said Holmes. "I naturally assume that you solicit my assistance under some conditions of difficulty. In such matters no details, however seemingly obscure, can be regarded as inessential, and I beg you to omit none of them."

The American flicked the ash from his cigar and began his story. "My friend and I landed at Liverpool ten days or more ago, for a summer's motoring in your country. We journeyed by easy stages up to London, stopping here only long enough to visit our bankers and to mail two or three letters of introduction[1] that we had brought from home."

"To mail—" interrupted Holmes; then he added with a laugh: "Ah yes, you posted your letters. Pardon me."[2]

"Long enough to post our letters," repeated the American, adopting the humorously proffered correction. "Then we pushed on for our arranged tour of the South of England. At Canterbury a note overtook us from the Lord M—, acknowledging receipt of

---

[1] A letter vouching for the bearer's character, describing their purpose in seeking a visit, and adding any private information that the recipient should know. It is a way for a person to seek a meeting with someone to whom they've not been formally introduced.

[2] A fine example of Oscar Wilde's comment that "we have really everything in common with America nowadays, except, of course, language." While Shaw has been credited with the more familiar, "Britain and America are two nations divided by a common language," the source of this *bon mot* has never been found.

our letter of introduction to that nobleman, and praying us to be his guests at dinner on Wednesday of the present week — yesterday — as later he should be out of the city. It seemed best, on a review of the circumstances, for us to return to London, as his Lordship was one whom we particularly desired to meet. So Wednesday found us again in the city, where we took rooms at the Langham, in Portland Place.[1] It wanting several hours of dressing time, we strolled out in a casual way, bringing up in Wardour Street.[2] I don't need to tell you that in its abounding curio shops, which have extraordinary fascination for all American travelers, we found the time pass quickly.

"In one of the little shops, where I was somewhat known to the proprietor by reason of former visits, we were turning over a tray of curious stones, with possible scarf pins in mind, when the dealer came forward with a package that he had taken from his safe, and removing its wrappings said: 'Perhaps, sir, you would be interested in this?'

"It was a curious bit of antique workmanship — a gold bar bearing the figure of a boy catching a mouse, the whole richly set about with diamonds and rubies, with a large and costly pearl as a pendant. Even in the dingy light of the shop it sparkled with a sense of value.

" 'It is from the personal collection of the Countess of Warrington,' said the dealer. 'It belonged originally to the unfortunate Mary Queen of Scots,[3] and there is an accompany-

---

[1] A large luxury hotel in the Marylebone district that faces Portland Place in London. Opened in 1865, it became the favored spot for Americans such as Mark Twain, high-profile politicians, and members of the royal family. The Langham appears twice in the canon. In *The Sign of Four,* Mary Morstan's father asks to meet her at the Langham, and the King of Bohemia registers at the Langham as Count Von Kramm in "A Scandal in Bohemia."

[2] A one-way street in the Soho district that has existed under several names since Elizabethan times. It was known at this time for its antique shops, artists' supplies, and furniture stores, before becoming the center of the British film industry.

[3] The life of Mary Stuart, a.k.a., Mary I of Scotland (1542-1587) could be the

ing paper of authentication, showing its descent through various hands for the past three hundred and forty years. You will see engraved here, in the setting, the arms of Mary.'"

Holmes, a past master in the science of heraldry, his voice exhibiting a degree of interest with which I was quite familiar, here broke in:

"Or, a lion rampant within a double tressure flory and counter flory, gules. Mary, as Queen of Scotland and daughter of James I, would bear the arms of Scotland.[1] I know the jewel you are describing — indeed, I saw it one time when visiting at the country seat of the Countess, following a daring attempt at burglary there. You know the particulars, Watson. I have heard that since the death of the Countess, the family

---

stuff of fiction, with danger, plotting, and tragedy, if it hadn't been so well-documented. She was placed on the throne of Scotland when she was six days old, then raised in France while regents ruled the country. She married the Dauphin of France and became queen consort until he died a year later. Returning to Scotland, she married her first cousin and had a son who would later rule Scotland and Britain as James I (1566-1625). Her husband died two years later in mysterious circumstances — his house blown up and he found dead in the garden — and the chief suspect married Mary a month after his acquittal. Scotland didn't take this lying down and revolted, forcing Mary to abdicate in favor of her son. She tried to regain the throne, but failing that, fled to England and the protection of her first cousin once removed, Elizabeth I. Since many English Catholics favored Mary over Elizabeth, it's not surprising that the queen would imprison Mary and keep a close eye on her. This lasted for more than 18 years until Elizabeth suspected that Mary was plotting against her and had her executed. Historians have argued ever since over Mary's character and actions.

As a side note, while there are two possible Countesses of Warrington — the line went extinct after the 2nd earl died in 1758 without male issue — there's no indication that Mary's gold bar existed.

[1] Holmes is quoting the description of the royal arms of Scotland. Expressed in a mix of French words and heraldic technical terms, here's how it is translated: "Or [a gold shield] a lion rampant [standing on its back legs with one paw raised] within a double tressure flory and counter flory [two bands, one inside the other, with the fleurs-de-lys on the outermost band pointing away from the center, and the fleurs-de-lys on the innermost band pointing toward the center] gules [red]." It has been also more simply described as "the ruddy lion ramping in his field of tressured gold."

being straitened financially, some of her jewels have been put into discreet hands for negotiation."

"So the dealer explained," the visitor continued, "and he added, that as the jewels were so well known in England, they could be sold only to go abroad, hence the value of a prospective American customer. I confess that the jewel interested me. I had a newly married niece in mind for whom I had not yet found just the wedding gift that suited me, and this appeared to fit into the situation.

" 'What is the price?' I asked.

" 'We think one thousand pounds very cheap for it, sir,' said the dealer, in the easy manner with which your shopkeepers price their wares to Americans.

"After some further talk, our time being run out, my friend and I returned to the Langham and dressed for dinner. It was while dressing that a knock came at my room door. Opening it, I found a messenger from the curio dealer's, who, handing me a small package, explained that it was the jewel, which the dealer desired me to retain for more convenient examination. In the embarrassment of the moment I neglected to do the proper thing and return the package to the messenger, who indeed had touched his cap and gone while I yet stood in the door.

"'Look at this, Fuller,' I called, and stepped into his room — it is our traveling custom to have rooms connecting. 'Isn't this quite like an English shopkeeper, entrusting his property to a comparative stranger? It's a dangerous thing to have credit with these confiding tradesmen.'

"My friend's reply very clearly framed the situation.

" 'It's a more dangerous thing,' he said, 'to be chosen as the safe deposit of priceless heirlooms. It is scarcely the sort of thing one would seek to be made the custodian of in a strange city.'

"This was true. The dinner hour was close on our heels, a taxi was in waiting, there was no time to arrange with the of-

---

[1] £1,000 in today's dollars would be worth £62,404, or $80,682 in 2019.

fice, and I dropped the package into my inner pocket. After all, it seemed a secure enough place. I could feel its gentle pressure against my side, which would be a constant guarantee of safety.

"We were received by Lord and Lady M— with the open-handed cordiality that they always accord to visitors from our country. The company at table was not so large but that the conversation could be for the most part general, running at the first to topics chiefly American, with that charming exhibition of English naiveté and ignorance — you will pardon me — in affairs across the water. From this point the talk trailed off to themes quite unrelated but always interesting — the Great War, in which his Lordship had played a conspicuous part; the delicious flavor of wall-grown peaches;[1] the health of the King; of her ladyship's recipe for barleywater;[2] the recent disposal of the library and personal effects of the notorious Lord Earlbank. This by natural steps led to a discussion of family heirlooms, which speedily brought out the jewel, whose insistent pressure I had felt all through the courses, and which was soon passing from hand to hand, accompanied by feminine expressions of delight.

"The interest in the jewel appeared to get into the air. Even the servants became affected by it. I noticed the under butler, while filling the glass of Captain Pole-Carew, who was holding the trinket up to catch the varying angles of light, in which it flashed amazingly, fasten his eyes upon it. For an instant he breathed heavily and almost leaned upon the captain's shoulder, forgetting the wine he was in the act of de-

---

[1] About the time Europe was gripped in the Little Ice Age (1550-1850), French farmers developed ways to use stone walls to grow peaches and grapes. Not only did the walls shield the trees from cold winds, it trapped the heat during the day, releasing it slowly at night and prevented frost damage. There were two methods: mazes of walls were built around the trees, and the espalier technique, in which branches were attached to wooden frames on the walls, providing enough space for roots and air circulation.

[2] A drink made from boiled pearl barley with helpings of lemon, fruit juice and sugar to taste.

canting, and which, overflowing the glass, ran down upon the cloth. The jewel continued its circuit of the table and returned to my inner pocket.

" 'A not over-safe repository, if I may venture the opinion,' said the captain, with a smile. I had occasion later to recall the cynical remark.

"We returned to our hotel at a late hour, and fatigued with the long day went directly to bed. Our rooms, as I have said, adjoined, and it is a habit in our travels at the day's end to be back and forth, talking as we disrobe. I allude to this fact as it bears upon the case. I was first in bed, and remember hearing Mr. Fuller put up the window before his light went out. For myself, I dropped off at once and must have slept soundly. I was awakened by hearing my name called loudly. It was Fuller's voice and I rushed at once into his room, hastily switching on the electric light. Fuller sat on the edge of the bed, in his pajamas — and as this part of the story is his, perhaps he would best tell it."

The visitor in the Pickwickian spectacles, thus appealed to, took up the narrative.

"I also had gone instantly to sleep," he said, "but by-and-by came broad awake, startled, with no sense of time, but a stifled feeling of alarm. I dimly saw near the side of my bed a figure, which on my suddenly sitting up made a hurried movement. With no clear idea of what I was doing, I made a hasty clutch in the dark and fastened my hand on the breast of a man's coat. I think my grip was a frenzied one, for as the man snatched himself away, I felt the cloth tear. In a second of time the man had crossed the room and I heard the window rattle as he struck the sash in passing through it.[1] It was then I cried out, and Mr. Richardson came running in."

"We made a hasty examination of the room," the first speaker resumed. "My evening coat lay on the floor, and I remembered that when taking it off I had hung it on the post of

---

[1] The wooden frame that holds a window in place.

Fuller's bed. It is to prolong an already somewhat lengthy story not to say at once that the jewel was gone. We stared at each other with rueful faces.

" 'The man has gone through that window with it!' cried Fuller. He pointed with a clenched hand. Then he brought his hand back, with a conscious air, and opened it. 'This is a souvenir of him,' he said, and he held out a button — this button."

Sherlock Holmes reached quickly for the little article that the speaker held out and carefully examined it through his lens.

"A dark horn button," he said, "of German manufacture and recent importation. A few strands of thread pulled out with it. This may be helpful." Then he turned to his callers. "And what else?"

"Well — that is about all we can tell you. We did the obvious thing — rang for the night clerk and watchman and made what examination was possible. The burglar had plainly come along a narrow iron balcony, opening from one of the hotel corridors and skirting the row of windows that gave upon an inner courtyard, escaping by the same channel. The night watchman could advance only a feeble conjecture as to how this might be done successfully. The burglar, he opined, could have made off through the servants' quarters, or possibly was himself a guest of the house, familiar with its passages and now snugly locked in his room and beyond apprehension."

"Did you speak of your loss?" asked Holmes.

"No; that did not appear to be necessary. We treated the incident at the moment as only an invasion."

"Exceedingly clever," approved Holmes. "You Americans can usually be trusted not to drive in too far."

"We breakfasted early, decided that you were our only resource and — in short," concluded the visitor, with an outward gesture of the hands, "that is the whole story. The loss is considerable and we wish to entrust the matter to the discreet hands of Mr. Sherlock Holmes."

My friend lay back in his chair, intently regarding the button poised between his forefingers.

"What became of that under butler?" he asked abruptly.

A little look of surprise slipped into the countenance of the visitor. "Why, now that you call attention to it," he returned, after a moment's reflection, "I remember seeing the head butler putting a spoonful of salt upon the red splotch[1] the spilled wine had made, then turning his awkward assistant from the room. It was so quietly done as to attract no special notice. Afterward, over our cigars in the library, I recall his lordship making some joking allusion to Watkins — so he called the man — being something of a connoisseur in jewelry — a collector in a small way. His Lordship laughingly conjectured that the sight of so rare a jewel had unnerved him. Beyond regarding the allusion in the way of a quiet apology for a servitor's awkwardness, I gave it no particular thought."

Sherlock Holmes continued to direct his gaze upon the button.

"Your story is interesting," he said after some moments of silence. "It will please me to give it further thought. Perhaps you will let me look in on you later at your hotel. It is possible that in the course of the day I shall be able to give you some news."

The visitors hereupon courteously taking their leave, Holmes and I were left alone.

"Well, Watson," he began, "what do you make of it?"

"There is an under butler to be reckoned up," I replied.

"You also observed the under butler, did you?" said Holmes abstractedly. After a pause he added: "Do you happen to know the address of Lord M—'s tailor?"

I confessed that this lay outside the circle of my knowledge of the nobility. Holmes put on his cap and raincoat.

"I am going out on my own, Watson," he said, "for a stroll

---

[1] A heavy layer of salt is a traditional remedy, as it easily absorbs red wine and can be swept away.

among the fashionable West End tailor shops.[1] Perhaps you will do me the honor to lunch with me at the Club. I may want to discuss matters with you."

Sherlock Holmes went out and I returned home. It was a dull day for patients, for which I was glad, and the lunch hour found me promptly at the Athenaeum,[2] waiting at our accustomed corner table — impatiently waiting, for it was long past the lunch hour when Holmes came in.

"A busy morning, Watson," was his brief remark as he took his chair.

"And successful?"

To this Holmes made no reply, taking his soup with profound abstraction and apparently oblivious of his guest across the table. While I was accustomed to this attitude of preoccupation, it piqued me to be left so entirely out of his consideration. A review of his morning investigations seemed, under the circumstances, to be quite my due.

"I am going to ask you," began Holmes, when the meal had gone on to its close in silence, "to get tickets for the Alhambra[3] tonight — four tickets. In the middle of the house, with an aisle seat. Then kindly drop around to the hotel and arrange with our friends to go with us. Or, rather, for us to go with them — in their motorcar, Watson. Request them to pick us up at Baker Street. You will undertake this? Very good, Watson. Then — till I see you at my rooms!" And tossing off his coffee

---

[1] An unofficial area west of the City of London and north of the Thames. It has always been a fashionable and wealthy area to live, due to it being upwind from the City's smoke, and close to Parliament and other government offices.

[2] A club founded in 1824 and open to intellectuals, especially in the arts, engineering and literature. Its more notable members included Thomas Carlyle (1795-1881), Charles Dickens (1812-1870), Lewis Carroll (1832-1898), Rudyard Kipling (1865-1936), Arthur Conan Doyle (1859-1930), and Alec Guinness (1914-2000).

[3] A theatre and music hall that operated under a number of different names in the West End. Designed in the Moorish style, it operated from 1854 to 1936, when the building was demolished.

in the manner of a toast, Sherlock Holmes abruptly arose and left me, waving his cap as he went through the door.

It was useless to demur at this cavalier treatment. I had to content myself with the reflection that, as my friend mounted into the atmosphere of criminal detection, the smaller obligations fell away from him. During what was left of the day I was busy in executing the commissions which he had entrusted to me, and night found me at Baker Street, where I discovered Holmes in evening clothes.

"I was just speculating, Watson," he began, in an airy manner, "upon the extraordinary range and variety of the seemingly insignificant and lowly article of commerce known as the button. It is a device common in one form or another to every country. Its origin we should need to seek back of the dimmest borders of recorded history. Its uses and application are beyond calculation. Do you happen to know, my dear Doctor, the figures representing the imports into England for a single year of this ornamental, and at times highly useful, little article? Of horn buttons, for example it were curious to speculate upon the astonishing number of substances that masquerade under that distinguishing appellation. Indeed, the real horn button when found — if I may quote from our friend Captain Cuttle — is easily made a note of." [1]

It was in this bantering vein that Holmes ran on, not suffering interruption, until the arrival of our callers of the

---

[1] *Captain Cuttle:* A major comic character from Charles Dickens' *Dombey and Son* (1848). The retired sea captain with a hook for a hand portrays himself as a rough customer, but he's afraid of his landlady and proves to be a willing friend and ally. He is fond of quoting aphorisms, finishing with "when found, make a note of." His catchphrase was adopted by William Thoms (1803-1885) as the motto for *Notes and Queries*, a weekly periodical launched in 1849 devoted to collecting and researching miscellaneous information. *Note of:* For example, consider the button. While its existence has been traced as far back as the Indus Valley civilization (2800-2600 B.C.), it was used solely for decoration. It wasn't until the 13th century and the invention of the buttonhole that form-fitting garments were possible (even the simpler hook and eye clasp didn't appear until the 14th century).

morning, in their motorcar, which speedily conveyed us to the Alhambra, that gorgeous home of refined vaudeville. The theater was crowded as usual. A few moments after our arrival, one of the boxes filled with a fashionable party, among whom our American friends recognized some of their dinner acquaintances of the previous evening. Later I perceived Captain Pole-Carew, as he looked over the house, bow to our companions. Then his glance ranged to Sherlock Holmes, where I may have imagined it rested a moment, passing thence to a distant part of the galleries. Why we had been brought to this public amusement hall it was impossible to conjecture. That in some manner it bore upon the commission Holmes had undertaken I was fain to believe, but beyond that conclusion it was idle to speculate. At one time during the evening Holmes, who had taken the aisle seat, suddenly got up and retired to the lobby, but was soon back again and apparently engrossed in what went on upon the stage.

At the end of the performance we made our way through the slowly moving audience, visibly helped along by Holmes. In the lobby we chanced to encounter Captain Pole-Carew, who had separated from the box party. He greeted the Americans with some reserve, but moved along with us to the exit, near which our motorcar already waited. The captain had distantly acknowledged the introduction to Holmes and myself, and knowing how my friend resented these cool conventionalities, I was unprepared for the warmth with which he seconded the suggestion that the captain make one of our party in the drive home.

"Sit here in the tonneau," he said cordially, "and let me take the seat with the chauffeur. It will be a pleasure, I assure you."

The captain's manifest reluctance to join our party was quite overcome by Holmes's polite insistence. His natural breeding asserted itself against whatever desire he may have entertained for other engagements, and in a short time the car had reached his door in Burleigh Street.

Sherlock Holmes quickly dismounted. "We have just time

for a cigar and a cocktail with the captain," he proposed.

"Yes, to be sure," said Captain Pole-Carew, but with no excess of heartiness. "Do me the honor, gentlemen, of walking into my bachelor home. I — I shall be charmed."

It was Sherlock Holmes who carried the thing off; otherwise I think none of us would have felt that the invitation was other than the sort that is perfunctorily made and expected to be declined, with a proper show of politeness on both sides. But Holmes moved gayly to the street door, maintaining a brisk patter of small talk as Pole-Carew got out his latchkey. We were ushered into a dimly lighted hall and passed thence into a large apartment, handsomely furnished, the living room of a man of taste.

"Pray be seated, gentlemen," said our host. "I expected my valet here before me — he also was at the theater tonight — but your motorcar outstripped him. However, I daresay we can manage," and the captain busied himself setting forth inviting decanters and cigars.

We had but just engaged in the polite enjoyment of Captain Pole-Carew's hospitality when Sherlock Holmes suddenly clapped his handkerchief to his nose, with a slight exclamation of annoyance.

"It is nothing," he said, "a trifling nose-bleed to which I am often subject after the theater." He held his head forward, his face covered with the handkerchief.

"It is most annoying," he added apologetically. "Cold water — er — could I step into your dressing room, Captain?"

"Certainly — certainly," our host assented; "through that door, Mr. Holmes."

Holmes quickly vanished through the indicated door, whence presently came the sound of running water from a tap. We had scarcely resumed our interrupted train of conversation when he reappeared in the door, bearing in his hand a jacket.

"Thank you, Captain Pole-Carew," he said, coming forward, "my nose is quite better. It has led me, I find, to a singular discovery. May I ask, without being regarded as impolite, if this is your jacket?"

I saw that Captain Pole-Carew had gone pale as he answered haughtily: "It is my valet's jacket, Mr. Holmes. He must have forgotten it. Why do you ask?"

"I was noticing the buttons," returned Holmes; "they are exactly like this one in my pocket," and he held the dark horn button up to view.

"What of that?" retorted our host quickly; "could there not be many such?"

"Yes," Holmes acknowledged, "but this button of mine was violently torn from its fastening — as it might have been from this jacket."

"Mr. Holmes," returned Captain Pole-Carew with a sneer, "your jest is neither timely nor a brilliant one. The jacket has no button missing."

"No, but it had," returned Holmes coolly; "here, you will see, it has been sewn on, not as a tailor sews it, with the thread concealed, but through and through the cloth, leaving the thread visible. As a man unskilled, or in some haste, might sew it on. You get my meaning, Captain?"

Sherlock Holmes as he spoke had crossed the room to where Captain Pole-Carew, his face dark with passion, was standing on the hearthrug. Holmes made an exaggerated gesture in holding up the jacket, stumbled upon the captain in doing so, and fell violently against the mantel. In an effort to recover himself his arm dislodged a handsome vase, which fell to the floor and shivered into fragments. There was a cry from Captain Pole-Carew, who flung himself amid the fractured pieces of glass. Swift as his action was, Sherlock Holmes was quicker, and snatched from the floor an object that glittered among the broken fragments.

"I think, Mr. Richardson," he said calmly, recovering himself, "that, as a judge of jewelry, this is something you will take particular interest in."

Before any one of us was over the surprise of the thing, Captain Pole-Carew had quite regained his poise, and stood lighting his cigar.

"A very pretty play, Mr. Sherlock Holmes," he said. "I am indebted to you and your itinerant friends for a charming evening. May I suggest, however, that the hour is now late, and Baker Street, even for a motorcar, something of a distance?"

"Naturally," said Sherlock Holmes, when we had reached his rooms and joined him in a good-night cigar, "you expect me to lay bare the processes and so rob my performance of its sole element of fascination. Watson has taught you in his memoirs to expect it. My button quest was certainly directed against his Lordship's under butler, but at the first inquiry it turned up, to my surprise, the entirely unexpected valet of quite another person. It was a curious fact, the tailor declared, that he should twice in one day have calls for that identical button, and he innocently alluded to the valet of Pole-Carew. This was sufficient clue to start upon.

"Investigation in proper quarters not only established the palpable innocuousness of the under butler, but afforded such insight into the existent relations between the captain and his valet as I doubt not will again bring them into the sphere of my attentions. It was plainly the brain of the master that conceived the robbery, but the hand of the valet executed it. I even paid a most enjoyable visit to our friends at the Langham, as I had promised."

The Americans looked at each other.

"That could hardly be," they said. "We were not out of our rooms, and our only caller was a clerk from the curio shop with a message from the dealer, an impertinent old fellow he was, too, who followed us about the rooms with many senile questions as to our tour.'

"In this profession I have to adopt many disguises," Holmes smilingly explained. "Of course I could have called on you openly, yet it amused me to fool you a bit. But a disguise would not serve my purpose in getting into Captain Pole-Carew's apartments, which was the thing now most desired. Looking back upon the achievement, I flatter myself that it was rather ingeniously pulled off. You know, Watson, of my association with the theaters and how easily under such a connection one can learn who has reserved boxes.

"I confess that here things played into my hand. I perceived that Pole-Carew recognized me — that is your doing, Watson — and I was not surprised when I saw his glance single out a person in the gallery, with whom he presently got into conversation. I say conversation, for Pole-Carew I discovered to be an expert in the lip language, an accomplishment to which I myself once devoted some months of study and which I have found very helpful in my vocation. It was an easy matter to intercept the message that the captain from his box, with exaggerated labial motion, lipped above the heads of the audience.

" '*Hide the vase!*' was the message, several times repeated. '*Hide the vase!*'

"That was the moment when I left the theater for consultation with a friendly detective in the lobby. I strongly suspect," said Sherlock Holmes, with a chuckle, "that the reason the captain failed to find his valet at home could be traced to the prompt and intelligent action of that friendly detective. Our foisting ourselves upon the reluctant captain was merely a clever bit of card forcing, arranged quite in advance, but the rest of it was simplicity itself.

"Inasmuch as you declare that it is the property only, and not a criminal prosecution, that you desire, I do not think anything remains?"

"Except," said the gentleman warmly, taking the jewel from his pocket, "to pay you for this extraordinary recovery."

Sherlock Holmes laughed pleasantly.

"My dear American sir," he replied, "I am still very much in your debt. You should not lose sight of Edgar Allan Poe." [1]

---

[1] Conan Doyle credited Poe's detective Dupin as one of the inspirations of Holmes, despite the detective's dismissal of his abilities in *A Study in Scarlet*.

The Indignant Lecturer and the Amateur Detective

H.H. Ballard

Harlan Hoge Ballard (1853-1934) is one of the few multiple contributors to the 223B Casebook series, with his "Sherlock Holmes' Daughter" appearing in the 1905-1909 edition. He was librarian for the Berkshire Athenaeum public library in Pittsfield, Mass., for nearly five decades. He also wrote books on a wide range of subjects, including an advice book for public speakers, a guide to chemistry and mineralogy, a translation of Virgil's Aeneid, *and a short-story collection,* Adventures of a Librarian, *from which this chapter was taken. While Sherlock does not appear in it, his deductive methods were used to a fruitful end. Ballard also drew on his knowledge and experiences as a Mason to write* The Tiler's Jewel *(1921), which stressed the fraternal organization's merits.*

If the narrator's description of the speaker's childhood reading seems far-fetched, it's remarkably similar to the childhood of best-selling mystery author Agatha Christie (1890-1976). Although not an only child, she was largely left alone and given free rein of her father's library, which contained the volumes mentioned below, as well as runs of popular magazines of the time.

At the time of this incident, our Library lacked a Children's Room.

As to the need for such a room, I had been rendered somewhat doubtful by the answer given to a question that I privately put to one of the earliest and most zealous protagonists of separate rooms for children.

"What is the underlying motive," I asked him, "in this agitation?"

"Why, to get rid of the children, of course. If they have the run of the Library, they are always under foot, and become a regular nuisance."[1]

---

[1] One of the earliest children's rooms, at the Brookline Public Library in Massachusetts in 1890, was established to get noisy children out of the

This reason did not seem to me convincing, for I loved children, and had done everything I could to attract them to the Library.

I was therefore delighted to learn that an eloquent lady who lived in another State was advocating children's rooms for the benefit of the children, and as I was then planning for a library convention, I was glad to secure her as one of the principal speakers.

She gave an excellent and impressive address. But the next morning she invaded my office in a mood that, in a less charming lady, I should be obliged to characterize as angry.

"I do not understand the way you treated me yesterday!" she said; "and I should like an explanation."

I was taken by surprise; I was puzzled. I hazarded something to the effect that, if I had done anything I was sorry for, I was willing to be forgiven, and asked what was on her mind.

"Why did you pass immediately from my subject to the next, without allowing time for the discussion of my paper?"

"That was no reflection upon you," I explained. "When you preside at any meeting, you have to follow the program very closely. Your paper, for which you had asked half-an-hour, extended beyond that limit and occupied all the time that had been reserved for the discussion. If I had not called the next speaker promptly at the time allotted to him, he would have been obliged either to curtail his address or miss his train to Boston."

"That is all very well," she persisted, "but you did not seem much interested in what I was saying."

"On the contrary, I was not only interested, but delighted."

"Well, you haven't any Children's Room, have you?"

"Not yet."

"Don't you know that you are a back number?" [1]

"Absolutely; yes!"

---

adult reading room. The janitor was tasked to oversee the children.

[1] An issue of a magazine earlier than the current one. She's implying that his beliefs are out of date.

"Well, why don't you start one, then?"

By this time her tension had relaxed, and I think she even smiled.

Responding to her changing mood, I ventured:

"If you will first allow me to ask you one or two personal questions, I will answer yours."

She nodded, a polite equivalent to my small grandson's "Shoot!"

Now I knew nothing of this lady's antecedents, circumstances, or history, but I had been reading Sherlock Holmes, and had made a few simple deductions during her address.

"You are the daughter of a professional man, are you not?" I began.

"I am."

"A clergyman, perhaps?"

"Yes."

"Your father, I think, was possessed of considerable wealth?"

"That is true, but I don't see how you—"

"Never mind," I said, "just guessing."

"He had a large and beautiful house in the city," I continued rapidly; "his ample study was on the ground floor." Her eyes were opening wider and wider. "His desk was in a corner of the room opposite a big fireplace, and on either side of the hearth there was a large case of books of a classical character, and among them some of considerable rarity?"

"This is positively uncanny!" She cried, drawing back a step. "When were you in our house?"

"Never even heard of it," I protested.

"Well, what else have you discovered?"

"Not so much," I confessed, "only that you were an only child, that your mother was an invalid, that while your father was busy with his sermons and your mother was confined to her room, you had the free run of your father's adult library; that before you were sixteen you had read the Bible at least once, *Pilgrim's Progress*, some of Macaulay's History, a few of Scott's novels, some of his poems, a good deal of Wordsworth,

Tennyson, Lowell, and Longfellow, nearly all of Dickens, at least one of Thackeray's, and a few French novels on the side; and, finally, that before you were twenty-four you had read pretty much all the really worthwhile literature[1] you have ever read! Am I right?"

"In the main, yes; I don't like to admit your last suggestion,— but I fear it is true!"

"Well, then," I concluded, "if you, through free access to an adult library and, through your early reading of great authors, acquired that mastery of English that you showed us yesterday, and that poise which enabled you to meet that audience and give us so charming a paper, why do you want me to shut our children up in a room by themselves, *and feed them on skimmed milk?*"

"I never thought of that," she said.

"I have been thinking a great deal about it," I replied, "and just as soon as we can get a suitable room, comfortable chairs and tables, good pictures, an open fire, a collection of books, including a fair proportion of the great books, and an attendant who knows both books and children and has the knack of bringing them wisely together, we shall open a Children's Room—and I much fear that we shall not wait quite so long as that!"

She offered her hand most cordially.

"I shall think it over," she said thoughtfully; "but please tell me how you learned all that about me and our family."

"Nothing simpler," I explained. "Your dress, your brooch of black pearls, your whole bearing, proclaimed you a lady of wealth. Your casual reference to a sermon by your father told

---

[1] This long list encompasses the high points of English literature. *Pilgrim's Progress* is a Christian allegory by John Bunyan (1628-1688); Thomas Babington Macaulay (1800-1859) was a historian and politician whose five-volume *History of England* was a landmark in historical writing; the novels and poetry of Walter Scott (1771-1832) were considered classics of Scottish literature; other major British and American authors include William Wordsworth (1770-1850), Alfred, Lord Tennyson (1809-1892), James Russell Lowell (1819-1891), Henry Wadsworth Longfellow (1807-1882), Charles Dickens (1812-1870), and William Makepeace Thackeray (1811-1863).

me his profession. Your expressed dissatisfaction with the appointments of the usual Children's Room, and your unusual suggestion for a more refined style of furniture gave me an inkling of your home interior; to which the library and books were a natural accompaniment. Your failure to speak of any brothers or sisters, while you discussed the needs and preferences of children, made me guess that you were an only child. Your emphasis on the importance of having children taught to read well enough to give pleasure to a shut-in mother told me of her illness. You quoted readily from two or three of the books I mentioned, and the others were merely such as any girl with your surroundings would naturally have read at the close of the Victorian era, and I judged that you could hardly have gained familiarity with so many modern books for children unless most of your time in recent years had been devoted to the study of juvenile literature."

"Good-bye, Sherlock," she said.

The Berkshire Athenaeum building and former library, now a government building.

1930

With his worsening health problems and his flagging energies, it was clearly time for Conan Doyle to take stock of his life and prepare for his death. Even now, he refused to go easily. Ordered by his doctors to rest, he compromised by cutting his golf to nine holes a day instead of eighteen. He exerted himself mentally by taking up painting, investigating reincarnation, and continuing to write.

He was still energetic enough about spiritualism to argue with the Society for Psychical Research over its skepticism. His resignation in March closed 36 years of membership.

One spring day, he snuck out of the house to hunt for the first snowdrop of the season, something he had done for Jean since they met in 1897. He roused the household when he collapsed in the hallway, one hand clutching his heart, the other the flower.

Besides, he had other activities to consume his interests. He passed his criminological library to Sotheby's for sale. He drew up his will. On July 1, he visited the Home Secretary in London to argue for reforming the Witchcraft Act, which was still being used to prosecute mediums. By this time, Conan Doyle was barely able to stand, and Jean stood by with smelling salts. The Home Secretary urged him to sit, and he did, reading his statement in a faltering voice as his fingers drummed against his chest. It was his last public appearance. Blade straight, steel true, he believed, and he lived by it until he couldn't will his body to obey anymore.

When it was clear the end was near, he didn't want to die in bed. He was moved to a chair where he could see his beloved Sussex countryside. On the morning of July 7, with his wife, Jean, and his children Adrian, Denis, and Jean by his side, Conan Doyle told his wife "You are wonderful," and died.

Four days later, after a brief service that seemed more like a garden party than a funeral, Conan Doyle was buried under a copper beech in Windlesham's rose garden.

To his second family, he left the majority of his estate, including the royalties from his books. To Mary, the daughter from his first marriage, he left only £2,000. It has been speculated that Mary's inheritances from her mother's family led Conan Doyle to write his will to balance the scales, but his decision clearly showed the family who he favored.

His wife Jean would follow him in 1940. When Windlesham was sold in 1955, they were moved to a cemetery in the New Forest in Hampshire.

During his life, Conan Doyle was a force of nature, fighting for causes he believed in and living the ideal of Chaucer's "veray parfit gentil knight." Today, he is remembered as the creator of Sherlock Holmes, an accomplishment which he treated as a curse. "I am rather tired of hearing myself described as the author of Sherlock Holmes," he said shortly before his death. "Why not, for a change, the author of Rodney Stone, or The White Company, or of The Lost World? One would think I had written nothing but detective stories."

Conan Doyle's presence in his family was as large as his impact on the culture. After his death, his family seemed to dissipate, tainted by the comfortable life Sherlock Holmes provided, and his children seemingly overawed by their father's accomplishments. His sons lived aimless lives as playboys; they married but had no children. Denis Conan Doyle died of a heart attack in 1955, age 45. His brother, Adrian, followed in 1970, age 59. His eldest daughter, Mary, did not marry and lived a quiet life until she died in 1976.

Only Denis and Adrian's sister, Jean Conan Doyle, lived a life of distinction, serving for 30 years in the Women's Royal Air Force, for which she was made a Dame Commander of the Order of the British Empire. Her death in 1997 ended the family's direct line to the man who founded it. Its as if Arthur Conan Doyle, through his writing, his activism, and his crusades, had lived for all of them.

Publications: The Edge of the Unknown (June).

Conan Doyle poses for sculptor Jo Davidson, 1930.

The Return of Herlock Sholmes

"Kittywyn"

This piece of seemingly stream-of-consciousness nonsense — a one-off by the pseudonymous author — appeared in the Feb. 2 edition of the Sunday Times' *comic section in Sydney, Australia.*

Herlock Sholmes, the great detective, was playing "patience"[1] when he heard a ring at the front door-bell.

"There must be somebody there," thought Herlock brightly. He waited until it rang again, and then, taking a pop-gun in his hands, he tiptoed to the door and opened it.

On the doorstep stood an old man, the tears were running down his cheeks.

"Oh-o-o," he sobbed to the tune of "Little Bo-Peep." "I've lost my chewing-gum and don't know where to find it."

"Lost your chewing-gum," cried Herlock in horrified tones. Then he was struck by a thought (but it didn't hurt him): "I will lend you mine," he said.

"No, thanks," replied the old man, "I want my own."

"Righto," replied Herlock, and then he had an inspiration. "Lead on, MacSniffles, and take me to your home. I know where it is."

MacSniffles obliged, and they soon arrived at their destination. Herlock and the old man entered the house by way of the underground chimney. Then the great defective sneaked into MacSniffles' bedroom, and pounced on the right-hand bed-post.

"Ah!" he cried, "Here is your chewing-gum, MacSniffles."

"However did you manage to find it?" asked the old man in tones of awe.

"Well," answered Herlock, as he patted himself on the back, "while walking down the street, that beautiful ballad ran

---

[1] A type of solitaire card game that arose in the 18th century of German or Scandinavian origin.

through my mind, 'Does the spearmint lose its flavor on the bedpost overnight.'[1] And that," he continued majestically, "gave me the clue, which was the reason for my success."

Having finished his speech, Herlock departed by falling down the stairs to the open door — which was closed.

On arriving home, he went to bed. Of course, he awoke in the morning, but that is another tale.

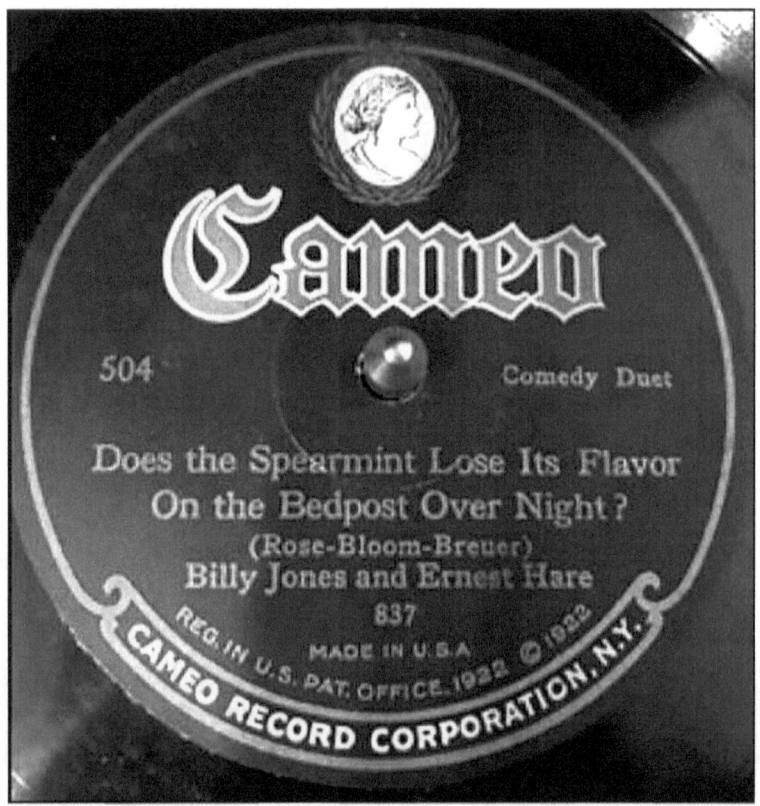

---

[1] The popular novelty hit of 1924 was written by Marty Bloom, Ernest Breuer, and a business-savvy newcomer named Billy Rose (1899-1966). The future theatrical producer was just starting out as a lyricist who already had a reputation for successfully promoting his songs. Its combination of nonsense lyrics and catchy title led one cultural critic to tie it to the then-popular Dada movement. A hit cover was recorded by Lonnie Donnigan in 1959.

Baffling, Mystifying Puzzle of Sunday News' Death

Great Circulation Secrets of Daily and Sunday Combine Papers

Sherlock Holmes Admits Defeat

Anonymous

Illustration by Anonymous

The story below represents a moment in Australian newspaper history, when the fierce competition for big news stories and for readers was matched behind the scenes by media companies striving to absorb their rivals.

At the center of it was Sir Hugh Denison (1865-1940), who parlayed his family's fortune in tobacco into an attempt to dominate the Sydney newspaper market against rivals Smith's Newspapers Ltd.. and the R.C. Packer family (whose descendants are still in the media business today). The rapacious Denison merged his Sun Newspapers Ltd. — which included the Evening News *and the* Sunday News — *with a rival to form Associated Newspapers Ltd. In a breathtaking move, he also bought the weekday and Sunday* Guardians *from Smith's Newspapers. By this time, he was running more than a dozen newspapers, many of them in Sydney.*

But the Depression that swept the world was biting deeper. Advertising was dropping, and attempts to reverse the decline through prices changes and buying high-profile articles and novels for serialization failed. As we see below, the Sunday News *was folded into the* Sunday Guardian. *Next year, more Associated newspapers were merged, the* Evening Sun *was gone, and the* Sunday Guardian *was absorbed into the* Sunday Sun. *Charting the decline (and getting a few kicks in of their own) was the* Truth, *a scandal sheet of dubious reputation, that printed this story in its April 6 edition.*

Ha! Ha! A case for Sherlock Holmes.

"My dear Watson," he would say, "probably you have not heard of the great circulation mystery.

"On the face of it, it concerns only the *Sunday News*, but — where did the big circulation — reputedly 98,000 papers — of the *Sunday News* go when the *Sunday Guardian* swallowed it?"

"Too simple," said Watson, reading a particularly lurid passage from the *Evening News'* new serial, and wondering when he would come to some of the "obscene" language the *News* had boasted about.[1]

"Nonsense," said the great Sherlock, rising and taking a couple of sniffs of cocaine. "This great circulation mystery has woven a web in which most of the great men of the newspaper world have become entangled. The circulation has been lost—vanished! Here one Sunday and gone the next. Fancy 98,000 Sunday papers suddenly being lost in a big State like N.S.W.!"[2]

Gnashing Teeth

"It is most intriguing, my dear Watson. The Denisons and the Knoxes[3] are most concerned, but think of the Editor of the

---

[1] Watson was reading a serialization of *Her Privates We*, a fictionalized account of the World War I experiences of Australian poet and novelist Frederic Manning (1882-1935). The novel was an expurgated version of *The Middle Parts of Fortune*, published anonymously the year before. The *Evening News* bragged that "the language of the solider is faithfully reproduced," including many "monosyllable and duosyllable expletives, which would make the hair of our Victorian grandmothers stand up straight." However, it promised its readers that many of them would be removed, so readers could avoid passages such as this:

"Where's Dixon?"

"Gone west. Blown to fuckin' bits as soon as we got out of the trench, poor bugger. Young Williams was 'it same time, 'ad most of an arm blown off, but 'e got back into the trench."

[2] New South Wales, one of six states that make up Australia. It lies on the Pacific coast, and its major cities include the capital, Sydney, and Canberra.

[3] Sir Hugh Denison (1865-1940) was a businessman and philanthropist who parlayed his family's tobacco business into a media empire including newspapers and a radio network. Sir Errol Galbraith Knox (1889-1949) rose through the ranks of the newspaper industry to become a director of Associated Newspapers Ltd. with Denison.

the *Sunday Guardian*, who suddenly expected his circulation to jump by 98,000 copies! He is tearing his hair and gnashing his teeth."

"And *Truth*, my dear Watson, has asked us to sally forth, and find this vanished circulation."

"But it is a mythical—."

"My dear Watson, do not raise objections. The now-defunct *Sunday News* would turn in its grave; its forlorn editor would rend you limb from limb if you insinuated for one moment that its circulation was mythical. We must look on it as tangible. The tangibility of mythology has always had my deepest consideration, and now we will put it to the test.

"Let us weigh the situation. The *Sunday Pictorial*, the little paper that talks so learnedly on birds, insects and New Guinea natives, has not shown any marked increase—. Let us rule the *Sunday Pictorial* out. And the *Sunday Times*. Ah, you will say, the *Sunday Times* says it put on 25,000 circulation when the *Sunday News* so nobly died in the interests of the *Sunday Guardian*.

Newest Paper

"Exactly, my dear Watson, do not mumble so much. I know you were going to hint that the Sunday Times must have more than doubled its existing circulation. That is beside the point.

"Let us take a look at the *Sunday Sun*. I know you, who jump at conclusions so naturally, are going to ask, without that finesse of the accomplished investigator, why the *Sunday Sun* has not published its circulation figures for some time! Well, Watson, that is easily explained. *Truth* has already told the story of how the *Sun* and Associated Newspapers Ltd. got panicky over the *Sunday Guardian* and bought the latter paper. It is whispered that the *Sunday Guardian* was the reason for the *Sunday Sun* not publishing its circulation figures. But the question is, did any of the *Sunday News* readers take to the *Sunday Sun*? The answer, my dear Watson, is one to which a negative answer is so easily returned that we will not go into it too deeply.

"And now, my dear Watson, take a look at the *Sunday Guardian*. That newest of Sunday papers, which dealt so concisely with birth control 'By a Mother of Eleven'[1] recently, boasted just prior to the time when Associated Newspapers Ltd. gobbled it up, that it had a circulation of over 100,000. Now, my dear Watson, by applying a few of the simplest rules of arithmetic, and not delving thoroughly into the question of registered insurance readers, it would appear that the *Sunday Guardian* circulation, plus the *Sunday News* circulation, would equal 198,000. But we would be quite safe in alleging that the *Sunday Guardian* circulation, the wish always being father to the thought, is not quite that.

"You are quite sure to ask, why not, my dear fellow. It is quite simple. Any new Sunday paper, just started out in life with a net audited circulation of over 100,000 copies per issue, would publish it; shout it; bawl it, my dear Watson.

"Well, I must say that this is the first time (and you have known me many years, Watson) that I have failed to elucidate a mystery. But the great mystery of the *Sunday News* circulation must go down in my records as unsolved. It is beyond me. It has baffled greater minds than mine in Associated Newspapers Ltd.

---

[1] The *Sunday Guardian* archives are not accessible, but could Holmes be referring to a "Mother of Eleven" birth control story that appeared in Australian newspapers in 1924? Even if he didn't, it's worth looking at, if only because the incident made the front page of newspapers across Australia.

During a debate on birth control at the National Conference of Labour Women in London, a woman stood up, declared that she was a mother of 11 children, and opposed teaching birth control to working women. She declared "What could be nicer than children?" and added that "economic conditions should be improved so that women can have more."

The women of the Labour Party didn't take kindly to this advice. One declared that birth control was "the only rational substitute for war, pestilence, and disease," and another with as good a grasp of theology as she did botany demanded that they "make the church alter its attitude to the question ... why should a woman go on bearing children like a fruit tree that goes on growing forever?"

Piles and piles of "Sunday News" that were under the microscope

"Advertisers are wondering. They have asked me when the *Sunday Sun, Sunday Guardian,* and *Sunday Pictorial* are going to publish their net circulation figures. Then, and then only, will the riddle of the *Sunday News* circulation be solved. Then only will there be unraveled before the great public a skein of unprecedented circulation mysteries.

"And, speaking of advertisers and circulation, and Associated Newspapers, Ltd., Watson, it brings to mind the fact that it is some time since we, as readers — and advertisers — have seen the circulation figures of the daily papers — Sun, News, Pictorial and Guardian.

On the first page of the two morning combine papers have stood figures that have remained stationary for many moons. Perhaps the type has become so fixed that it cannot be shifted!'[1]

"Still, Watson, the *Sun* still has with it that great advertising genius, Mr. Fordyce Wheeler.[2] He knows the value of circulation. He knows his advertisers, and even though he has severed his connection with the *News* advertising, he will, no doubt, urge the two evening papers to publish their figures. Watson, this Fordyce Wheeler has my greatest admiration. He is a man who knows the difference between net and machine circulation. Advertisers always like to know exactly how many papers are actually sold. It is hard to tell them sometimes when newsagents are not allowed returns and unsold *Sun*s and *News* go from the agents counters to the butchers' chopping blocks, to roll up the family sausages. Mr. Fordyce Wheeler knows that these papers should not be included in net circulation.

"And then, my dear Watson, there are those thousands of punters,[3] so prevalent in Sydney, who buy two or three evening papers each days for race results. Advertisers should know about them. Mr. Fordyce Wheeler is the man to keep them informed.

"It is complicated, this circulation business, my dear Watson. Printing machines register so many thousands — this is machine circulation — but when returns are not allowed it is almost impossible to show an audited net circulation. And net circulation, net circulation, I said Watson, is what the advertisers pay for.

"And Watson, I may be a bad judge, but when the *Sun*

---

[1] Newspaper pages were created with a linotype machine that used metal to form lines of type that were assembled. The writer is joking that the numbers haven't changed because they can't loosen the type so it can be replaced.

[2] Wheeler (1870-1937) was the longtime advertising manager for Sun Newspapers Ltd. He was also a member of the board, and highly influential in the affairs of the newspaper. He was remembered after his death as a pugnacious manager willing to fight for what he believed was right. In his obituary, *The Sun* noted "He was a driving force in advertising, and a natural journalist. He never made this boast, but it is a true one, that he evolved the advertising campaigns of this city for almost a quarter of the century, and others followed him and adapted his ideas."

[3] A gambler or investor who takes risks. The word is believed to be derived from the French *ponter*, to bet against the bank in card games.

and *News* go up to 1½ d to-morrow,¹ I believe the machine circulation, as well as the net circulation, of both papers will suffer. And, would you believe it, Watson? My heart aches for the *News*, I sympathise with Mr. Fordyce Wheeler, who has ceased to control the advertising.

Real Friendly

"It was of the evening papers I was speaking, Watson. The morning papers are different. The *Guardian* and *Pictorial* allow agents to return the 'unsolds' up to a certain percentage. So it should be quite easy for these papers to show their net circulations. The *Guardian* once called the *Pictorial*, the 'nasty-minded little brother of the *Sun*.'" Yes, it is a fact. Now the *Guardian* and *Pictorial* are brothers — real nice and friendly. So as to stop them from fighting the combine sent the *Pictorial* editor over to the *Guardian* to put an end to future brawls and they have got on well together ever since. Still fighting on the surface of things, as it were, but, you know, all fun beneath.

"Not so long ago, the *Pictorial* nearly crowed its head off as its circulation went up and up. It has not said a word about it for a long time. Even the *Guardian* is quiet. Not since coming under the wing of the combine has it shouted to the housetops its circulation.

"Not, my dear Watson, that I would suggest for one moment that the circulation of the *Sun* is not what it used to be, or that the *News* has dwindled away, or that the *Guardian* is ashamed to publish its figures, or that the *Pictorial* has not continued to forge ahead. Certainly not! But it appears strange that the combine newspapers should be so silent about it. The advertisers, my dear Watson, are the ones who count, and they have been inquisitive. It is not nice of the advertisers. They are

---

¹ To keep its investors happy, newspapers tested raising and lowering prices. A pence is a small amount in the old British coinage system, taking 240 of them to make a pound. A pence in 1930 is worth 9 pence or 18 U.S. cents today.

entitled to know, but why should they know?

"And after all, Watson, the mysterious disappearance of the *Sunday News* circulation might be cleared up, and a silver lining appear on the dark clouds. If Associated Newspapers, Ltd., published the circulation figures of the daily and Sunday papers under its control.

"Still, and I must say it before I turn in for the night — You have heard me repeat it often, Watson, when previously I have stubbed my toe in looking into matters appertaining to trusts and combines — the fellow who said a combine has 'no soul to be damned, or body to be kicked,'¹ knew his — forgive my lapse into that hated American slang — onions.

"And, Watson, an afterthought. I believe you knew Lord Rothermere,² English newspaper magnate? Quite so. Wasn't his slogan, 'Publish your circulation'? Didn't he make it a set policy to tell advertisers the circulation of his papers?"

"Yes, but ..."

"H ...," remarked Sherlock as he bounded into bed. "Funny, newspaper combines in Sydney never thought of it."

[The above is published with due apologies to Conan Doyle, Mark Antony, Dr. Watson, Ned Kelly, Sherlock Holmes and Cleopatra, and not excluding John Barleycorn.]³

---

¹ A spurious quote attributed to Baron Edward Thurlow (1731-1806). What he said was no less true: "Corporations have neither bodies to be punished, nor souls to be condemned; they therefore do as they like."
² Harold Harmsworth (1868-1940) was a leading British newspaper owner who with his brother Alfred helped build the *Daily Mail* and the *Daily Mirror* into leading newspapers. Although he was not known for saying "publish your circulation," there's no doubt he would have bragged about his paper's growing popularity when he would benefit from it.
³ *Conan Doyle, Dr. Watson,* and *Sherlock Holmes* of course you recognize. *Mark Antony* is better known as Marcus Antonius (83-30 B.C.), a Roman politician and general who helped rule Rome with Julius Caesar, carried on a torrid affair with Cleopatra, and paid with his life in the civil war after Caesar's death. *Ned Kelly* was an Australian outlaw and murderer who is celebrated as a national hero. *Cleopatra* (69-30 B.C.) was the ruler of Egypt and legendary lover. *John Barleycorn* is a character in a British folksong, the personification of the cereal crop and the beer and whiskey made from it.

Purple Peanut

A Tale of the Greyhound Track
Anonymous

This take on the short story "Silver Blaze" features numerous references to Leeds and Yorkshire, which should not be a surprise since this was published in The Tyke, *an undergraduate magazine at Leeds University on June 28.*

The word Tyke and its Yorkshire links deserves an explanation. The word is derived from the Old Norse tik *for a dog, particularly a female. It has several definitions, some of them derogatory. People with little fondness for Geordies — as people from Yorkshire are nicknamed — call them tykes, but it is also what they call themselves, their children, and their dialect. One soccer club in South Yorkshire even adopted it as one of their nicknames. In the manner of people everywhere, a rude name is adopted and turned into a source of pride.*

Sherlock Holmes and myself were seated in my apartment one dark, dreary and dank night in winter, playing snooker-pool, when a ring was heard at the door.

"Ha!" said Holmes, taking a nice pink[1] and a copious draught of chamomile tea, "a visitor."

"No," said I.

"Yes," said he, "and moreover a small man with bowlegs and a harelip, who is a freemason and probably plays the Jew's harp and beats his wife in his spare time."

"Wonderful," I cried.

"Elementary, my dear Watson, you know my methods, and so much is obvious. But list!"[2]

The door opened abruptly, and a tall man in a fur coat

---

[1] Snooker is played with 22 balls: the white cue ball, 15 red balls worth one point, and one ball of yellow (2 points), green (3 points), brown (4 points), blue (5 points), pink (6 points), and black (7 points).

[2] An archaic word meaning to listen. In Edgar Allan Poe's poem "Al Aaraaf" (1829), can be found the line "But, list, Ianthe! when the air so soft / fail'd, as my pennon'd spirit leapt aloft."

crawled in. He was wearing a black mask, and a cricket cap. He stood up suddenly and confronted us.

"Good evening, Professor," said Holmes, not a whit perturbed by this mode of entry.

Our visitor started. "I'm not a professor," he retorted in amazement.

Holmes smiled in superior fashion, and suddenly whipping out a coil of rope from his back-pocket, he dexterously bound our portly client hand and foot. The outraged man protested in vain for some time while Holmes inspected every inch of him with a powerful magnifying-glass, two electro-magnets, and a water diviner's rod, ending by running the vacuum cleaner over him. Then he released him.

"Pray be seated," said he in his suave tones. "Probably you are a little surprised, but it is a precaution I must take with all my clients. But to business. You have lost a great deal on the Turf lately, I see."[1]

Our visitor gasped until his uvula[2] was plainly visible. "Marvellous," he ejaculated at length. "How did you find out?"

"By the same deductive reasoning as I discovered that you are in the habit of beating your wife, since you smoke Empire Mixture[3] and your right arm and forearm are very strongly developed. *Ex-offico* and *his rebus factis*, since your right coat sleeve is shiny with writing out betting-slips and you wear a morose expression, it is easy to deduce that you have been gambling unsuccessfully."[4]

"Heaven knows you are right, Mr. Holmes! I am the Earl

---

[1] A slangy reference to horse-racing, which is sometimes run on grass.

[2] In the mouth, it's the bulb-like protrusion from the top of the soft palate.

[3] A type of shag tobacco for pipe smokers. It typically combined tobacco from several nations in the British Empire. One particular blend, Player's, used leaf from Rhodesia, Nyasaland, India, or Canada. Another advantage of Empire blends were their lower prices, since tobacco from within the Commonwealth was taxed at a lower rate than imports.

[4] *Ex-officio*: Latin for "from the office," it is applied to people who are members of a group because of their status in another area. *His rebus factis*: A Latin phrase meaning "with these things having been done."

of Beeston, and my home is at Cross Flatts Court,¹ Leeds—" He halted in amazement while Holmes sprang into a corner and hastily mounted a machine-gun, covering our noble client.

"Take down the index volume, Watson," said Holmes in a menacing voice, "and look up Cross Flatts." I did so, and read out:

"Cross Flatts. A beautiful piece of park-land in South Leeds, famed afar for its sylvan glades, which are the happy haunts of young courting couples."

"Good," said Holmes. "Pray continue your most interesting statement, sir."

"Well," continued the Earl, "as befits a nobleman I patronise every branch of sport, but my chief interest is in Greyhound Racing. I own Purple Peanut, the best bitch ever seen at Elland Road,² and she was entered for the Moortown Stakes last Saturday. She started a hot favourite, and I risked my all upon her." At this juncture the Earl broke into a paroxysm of sobbing, and it was only after the dexterous application of the hypodermic syringe, containing a strong dose of turkey-rhubarb and Kompo, and repeated blows from a sledge hammer, that he was able to continue.³

At length he resumed.

"She lost, gentlemen," said he, with distended epiglottis,⁴

---

¹ Located in Beeston, a suburb of Leeds. During the Victorian period, it was a residential area for industrial workers. There is also a 44-acre park there that later became a wasteland and dumping area, but has since been cleaned up and improved.
² A greyhound stadium that was demolished in 1982.
³ *Turkey-rhubarb*: A herbaceous perennial plant resembling the edible rhubarb. It is used in traditional medicine for stomach ailments, constipation, and as a poultice for fevers and swelling of the tissues. In high doses, it can cause the tongue and breathing canals to swell and cause suffocation. *Kompo*: Could not be identified. It was a common brand name for soap, silverware cleaners, and fabric.
⁴ The flap in the throat that keeps food from dropping down the windpipe and into the lungs. *Distended* means that it was swollen from inside.

"lost by 20 lengths, and I am convinced that there has been foul play. Half my kingdom if you can find the explanation of the mystery, Mr. Holmes. Farewell!"

And he rushed out with a curious rotary motion which did not pass unnoticed by the Baker Street sleuth.

Immediately he had gone, Holmes was galvanised into action.

"Come," said he, finishing off a chlorodyne[1] and soda, "we must sail for Leeds tonight."

Donning a Balaclava helmet[2] and gum-boots, and arming ourselves with a bow and arrow each, we chartered a taxi.

"A guinea[3] if you do it in time," screamed Holmes to the driver, and away we tore into the night. Ten minutes later we were battling our way north against a fearful gale which threatened to swamp the cruiser which Holmes had chartered from the Admiralty.

It was early next day when we docked at Leeds Bridge, and we arrived at Cross Flatts Court by means of a Beeston Tram which rocked and roared to its destination in record

---

[1] A popular patent medicine sold to treat cholera, insomnia, headaches, diarrhea, and other maladies. Its contents included chloroform, tincture of cannabis, and an alcoholic solution of opium. While it worked a treat to knock you out, it could also leave you addicted to opium, and taking too much could kill you. The much-reduced version of the original mixture developed by John Collis Browne (1819-1884) is sold outside the U.S. today as "J Collis Browne's Mixture." It consists of morphine and peppermint oil.

[2] A knitted garment that covers the head and neck, leaving space for the eyes and mouth. Also known as a ski mask. It was developed by British troops to keep warm when they were stationed near Balaclava near Sevastopol during the Crimean War (1853-1856). The style is widely favored today by outdoor sports enthusiasts and robbers of convenience stores.

[3] A coin worth one pound plus one shilling (or 21 shillings). The coin itself was originally made of gold from the Guinea region in West Africa, hence its name. Although the coin was replaced by the pound in 1816, guineas continued to circulate, and because of its aristocratic overtones (and hidden surcharge), many items were priced in guineas, such as professional fees, auctioned livestock and racehorses, art, bespoke tailoring and other luxuries.

time.¹ The Earl himself greeted us at the front door, and wiping our feet and clutching our bows and arrows we were ushered into the back kitchen.

After greeting the Earl, Holmes rushed upstairs. Half an hour elapsed before he reappeared disguised as a Highlander. With hastily muttered farewells he went forth into the night, with a sabre in one hand and a bridge-scoring pad in the other.

❖   ❖   ❖   ❖

It was just after breakfast when Holmes returned.

"I have found my man, Watson," said he triumphantly. "He is no other than the Count of Claypit Lane, who holds a mortgage over this fair estate. With devilish cunning he realised that the Earl had risked his all upon Purple Peanut in order to pay off his mortgage and thus save the Ducal halls. So he decided to stop the bitch at all costs. This he effected by the cunning expedient of placing — what do you think Watson? — lamp-posts — lamp-posts round the track in order to distract her attention. Our ordinary criminal would have been content with 'Drink, Puppy Drink,'² vessels, but this villain took no chances. He will swing for this. Come Watson, our duty is done.

---

¹ *Admiralty*: The department responsible for overseeing the Royal Navy. *Leeds Bridge*: A structure spanning the River Aire in Leeds. Originally a ferry crossing, a bridge has been at that site since medieval times. The current cast-iron structure was opened in 1870. The joke is that the depth of the Aire in Leeds is about 11 feet, so sending a cruiser there is impossible. *Beeston Tram*: Leeds ran a system of horse-drawn and later electric-powered trams from 1891 to 1959.

² A hunting song written by Scottish novelist and poet G.J. Whyte-Melville (1821-1878) in 1874. Whyte-Melville is also known for the opening line of "The Object of a Life": "To eat, drink, and be merry, because to-morrow we die."

The Great Flatbush Mystery

Ed Hughes

Illustrated by Ed Hughes

The Brooklyn Dodgers were known by many names, such as the Trolley Dodgers, the Bridegrooms, the Superbras, and the Robins. Sometimes, they were known by several names at the same time, and newspaper writers used them interchangeably in the same article. Under any name, they were the underdogs compared to the legendary Yankees and the New York Giants. In 1929, for example, in the eight-team National League, the Robins finished 6th for the fifth year in a row. This depressing state of affairs was parodied in the Brooklyn Eagle *newspaper of Sept. 3.*

Ed Hughes was a cartoonist, sportswriter and columnist for newspapers in New York and San Francisco.

Flatbush,[1] in fact all Brooklyn, has been shocked to the marrow of its soul by what appears to be the boldest and most dastardly of all the racketeer crimes committed in the country. "The Flatbush Robin," a well-known diamond racketeer, also a prominent National League clubman, was found dead in his palatial residence on Bedford and Flatbush Aves.[2] This latest outrage and manifestation of gang power has roused the community as nothing before. Various deeds of violence, gangster killings, even the challenge of the laundry racketeers have been all been shunted into the shadow by the Great Flatbush Mystery.

The righteous citizenry of Brooklyn are stirred to the roots over the case. They demand that Mulrooney get to the bottom of this at any cost, even to laying aside the Rothstein case[3] for the time being.

---

[1] A neighborhood in the borough of Brooklyn. The area closely identified with the Dodgers, and its famous centerfielder Duke Snider was called "the Duke of Flatbush."
[2] Two major streets that intersected in Brooklyn.
[3] *Mulrooney:* Edward P. Mulrooney (1874-1960) was New York City Police Commissioner from 1930 to 1933. *Rothstein Case:* Arnold Rothstein (1882-

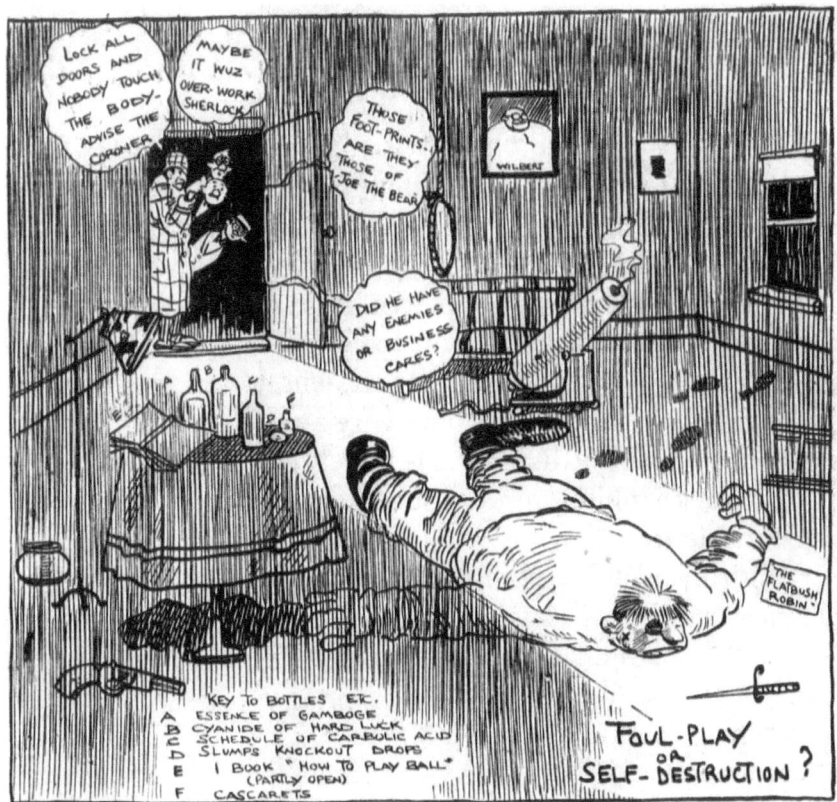

Commissioner Mulrooney was exercised over the tragedy. He means to ferret out the criminal — if there was one — and punish him to the full extent of the law.

The commissioner has already decided one thing. He is sure Legs Diamond[1] didn't do it. When asked about that yesterday, he said: "We do not want Diamond for the Flatbush

---

1928) was a racketeer and gambler who headed the Jewish mob in New York City. He was believed to be among those who conspired to fix the 1919 World Series. Mulrooney could afford to lay aside the Rothstein inquiry, as the gangster had been murdered two years before.
[1] Jack "Legs" Diamond (1897-1931) was a gangster and associate of Arnold Rothstein. He profited from Prohibition by smuggling liquor into the U.S., and survived several assassination attempts before finally being gunned down in his rooming house. At the time of the story, Diamond had been in Europe for a month. He was visiting Germany looking for rye whiskey to import into the U.S.

Mystery. We have nothing on him. In fact he has a lot on us. He is enjoying a trip in Europe. Ha! Ha!"

Famous Sleuth Engaged

With its usual zeal and public spiritedness the *Eagle* has already enlisted its aid in the case. This paper has assigned its star crime reporter, Sherlock Holmes, to work on this case in conjunction with the special pieces he is now submitting.

That Holmes, working elbow to elbow with Dr. Watson and Thomas Holmes,[1] our baseball expert, will do much goes without saying. Both the Holmes boys have a reputation to preserve, but Watson is a little different. He merely cleans the needles.

Sherlock Holmes approaches the case with his characteristic confidence.

With his usual dynamic energy he is already hip-deep in the mess. When seen last night he said:

"This is a singular case, of course, but I have no great fear of it."

"What! You have solved it already?"

Holmes looked up slowly and then took his bottle from the mantelpiece and his hypodermic syringe from its morocco case.[2] Then he filled his old briar pipe with his long, white, nervous fingers.

"That is a little too much to say," he drawled. And then, "But I have certain opinions."

"What are they?" I ventured.

'The watch has been recently cleaned, which robs me of my most suggestive facts — no, no, that is another case," he explained, languidly. "I'm a little tired, I imagine."

---

[1] Holmes (1903-1975) covered the Brooklyn Dodgers for the *Brooklyn Eagle* and the *New York Herald-Tribune* from 1924 to 1957.

[2] Goatskin originally imported from Morocco that's been dyed red on the grain side and then tanned to bring out its characteristic bird's-eye pattern. It was the subject of a pun in the Bob Hope-Bing Crosby movie "The Road to Morocco" where they sing that "like Webster's Dictionary / we're Morocco bound."

Holmes' Opinions

Then the great detective gathered himself together and told me what he knew of the Great Flatbush Mystery.

"Now, my dear doctor, we have an hour to ourselves, and you are not on the Surrey Side or near the Vauxhall Bridge Road.[1] You are in Flatbush."

"How simple," returned Watson. "Right on both points!"

"You have an extraordinary genius for minutiae," I remarked.

"I have the power of observation and that of deduction, and this leads me to believe that the man Robin either died from self-destruction or he was a victim of foul play."

Holmes lit his pipe and continued: "However, there are certain things I must know before I can get anywhere with this cast.

"Who were this man's enemies and to what extent? I think they will play a great part in the clearing up of this mystery. There is that man named McCarthy, sometimes called 'Joe the Bear.'[2] He may have had a lot to do with this case. They had many combats, and I am led to believe Robin fared ill. McCarthy will bear watching."

It was half-past 5 before Holmes returned. "There is no great mystery in this matter," he said, taking the cup of tea which I poured for him.

"The victim's personal characteristics interest me strangely, my dear Doctor. He may have had business or professional worries. He was up in the world and then went down. That may have induced melancholia. He had a hard life schedule mapped out and it may be he wasn't up to it. Maybe he was a loafer."

Watson Dozes

Holmes unfolded the paper carefully and smoothed it on his knee.

---

[1] *Surrey Side:* A county southwest of Greater London. *Vauxhall Bridge Road:* A major road running southeast from the Buckingham Palace area, across Vauxhall Bridge on the Thames, to Vauxhall Park.

[2] Joe McCarthy (1887-1978) managed the New York Yankees from 1931 to 1946, winning nine league titles and seven World Series.

"Was this man a moral weakling? That I shall have to look into. He may have destroyed himself, thrown up the sponge[1] — but that I do not yet know.

'The condition of his study when we found him was interesting, too. The room I ordered locked and I instructed that nobody touch the body. There was a pistol, a cannon, a noosed rope hanging from the chandelier and various bottles of powerful poisons on the table. As I say, it may have been suicide. But to confound the situation there were footprints leading to an open window."

"Who is there?" cried a gruff voice from without, followed by a shrill whistle.

Holmes immediately answered: "There are apparently no women in this case. But I am interested in a man who signs himself 'Wilbert R.'[2]

"I'm also interested in a person known as 'Babe H.'[3] There is another item that puzzles me. What is second base? Did this man have a physical breakdown? I wonder. Maybe his work was too hard for him, though he seems to have had assistants enough.

"I must ask that any one in Brooklyn who knows anything about this case come forward and give me in the facts."

"What time was that?" asked Watson, who had been dozing.

---

[1] A phrase from boxing. When a fighter is losing and it's time to quit, the manager literally throws the sponge into the ring. A slang dictionary dates the phrase from the 1860s: " 'To throw up the sponge,' to submit, give over the struggle, - from the practice of throwing up the sponge used to cleanse the combatants' faces, at a prize-fight, as a signal that the 'mill' is concluded." By 1913, the phrase had changed to "throw in the towel."
[2] Wilbert Robinson (1863-1934) was a ballplayer who managed Brooklyn from 1914 to 1934. In his honor the team was referred to as the Robins, and he was nicknamed "Uncle Robbie."
[3] Floyd "Babe" Herman (1903-1987) played right field for nearly 20 years for the Brooklyn Dodgers. Although he was an excellent power hitter setting several team records, this was counterbalanced by his below-average fielding. He had a genius for committing errors. During the 1930 season, he twice stopped while running the bases to watch a home run and was passed by the batter, causing the runs to count as a single.

The Bound of the Haskervilles

An Unpublished Memoir of Herlock Sholmes, the Famous Detective. As told by Dr. Jotson.

" T.P.J."

Published by the Sarawak Oilfields, Mirage *was a blatant copy of* Punch *magazine. Sarawak today is a state in Malaysia, located on the northwest side of Borneo Island. But in 1930, it was the property of the Brooke family, which had governed it since 1841. After World War II, the family ceded control to the British, which granted the territory independence in 1963. The first oil well was drilled in 1910.*

Chapter I

It was a typical London day of rain and fog. In our cosy sitting room in Shaker Street also the fog was terrific due to Sholmes smoking a hookah given him by the Nabob of Iam for recovering one of his wives whom he (the Nabob I mean) afterwards beheaded.

Sholmes was in one of his pensive moods; all was not well with him, and as he brooded over the events of the day I concluded he was best left alone, so I continued writing my eighteenth volume on the habits and pastimes of the common wood-louse.

Suddenly a squeaking of brakes was followed by a knock and a rushing of feet, and an excited figure rushed in upon us accompanied by our landlady, Mrs. Bloomer. "Mr. Herlock Sholmes?" he cried.

Sholmes left off picking the winners for the morrow's 2.30, removed his left foot from the clock on the mantel, and his right one from the coal bucket, took a final pull at his flask of cocaine, turned, and replied, "Well, Doctor, what can I do for you?"

"Doctor?" I echoed.

"Yes, Doctor," replied Sholmes. "From his blue shirt, his black bag, his stethoscope protruding from his pocket, and, I imagine, his unlimited supply of bedside stories, I deduce that our client is of the medical profession. Elementary, my dear Jotson."

"Marvellous, Sholmes! Marvellous!"

Our visitor had collapsed into the only available arm chair and was engaged in wiping his brow with boracic lint,[1] thus supporting Sholmes' deduction.

In view of the distressed condition of our visitor I did not like to mention that he was also sitting on the remains of our supper.

With an effort, the figure huddled in the seat pulled himself together and, glancing round the room, began, "Have you heard this one? — er— I mean, Mr. Sholmes I have come to consult you on a matter that is worrying me. I am as you presumed, a doctor, a family doctor." (Sholmes' face brightened and, glancing at me, he wagged his left ear in an old familiar manner.) "And as a doctor I receive a lot of confidences.

"There is at Little Wartlebury-in-the-Marsh the old family of Haskervilles who can trace their descent to the forefather who lit the fire at which Alfred burnt the cakes.[2] It is the custom that when the eldest son of the Haskervilles attains his majority a secret is told him and a task set him. This test is known as the Bound of the Haskervilles," continued our visitor, "and consists in leaping a dyke which separates Little Wartlebury-in-the-Marsh from Greater Wattlebury-on-the-Hill.

"All the eldest sons of the Haskervilles have been told this dire secret and have kept the Bound, but" — here the doctor paused and with a dismal look slowly stated — "the present scion, the Hon. Horace Marmaduke, who attains the age of twenty-one tomorrow cannot jump."

A silence that could be felt followed, broken at last as Sholmes put his violincello[3] under his chin and slowly played

---

[1] (The first word is pronounced "brass-sic".) A medical dressing made from surgical lint soaked in boracic acid and glycerin. Used as an antiseptic for burns and cuts and especially effective on leg ulcers.
[2] A legend about Alfred the Great (847 to 849-899), who considered Britain's first ruler. Fleeing the Danes after their successful attack on Chippenham in 878, a disguised Alfred took shelter with a peasant woman while he organized a guerilla-style resistance against the Vikings. She was cooking wheaten cakes near a fire, and tasked him with watching them while she did her chores. Preoccupied with his problems, Alfred let them burn, for which he was scolded.
[3] A member of the viol family of stringed instruments that were played

his masterpiece "Oh Father, Dear Father Come Home With Me Now."[1]

Tired of his melody, he kicked the cat on the hearth rug and resumed the gas attack on the hookah.

For several minutes no one spoke and as I watched Sholmes' face it slowly brightened till, with beaming smiles, he announced, "Doctor, your worries are over. Tomorrow, we will proceed to Little Wartlebury-in-the-Marsh; produce your Horace Marmaduke who will, I guarantee, live up to the old traditions of the ancient Haskervilles."

With grateful thanks the doctor departed, leaving us to muse on tomorrow's events while sipping the evening hogshead.[2]

Chapter II

The day broke fine and warm. We had an uneventful journey down from London to Little Wartlebury-in-the-Marsh, where a small carriage, emblazoned with the arms of the Haskervilles (two dormice[3] rampant surrounded by the family motto "Dum Novio Sanitas"—What Ho She Bumps), awaited us.[4]

An episode which might have led to serious consequences was only averted by the sang-froid[5] of Sholmes. The guard of

---

upright. The popularity of the violin led to the rest of the family fading from use in Europe by the middle of the 18th century.

[1] A popular 1864 temperance song written by Henry Clay Work (1832-1884), an anti-slavery activist and songwriter. A child is in the pub beseeching her father to come home because his son is ill and calling for him. With each succeeding verse, the child declines until he cries out "I want to kiss Papa goodnight," and dies. Work also wrote "Marching Through Georgia" (1865), inspired by Gen. William Tecumseh Sherman's march to the sea the year before.

[2] A large cask used to transport goods such as tobacco, wine, beer, sugar or molasses. Depending on the law, its size ranged from 50 to 70 U.S. gallons.

[3] A small rodent known for hibernating for as long as six months.

[4] *Dum Novio Sanitas*: Latin for "When the new health." *What Ho, She Bumps* was a music hall song written by Harry Castling and A.J. Mills about a boat moving through a choppy sea. The title became a phrase for anyone or anything displaying energy.

[5] Composure or coolness, especially in times of danger. From the French words for "cold blood."

the train, suspecting that Sholmes' hookah was either a sea-serpent or a diabolic machine, insisted on its being put in the guard's van; but Sholmes, tipping the guard a half-penny with the air of a bon viveur,[1] was allowed to retain it on the assumption it was a musical instrument.

The drive along pleasant rural roads was quite in keeping with Sholmes' country clothes which consisted of a deerstalker's hat, frock coat, green striped plus fours, blue socks, white spats, and brown boots. An alpenstock, butterfly net, and a mysterious parcel completed his outfit.[2]

Sholmes has always insisted that, to allay suspicion, it was necessary to dress and act the part.

Soon the turreted towers of Haskerville House appeared and, with a sharp turn from the main road, we were speeding along the drive to the portico where our host awaited us.

The doctor introduced us to the Earl of Haskerville and his son the Hon. Horace Marmaduke.

Horace Marmaduke, just down from Oxford, where he had got his Blue for Shove Ha'penny and Pushing the Ace,[3] was one of the usual public school type.

After a desultory conversation about the crops, the price of chewing gum and the servant problem,[4] we were led by our host

---

[1] A pseudo-French word adapted from *bon vivant* to mean "one who lives well." The phrase also suggests overindulgence and pretentiousness.

[2] *Plus fours:* Trousers that closed on the leg below the knee. Because they were four inches longer than the short pants called knickerbockers, they were called plus fours; *spats:* An footwear accessory that consisted of a piece of felt or leather that covered the instep and ankle; *alpenstock:* A long wooden pole with an iron tip, used to stabilize a mountain climber.

[3] *Blue:* An award earned by athletes performing at the highest level. The custom appears to have started at Cambridge, which awarded the university's official color (light blue) to eligible participants in the school's senior sports (rowing, cricket and track and field) in the 1860s. The custom spread to Oxford, and other universities; *shove ha'penny:* A pub game resembling shuffleboard, in which coins or discs are pushed across a tabletop to score points; *pushing the ace:* Unidentified.

[4] The problem was that there were fewer of them to go around. After the war, the demand for women in certain professions grew. Many women

towards a formidable dyke, which we now knew as the Bound.

I noticed during this little walk that Sholmes, carrying his mysterious parcel, had tarried somewhat and was deeply engaged in conversation with the doctor.

While we stood gazing at the deep forbidding abyss that lay before us Sholmes had quietly approached Horace Marmaduke and, under the pretence of removing a dead earwig, silently poured a colourless liquid down his neck.

With a yell of agony that would have awakened the dead, the Honourable Horace Marmaduke, rushing madly in a circle, found himself near the edge of the notorious Bound.

The sweat broke out on his terror-stricken brow as he realised that he could not stop in time. Life or death lay before him. Could he, with a mighty effort, clear the chasm, or would he fail and fall into its bottomless depths? Up, up he soared till with a thud he found he was on solid earth. With the intense and tingling pain in his neck he was to be seen disappearing in the distance towards Greater Wartlebury-on-the-Hill in search of relief.

Sholmes, smiling to himself, looked towards me and, in a contented voice said, "Elementary, my dear Jotson, elementary."

"Marvellous, Sholmes, but how. . .?" I queried.

"During my numerous travels in the East," began Sholmes, "I had occasion to render a small service in a poker game to an oil magnate, who in return gave me his secret called "high-life." A little of this mixture, he assured me, had been known to make lame dogs jump like grass-hoppers."

"Wonderful! Sholmes," I replied, "but the secret."

Furtively glancing round, Sholmes came closer and whispered in my ear.

I shuddered as I heard his words. A dizziness came over me, a mist before my eyes, and everything went black. I had fainted.

---

decided that even factory work with regular hours was preferable to working in someone else's home.

The Clue of the Six Pips

Sherlock Holmes Solves a Lincoln Mystery
"Sir A. Roastan Boil"

We have seen ads that contained parodies. Here's one in which the parody is the ad. Tucked in this 2,000-word story that appeared in the Dec. 19 edition of the Lincolnshire Echo *are more than twenty local stores. Lincolnshire is a county that shares a view of the North Sea with Yorkshire to the north, and the* Echo *has been reporting the news from its headquarters in Lincoln since 1893. The title, of course, is a reference to "The Five Orange Pips," although here pips do not refer to orange seeds, but to a form of counting that's familiar to Brits.*

Chapter I
We Have a Visitor

One night I was returning from a journey to a patient, when my way led me through Baker-street. As I passed the well-remembered door, I was seized with a keen desire to see Holmes again. His rooms were brilliantly lit, and even as I looked up, I saw his tall spare figure pass twice in a dark silhouette against the blind.

He was pacing the room swiftly, eagerly, with his head sunk on his chest, and I knew that something must have disturbed him greatly, for he dearly loved his deep arm chair. It was a *Buoyant* which had caught his eyes when passing CURTIS AND MAWER'S windows in Silver-street some months before and he had bought it on the impulse — and never regretted the purchase.[1]

I entered his study and with hardly a word spoken, but

---

[1] Buoyant chairs were low-slung armchairs with wide arms and leather upholstery. They resembled chairs you might find in a club and, as one ad described, with near-erotic overtones: "The Buoyant Chair is designed for utter relaxation. It takes away all temptations to be up and doing. It resists even the minor motions of muscle and mind. It beguiles you into giving yourself, body and almost soul, into the deep embrace of those springs." *Curtis and Mawer's:* Furniture manufacturers in Lincoln.

with a kindly eye, he waved me to the chair and passed across a box of cigars.

"Try these," he said, "SHARMAN AND LONG'S told me they were good and after trying one I think you'll agree with them — and with me, that never have you smoked a more excellent brand. Or you can try some of HIGGS' tobacco in your pipe. It is a delightful blend."

"Well," I remarked, as I pocketed a cigar and filled my pipe and reclined at ease in the *Buoyant*, "why this agitated consternation?"

At A Loss

"I have broken my high-power magnifying glass," replied Holmes, "and BATTLES closed at seven."

"Aren't there any more opticians in the town?" I asked.

"There are — several — but I shall get a new one from BATTLES. I had had that one for years and it was far superior to any I had previously. You remember that little incident which you chronicled as "A Scandal in Bohemia"? I was defeated there by a woman — but I should not have been had I had a good glass to work with. Since buying my glass from BATTLES I have never been defeated in any case."

There came a sudden ringing of the door bell.

"We have a visitor," remarked Holmes, and a minute later the door burst open and a man entered. He looked about him anxiously in the glare of the lamp, and I could see that his face was pale and his eyes heavy, like those of a man who is weighed down with some great anxiety.

"Ah, come in," welcomed Holmes. "Have you been losing some trains or mislaying a station?"

Our visitor started. "How did you know I was connected with the railway?" he asked in amazement.

Holmes laughed. "Merely by the fact that you are wearing a railwayman's tie[1] of bright red and that in your breast pocket

---

[1] In the early days of railroading, before sophisticated signaling systems

et is a handkerchief of vivid green. Apart from that and the facts that you are a Methodist, married, with a small child, and take a great pride in the manner in which you dress, I know nothing at all about you."

"Marvellous," exclaimed our visitor, "quite true, but how ...?"

"Yes, Holmes," I said, "I know your methods, but I am afraid you beat me this time."

"Elementary! my dear Watson, elementary. Our visitor has a copy of *Joyful News*[1] sticking out of his coat pocket, traces of toffee apple on his cheek. I cannot think that our man indulges in the eating of toffee apples, ergo, a child is indicated — and I recognize your handsome fur gloves as coming from WINGAD'S and your coat from DIXON AND PARKER'S. By those last two indications I deduce that you take pride in your appearance. I always go to MR J.P. WINGAD in Silverstreet for my gloves, and although I only wear an overcoat in the coldest weather, I have always bought them from DIXON AND PARKER'S. And that beautiful silk scarf could have come from nowhere except ARMSTRONG'S in Ballgate, I'll warrant.

Ah! and I also see that you have been to PENNELL'S for your buttonhole, and I hope you'll pardon me for saying it, but it is the finest specimen of *Dianthus Caryophyllaceae*[2] I have seen for some time. I must persuade Mrs. Hudson, my landlady, to procure me some.

Well, well, to return to business, what is troubling you?"

Lost the Level Crossings

Our visitor looked worried again.

"I fear we have lost our level-crossing gates,"[3] he mut-

---

were invented, crews were issued red neckerchiefs to use as a warning signal in an emergency. This practice carried over to the wearing of ties. When the railroads were nationalized in 1948, red ties were mandatory. However, no information was found about green handkerchiefs.

[1] A Methodist magazine founded by the Rev. Thomas Champness (1832-1905).
[2] The scientific name for a carnation or clove pink flower.
[3] The system of stopping traffic at railway crossings is far more complicat-

tered, and sinking his head into his hands, he wept bitterly.

"Lost your level crossings?" I cried, "however could you lose level crossings?"

"They have been stolen, you mean?" queried my friend.

"Yes," replied the sad man. "During the night, the gates — all four of them — were removed without a trace being left. Find them and we will give you anything you like — an engine, miles of lines, a signal box, or a case of fog signals — but find them, please. I have worked with them for years and have become quite attached to them."

Holmes smiled. "If I find your gates for you — and I have no doubt that I shall find them — you can give me a sweet little oak bureau I saw in G.H. SHAW'S windows at 126, High-street. It is quite cheap, but I want it to file the data collected during my investigations in the case chronicled by my friend, Dr Watson, as "The case of the North Hykeham Builder." Then I need not trouble you for any of your rolling stock or tunnels, but if I am successful, you may purchase for a young nephew of mine, a clockwork train, so long as you buy it at HARTWELL'S."

"It's a bargain," said our visitor.

Chapter II
The Six Pips

A pale moon shone down in the High-street and the metals of the railway lines shined silvery in its rays. As we neared the crossing, the figure of a woman approached from the opposite direction. Tall and dark and expensively dressed in a charming green dress under her green coat, with a small but becoming fur around her throat, she glided up to Holmes and whispered something in his ear. I could not catch what she said, but could only guess from my friend's whistle of aston-

---

ed than in the United States. There are automated systems where gates are raised and lowered. Some of them have a barrier — a low wall — that rolls across the road to keep vehicles and pedestrians from crossing. Roads and paths where farm animals cross require special gate-type barriers to ensure that they don't wander onto the rail bed.

ishment that her words had made an impression.

The woman glided away as silently as she had approached and we were left alone. What a witch! I thought.

Deduction

My eyes followed her. "What wonderful clothes," I remarked, "and how well she wears them."

"True," replied my friend, "that coat and dress came from C.J. FOX'S, and if ever I marry, my wife will have all the clothes she wants — so long as she gets them from C.J.'s."

Sherlock Holmes chuckled to himself as he thought of marriage. He, the greatest detective the world had ever known, married! Ha! ha! He chuckled again and slowly shook his head.

"You saw that fur she was wearing?" he asked me. "That came from HEBDON'S, on Monks-road. A marvelous piece of work — a genuine silver fox.

We proceeded on our way and halted at the level crossing, now looking oddly bare without its familiar gates.

Holmes dropped to his knees and closely examined the ground and the gate posts. Repeatedly he picked up small articles, only to drop them again with a gesture of annoyance. He had crawled halfway across the road when he suddenly came upon a number of small objects which he placed in an envelope. Then he straightened himself up and smilingly beckoned me to follow him.

An Inspiring Secret

We returned to Baker-street and Holmes seated himself in his arm chair, while I threw myself on a settee which Mrs Hilton Cubitt, whom he assisted in the case of the Dancing Men,[1] had given to Holmes. In his own inimitable fashion he had demonstrated to me his proofs that this artistic and comfortable piece of furniture had come from CROSSLEY'S.

---

[1] While Holmes did help Elsie Cubitt in "The Adventure of the Dancing Men," Watson did not record that Holmes had received a settee for his troubles.

Holmes took out the envelope into which he had thrust the articles he had picked up, and tossed them out on to a small table of curious design which I congratulated myself on my powers of observation — I remembered to have seen it in BAINBRIDGE'S window a few days previously. What I saw instantly brought to mind the case which I recorded as "The Adventure of the Five Orange Pips." Here, however, on the table there were six pips.

"Six pips," mused Holmes, as he sprayed a sweet-smelling perfume over himself. He always did this when thinking out a case, instead of injecting drugs as before. Drug injection was, I had pointed out to him, dangerous, and he had thereafter refrained from indulging in that rather foolish proceeding and had instead purchased from KEMP AND ELMITT'S a regular supply of Yardley's perfume.[1]

"Six pips," muttered Holmes, "what do they remind you of my friend?"

"The case of the Five Orange Pips," I answered immediately.

"Yes, yes," said Sherlock Holmes impatiently, "but don't they call to your mind anything else?"

I thought for some minutes. Six pips? No, they conveyed nothing to me, and I very reluctantly had to confess this to Holmes, who saw in my ignorance some subtle joke, for he chuckled again.

"Enough of work for to-day," he said. "Let us have some music. ASHLEY'S sent me a supply of new records to-day, and they are pretty good. You really must get one of their 'Gilbert' Gramophones, Watson. You know I've..."

"I have had one for nearly a month," I retorted, for Holmes had advised me on several previous occasions to buy one of Ashley's gramophones.

"Do you like it?" Holmes asked.

"Like it?" I retorted. "it's 'on' whenever I am in the house."

I put on a record and we spent the rest of the night in harmony, helped along by a box of chocolates which Holmes had had sent him from BEAN'S Candy Stores in Sincil-street.

---

[1] A British company, established in 1770, that specializes in cosmetics, fragrances, and soap.

Chapter III
A Long Quest

The following night Holmes and I set out on a tour of the city. What we were in search of I did not know, for Sherlock Holmes had not yet taken me into his confidence.

We went down many streets and into many passages and back yards, my friend making great use of a powerful electric torch, which he had that morning purchased from MR C.R. SPOUGE, on the Cornhill. It was an Ever Ready spotlight and cost only 7s, but it threw a brilliant beam of light for nearly a hundred yards. We had visited seven hundred and fifty-six back yards when I heard Holmes give an exclamation of delight and satisfaction.

"At last," he murmured to himself, "at last. Our quest is ended. Come here, Watson, and listen." We both crept to a window and listened...

"That is the end of the programme of music given by Jack Payne and his B.B.C. dance orchestra.[1] The weather and news will follow in approximately two minutes time."

We slipped away in the gloom. Holmes whistling a snappy little piece called "Gorgonzola."[2]

Holmes Solves the Mystery

"You see, Watson," he explained the following night, as we sat over a glass of whisky and soda from WHITTON AND ASHLEY'S. "the whole thing was perfectly clear almost from the first."

---

[1] Jack Payne (1899-1969) was a dance music bandleader who moved from leading the band at the Hotel Cecil starting in 1925 to becoming the BBC Director of Dance Music and leader of the orchestra in 1929. His subsequent music career included leading a touring dance band, returning to the BBC as director of Dance Music (1941-1946), and television appearances in the 1950s.

[2] A novelty song sung in praise of that noble, pungent cheese, recorded in 1930 by British entertainer Leslie Sarony (1897-1985). A sample stanza: "It's very labour-saving when a dinner party comes / You leave it on the table and it eats up all the crumbs / Gorgonzola, Gorgonzola / Three cheers for the green, white and blue."

"I must confess I do not yet see a glimmer of light on the problem," I replied with some natural impatience.

Holmes laughed. "You remember the six orange pips and the lady in green?"

"Yes," I said, "but I still cannot see the significance of them."

Sherlock Holmes looked at his watch. "Switch on the wireless," he said.

"Wireless?" I queried. "I did not know you had a wireless."

"I hadn't until to-day," Holmes remarked with a smile, "but after hearing that one last night, I called in to see MRS. WOODHEAD in the Exchange Arcade, and bought that portable you see there. Switch it on. The tone is marvellous."

I turned the knob, but there was only silence for a few moments, and then, clearly over the ether came the sound.

Pip! pip! pip! pip! pip! pip!

Six pips! How dense of me.

"The woman — the Green Witch — gave me the first clue," explained Holmes, "and immediately I saw the six pips I knew we had a wireless fiend to deal with. What should a wireless fiend want with level crossing gates? Obviously he wanted a pole for his aerial, and had taken the gates for that purpose. I must confess the long staves of the gates made an excellent aerial, and they are out of the way in that garden. I think I'll let them stay there and tell our friend the railwayman that the gates have been collected by an American curio hunter, who has shipped them to the States. It might encourage the railway company to do away with the crossings altogether. I'll buy the bureau from SHAW's myself and send Mrs Hudson across to HALLIWELL'S for that clockwork train. I'll tell her to bring it here so that we can see that it works alright, eh, Watson?"

"Good idea," I returned, "but one thing is not yet clear, Holmes. What did that woman in green say to you?"

"Oh, she told me that if I wanted one of INKLEY'S pork pies for Christmas I would have to hurry, because there was such a demand for them."

The Great Detective

Stephen Leacock

The great Canadian humorist Stephen Leacock (1869-1944) has appeared in this series twice before, with "Maddened by Mystery" in the 1910-1914 volume and "An Irreducible Detective Story" in the 1915-1919 book. This time, he casts a comic eye at the overused mystery tropes during this golden age of detective fiction. How many connections to Holmes can you spot?

"'Ha!' exclaimed the Great Detective, raising himself from the resilient sod on which he had lain prone for half an hour, 'what have we here?'
"As he spoke, he held up a blade of grass he had plucked.
"'I see nothing,' said the Poor Nut.
"'No, I suppose not,' said the Great Detective; after which he seated himself on a stone, took out his saxophone from its case, and for the next half hour was lost in the intricacies of Gounod's 'Sonata in Six Flats with a Basement.'"
—Any Detective Story

I.

The publishers tell us that more than a thousand detective stories are sold every day — or is it every hour? It does not matter. The point is that a great many are sold all the time, and that there is no slackening of the appetite of the reading public for stories of mysterious crime.

It is not so much the crime itself that attracts as the unraveling of the mystery by the super-brain of the Great Detective, as silent as he is efficient. He speaks only about once a week. He seldom eats. He crawls around in the grass picking up clews. He sits upside down in his armchair forging his inexorable chain of logic.

But when he's done with it, the insoluble mystery is solved, justice is done, the stolen jewels are restored, and the criminal is either hanged or pledges his word to go and settle on a ranch in Saskatchewan; after which the Great Detective takes a night off at the Grand Opera, the only thing that really reaches him.

The tempting point about a detective story — both for the writer and the reader — is that it is so beautifully easy to begin. All that is needed is to start off with a first-class murder.

"*Mr. Blankety Blank sat in his office in the drowsy hour of a Saturday afternoon. He was alone. Work was done for the day. The clerks were gone. The building, save for the janitor, who lived in the basement, was empty.*

"*As he sat thus, gazing in a sort of reverie at the papers on the desk in front of him, his chin resting on his hand, his eyes closed and slumber stole upon him.*"

Quite so. Let him feel just as drowsy as ever he likes. The experienced reader knows that now is the very moment when he is about to get a crack on the nut. This drowsy gentleman, on the first page of a detective story, is not really one of the characters at all. He is cast for the melancholy part that will presently be called The Body. Some writers prefer to begin with The Body itself right away — after this fashion:

"*The Body was that of an elderly gentleman, upside down, but otherwise entirely dressed.*"

But it seems fairer to give the elderly gentleman a few minutes of life before knocking him on the head. As long as the reader knows that there is either a Body right away, or that there is going to be one, he is satisfied.

Sometimes a touch of terror is added by having the elderly gentleman killed in a country house at night. Most readers will agree that this is the better way to kill him.

"*Sir Charles Althorpe sat alone in his library at Althorpe Chase. It was late at night. The fire had burned low in the grate. Through the heavily curtained windows no sound came from outside. Save for the maids, who slept in a distant wing, and save for the butler, whose room was under the stairs, the Chase, at this time of the year, was empty. As Sir Charles sat thus in his arm-chair, his head gradually sank upon his chest and he dozed off into slumber."*

Foolish man! Doesn't he know that to doze off into slumber in an isolated country house, with the maids in a distant wing, is little short of madness? Apparently he doesn't and his fate, to the complete satisfaction of the reader, comes right at him.

Let it be noted that in thus setting the stage for a detective story, the Body selected is, in nine cases out of ten, that of an "elderly gentleman." It would be cowardly to kill a woman, and even our grimmest writers hesitate to kill a child.[1] But an "elderly gentleman" is all right, especially when "fully dressed" and half asleep. Somehow they seem to invite a knock on the head.

After such a beginning, the story ripples brightly along with the finding of the Body, and with the Inquest, and with the arrest of the janitor, or the butler, and the usual details of that sort.

Any trained reader knows when he sees that trick phrase, *"save for the janitor, who lived in the basement,"* or *"save for the butler, whose room was under the stairs,"* that the janitor and the butler are to be arrested at once.

Not that they really did commit the murder. We don't believe they did. But they are suspected. And a good writer in the outset of a crime story throws suspicion around like pepper.

In fact, the janitor and the butler are not the only ones. There is also, in all the stories, a sort of Half Hero (he can't be a whole hero, because that would interfere with the Great Detective), who is partly suspected, and sometimes even arrested. He is the young man who is either heir to the money in the story, or who had a "violent quarrel" with the Body, or who was seen "leaving the premises at a late hour" and refuses to say why.

Some writers are even mean enough to throw a little sus-

---

[1] Not always. See Agatha Christie's *Hallowe'en Party* (1969).

picion on the Heroine — the niece or ward of the elderly gentleman — a heedless young woman dragged in by convention into this kind of novel. She gets suspected merely because she bought half a gallon of arsenic at the local chemist shop. They won't believe her when she says, with tears, in her eyes, that she wanted it to water the tulips with.[1]

The Body being thus completely dead, Inspector Higginbottom of the local police having been called in, having questioned all the maids, and having announced himself "completely baffled," the crime story is well set and the Great Detective is brought into it.

Here, at once, the writer is confronted with the problem of how to tell the story, and whether to write it as if it were told by the Great Detective himself. But the Great Detective is above that. For one thing, he's too silent. And in any case, if he told the story himself, his modesty might hold him back from fully explaining how terribly clever he is, and how wonderful his deductions are.

So the nearly universal method has come to be that the story is told through the mouth of an Inferior Person, a friend and confidant of the Great Detective. This humble associate has the special function of being lost in admiration all the time.

In fact, this friend, taken at his own face value, must be regarded as a Poor Nut. Witness the way in which his brain breaks down utterly and is set going again by the Great Detective. The scene occurs when the Great Detective begins to observe all the things around the place that were overlooked by Inspector Higginbottom.

"'But how,' I exclaimed, 'how in the name of all that is incomprehensible, are you able to aver that the criminal wore rubbers?'

"My friend smiled quietly.

"'You observe,' he said, 'that patch of fresh mud about ten feet square in front of the door of the house. If you would look,

---

[1] True, arsenic has agricultural uses as an insecticide. Its organic form is also fed to chickens and turkeys to promote growth.

you will see that it has been freshly walked over by a man with rubbers on.'

"I looked. The marks of the rubbers were there plain enough — at least a dozen of them.

"'What a fool I was!' I exclaimed. 'But at least tell me how you were able to know the length of the criminal's foot?'

"My friend smiled again, his same inscrutable smile.

"'By measuring the print of the rubber,' he answered quietly, 'and then subtracting from it the thickness of the material multiplied by two.'

"'Multiplied by two!' I exclaimed. 'Why by two?'

"'For the toe and the heel.'

"'Idiot that I am,' I cried, 'it all seems so plain when you explain it.'"

In other words, the Poor Nut makes an admirable narrator. However much fogged the reader may get, he has at least the comfort of knowing that the Nut is far more fogged than he is. Indeed, the Nut may be said, in a way, to personify the ideal reader, that is to say the stupidest — the reader who is most completely bamboozled with the mystery, and yet intensely interested.

Such a reader has the support of knowing that the police are entirely "baffled" — that's always the word for them; that the public are "mystified," that the authorities are "alarmed," the newspapers "in the dark," and the Poor Nut altogether up a tree. On those terms, the reader can enjoy his own ignorance to the full.

A first-class insoluble crime having thus been well started, and with the Poor Nut narrating it with his ingenuous interest, the next stage in the mechanism of the story is to bring out the personality of the Great Detective, and to show how terribly clever he is.

II.

When a detective story gets well started — when the "body" has been duly found — and the "butler" or the "janitor" has been arrested — when the police have been completely "baffled" — then is the time when the Great Detective is brought in and gets to work.

But before he can work at all, or at least be made thoroughly satisfactory to the up-to-date reader, it is necessary to touch him up. He can be made extremely tall and extremely thin, or even "cadaverous." Why a cadaverous man can solve a mystery better than a fat man it is hard to say; presumably the thinner a man is, the more acute is his mind.[1] At any rate, the old school or writers preferred to have their detectives lean. This incidentally gave the detective a face "like a hawk," the writer not realizing that a hawk is one of the stupidest of animals. A detective with a face like an ourang-outang[2] would beat it all to bits.

Indeed, the Great Detective's face becomes even more important than his body. Here there is absolute unanimity. His face has to be "inscrutable." Look at it though you will, you can never read it. Contrast it, for example, with the face of Inspector Higginbottom, of the local police force. Here is a face that can look "surprised," or "relieved," or, with great ease, "completely baffled."

But the face of the Great Detective knows of no such changes. No wonder the Poor Nut, as we may call the person who is supposed to narrate the story, is completely mystified. From the face of the great man you can't tell whether the cart in which they are driving jolts him or whether the food at the Inn gives him indigestion.

To the Great Detective's face there used to be added the old-time expedient of not allowing him either to eat or drink. And when it was added that during this same period of about eight days the sleuth never slept, the reader could realize in

---

[1] To which Nero Wolfe, all one-seventh of a ton of him, would reply, "Pfui."

[2] An early spelling of a species of great ape found in Borneo and Sumatra. The hyphenation reflects the two Malay and Indonesian words that mean "person of the forest": *orang* (person) and *hutan* (forest).

what fine shape his brain would be for working out his "inexorable chain of logic."

But nowadays this is changed. The Great Detective not only eats, but he eats well. Often he is presented as a connoisseur in food. Thus:

"'Stop a bit,' thus speaks the Great Detective to the Poor Nut and Inspector Higginbottom, whom he is dragging around with him as usual; 'we have half an hour before the train leaves Paddington. Let us have some dinner. I know an Italian restaurant near here where they serve frogs' legs a la Marengo better than anywhere else in London.'

"A few minutes later we were seated at one of the tables of a dingy little eating-place whose signboard with the words 'Restauranto Italiano' led me to the deduction that it was an Italian restaurant. I was amazed to observe that my friend was evidently well known in the place, while his order for 'three glasses of Chianti with two drops of vermicelli in each,' called for an obsequious bow from the appreciative padrone. *I realized that this amazing man knew as much of the finesse of Italian wines as he did of playing the saxophone."*[1]

We may go no further. In many up-to-date cases the detective not only gets plenty to eat, but a liberal allowance of strong drink. One generous British author of today is never tired of handing out to the Great Detective and his friends what he calls a "stiff whiskey and soda." At all moments of crisis they get one.

For example, when they find the Body of Sir Charles Althorpe, late owner of Althorpe Chase, a terrible sight, lying on the floor of the library, what do they do? They reach at once to the sideboard and pour themselves out a "stiff whiskey and soda." Or when the heroine learns that her guardian

---

[1] The humor in this paragraph comes from the number of errors. "Restauranto" does not mean "Restaurant" (it's "Ristorante"). *Vermicelli* is not a liquid but pasta we know better as spaghetti. *Padrone* is a close-enough word, meaning business owner, host, or landlord. And finesse has nothing to do with a knowledge of wines.

Sir Charles is dead and that she is his heiress and when she is about to faint, what do they do? They immediately pour "a stiff whiskey and soda" into her. It is certainly a great method.

But in the main we may say that all this stuff about eating and drinking has lost its importance. The great detective has to be made exceptional by some other method.

And here is where his music comes in. It transpires — not at once but in the first pause in the story — that this great man not only can solve a crime, but has the most extraordinary aptitude for music, especially for dreamy music of the most difficult kind. As soon as he is left in the Inn room with the Poor Nut out comes his saxophone, and he tunes it up.

"'What were you playing?' I asked, as my friend at last folded his beloved instrument into its case.

"'Beethoven's Sonata in Q,' he answered modestly.

"'Good Heavens!' I exclaimed."[1]

Another popular method of making the Great Detective a striking character is to show him as possessing a strange and varied range of knowledge. For example, the Poor Nut is talking with a third person, the Great Detective being apparently sunk in reveries. In the course of the conversation the name of Constantinople is mentioned.

"I was hardly aware that my friend was hearing what was said.

"He looked up quietly.

"'Constantinople?' he said. 'That was the capital of Turkey, was it not?'

"I could not help marveling again how this strange being could have acquired his minute and varied knowledge."[2]

The Great Detective's personality having been thus ar-

---

[1] Absurdity piled upon absurdity. A saxophone can't be folded except with the aid of a very large hammer. Finally, neither Ludwig van Beethoven (1770-1827) nor any other composer ever wrote a sonata in the key of Q, if only because the key of Q doesn't exist.

[2] As of 1930, the year Constantinople was officially renamed Istanbul, Ankara had been the capital of Turkey for only seven years.

ranged, he is brought along with the Poor Nut and Inspector Higginbottom to Althorpe Chase and it is now up to him to start to "solve" the mystery. Till a little while ago, the favorite way of having him do this was by means of tracks, footprints, and other traces. This method, which has now worn threadbare, had a tremendous vogue. According to it, the Great Detective never questioned anybody.

But his real work was done right at the scene of the crime, crawling round on the carpet of the library, and wriggling about on the grass outside. After he has got up after two days of crawling, with a broken blade of grass, he would sit down on a stone and play the saxophone and then announce that the mystery is solved and tell Inspector Higginbottom whom to arrest. That was all. He would not explain anything but what the Poor Nut, half crazy with mystification, begged him to do.

"'The case,' he at last explained very airily, 'has been a simple one, but not without its features of interest.'

"'Simple!' I exclaimed.

"'Precisely,' said he; 'you see this blade of grass. You tell me that you see nothing. Look at it again under this lens. What do you see? The letters ACK clearly stamped, but in reverse, on the soft green of the grass. What do they mean?'

"'Nothing,' I groaned.

"'You are wrong,' he said, 'they are the last three letters of the word DACK, the name of a well-known shoemaker in Market Croydon four miles west of the Chase.'"[1]

"'Good Heavens,' I said.

"'Now look at this soft piece of mud which I have baked and

---

[1] *Market Croydon:* While Leacock didn't have a particular place in mind, there is a Croydon in Britain. Now a large borough in south London, in the Middle Ages it was a village that was given market status, meaning it could hold a weekly market. By 1930, Croydon was a major industrial area for car manufacturing and metal working. It was absorbed into London in 1965. The Chase is an area of unenclosed common land that was reserved for hunting by one or more persons. There is also a Royal Chase which would be reserved for the British royal family.

which carried a similar stamp — ILTON.'

"'Ilton, Ilton,' I repeated, 'I fear it means less than ever.'

"'To you,' he said. 'Because you do not observe. Did you never note that makers of trousers nowadays stamp their trouser buttons with their names? These letters are the concluding part of the name BILTON, one of the best-known tailors of Kings Croft, four miles east of the Chase.'[1]

"'Good Heavens!' I cried, 'I begin to see.'

"'Do you?' he said drily. 'Then no doubt you can piece together the analysis. Our criminal is wearing a pair of trousers, bought in Kings Croft, and a shoe bought in Market Croydon. What do you infer as to where he lives?'

"'Good Heavens,' I said, 'I begin to see it!'

"'Exactly,' said the Great Detective. 'He lives halfway between the two!'

"'At the Chase itself!' I cried. 'What a fool I have been.'

"'You have,' he answered quietly."

But unfortunately the public has begun to find this method of traces and tracks a "bit thick." All these fond old literary fictions are crumbling away.

The Method of Recondite Knowledge

In fact, they are being very largely replaced by the newer and much more showy expedient that can be called the Method of Recondite Knowledge. The Great Detective is equipped with a sort of super-scientific knowledge of things, materials, substances, chemistry, actions, and reactions that would give him a Ph.D. degree in any school of applied science.

Some of the best detectives of the higher fiction of today even maintain a laboratory and a couple of assistants. When they have this, all they need is a little piece of dust or a couple of micrometer sections and the criminal is as good as caught.

---

[1] The town doesn't exist, although there are plenty of roads in Britain and the U.S. that use that name.

Thus, let us suppose that in the present instance Sir Charles Althorpe has been done to death — as so many "elderly gentlemen" were in the fiction of twenty years ago — by the intrusion into his library of a sailor with a wooden leg newly landed from Java. Formerly the crime would have been traced by the top heaviness of his wooden leg — when the man drank beer at the Althorpe Arms, his elbow on the side away from his leg would have left an impression on the bar, similar to the one left where he climbed the window sill.

But in the newer type of story the few grains of dust found near the Body would turn out to be specks from the fiber of Java coconut, such as is seen only on the decks of ships newly arrived from Java, and on the clothes of the sailors.

But, by the one method or the other method, the "inexorable chain of logic" can be completed to the last link. The writer can't go on forever; sooner or later he must own up and say who did it. After two hundred pages, he finds himself up against the brutal necessity of selecting his actual murderer.

So, now, who did it? Which brings us to the final phase of the Detective Story. Who really killed Sir Charles?

III.
The Tramp Solution

According to one very simple expedient, the murder was not committed by any of the principal characters at all. It was committed by *a tramp*. It transpires that the tramp was passing the Chase late that night and was attracted by the light behind the curtain (as tramps are apt to be), and came and peered through the window (as tramps love to do), and when he saw Sir Charles asleep in his chair with the gold watch on the table beside him, he got one of those sudden impulses (such as tramps get when they see a gold watch), and, before he knew what he had done, he had lifted the window and slipped into the room.

Sir Charles woke — and there you are. All quite simple. Indeed, but for the telltale marks on the grass, or the telltale fiber on the carpet, or the telltale something, the murderer would never have been known.

And yet the solution seems paltry. It seems a shame to drag in the poor tattered creature at the very end and introduce and hang him all in one page.

So we have to look round for some other plan.

The Murder Was Committed By Somebody Else Altogether Different

A solution, which is a prime favorite with at least one very distinguished contemporary author, is to have it turn out that the murder has been committed by somebody else altogether different. In other words, it was committed by some casual person who just came into the story for about one half a second.

Let us make up a simple example. At the Althorpe Arms Inn where the Great Detective and the Poor Nut are staying while they investigate the death of Sir Charles, we bring in, just for one minute, "a burly-looking man in a check suit[1] drinking a glass of ale in the bar." We ask him quite casually, if he can tell us anything about the state of the road to Farringham. He answers in a surly way that he's a stranger to these parts and knows nothing of it. That's all. He doesn't come in any more till the very end.

But a really experienced reader ought to guess at once that he committed the murder. Look at it: he's burly; and he's surly; and he has a check suit; and he drinks ale; and he's a stranger; that's enough. Any good law court could hang him for that — in a detective story, anyway.

When at last the truth dawns on the Poor Nut.

"'Great Heavens," I exclaimed, 'the man in the check suit!'
"The Great Detective nodded.
"'But how on earth!' I exclaimed, more mystified than ever,

---

[1] A suit in a loud checkered pattern was a distinctive choice at this time. A man who wore one was not a gentleman, but a gambler, a card sharp, or a con man.

'were you ever led to suspect it?'

"'From the very first,' said my friend, turning to Inspector Higginbottom, who nodded in confirmation, 'we had a strong clew.'

"'A clew!' I exclaimed.

"'Yes, one of the checks on his coat had been cached.'

"'Cashed,' I cried.

"'You misunderstand me; not "cashed," CACHED. He had cut it out and hidden it. A man who cuts out a part of his coat and hides it on the day after a crime is probably concealing something.'

"'Great Heavens!' I exclaimed, 'how obvious it sounds when you put it that way. To think that I never thought of it!'"

The Solution of the Thoroughly Dangerous Woman

According to this method, the crime was committed by a thoroughly bad, thoroughly dangerous woman, generally half foreign — which is supposed to account for a lot. She has just come into the story casually — as a nurse, or as an assistant bookkeeper, or, more usual and much better, as a "discarded flame" of somebody or other.[1]

These discarded flames flicker all through detective literature as a terrible warning to persons of a fickle disposition. In any case, great reliance is placed on foreign blood as accounting for her. For Anglo-Saxon readers, if you put a proper quantity of foreign blood into a nurse and then discard her, that will do the trick every time.

To show how thoroughly bad she is, the Dangerous Woman used to be introduced by the writers of the Victorian age as smoking a cigarette. She also wore "high-heeled shoes and a skirt that reached barely to her ankles." In our time, she would have to do a little better than that. In short, as the key to a murder, we must pass her by. She would get acquitted

---

[1] A lover has been called a flame as far back as 1651, while calling a former lover an old flame dates as far back as William Makepeace Thackeray's *Vanity Fair* (1848).

every time.

Let us try something else.

The Solution that the Murder Was Committed by Blue Edward

According to this explanation of the mysterious crime, it turns out, right at the end of the story, that the murder was not done by any of the people suspected — neither by the Butler, nor the Half Hero, nor the Tramp, nor the Dangerous Woman. Not at all. It was the work of one of the most audacious criminals ever heard of (except that the reader never heard of him till this second), the head and brain of a whole gang of criminals, ramifying all over Hades.

This head criminal generally goes under some such terrible name as Black Pete, or Yellow Charlie, or Blue Edward. As soon as his name is mentioned, then at once not only the Great Detective but everybody else knows all about him — except only the reader and the Nut, who is always used as a proxy for the reader in matters of astonishment or simplicity of mind.

At the very height of the chase, a new murder, that of a deputy police inspector (they come cheap; it's not like killing one of the regular characters), is added to the main crime of killing Sir Charles. The manner of the murder — by means of a dropping bullet fired three miles away with its trajectory computed by algebra — has led to the arrest. The Great Detective, calculating back the path of the bullet, has ordered by telephone the arrest of a man three miles away. As the Detective, the Nut, and the police stand looking at the body of the murdered policeman, word comes from Scotland Yard that the arrest is made:

"The Great Detective stood looking about him, quietly shaking his head. His eye rested a moment on the prostrate body of Sub-Inspector Bradshaw, then turned to scrutinize the neat hole drilled in the glass of the window.

"'I see it all now, he murmured. 'I should have guessed it

sooner. There is no doubt whose work this is.'

"'Who is it?' I asked.

"'Blue Edward,' he announced quietly.

"'Blue Edward!' I exclaimed.

"'Blue Edward,' he repeated.

"'Blue Edward!' I reiterated, 'but who then is Blue Edward?'"

This, of course, is the very question that the reader is wanting to ask. Who on earth is Blue Edward? The question is answered at once by the Great Detective himself.

"'The fact that you have never heard of Blue Edward merely shows the world that you have lived in. As a matter of fact, Blue Edward is the terror of four continents. We have traced him to Shanghai, only to find him in Madagascar. It was he who organized the terrible robbery at Irkutsk in which ten mujiks were blown up with a bottle of Epsom salts.[1]

"'It was Blue Edward who for years held the whole of Philadelphia in abject terror, and kept Oshkosh, Wisconsin, on the jump for even longer. At the head of a gang of criminals that ramifies all over the known globe, equipped with a scientific education that enables him to read and write and use a typewriter with the greatest ease, Blue Edward has practically held the police of the world at bay for years.

"'I suspected his hand in this from the start. From the very outset, certain evidences pointed to the work of Blue Edward.'"

After which all the police inspectors and spectators keep shaking their heads and murmuring, "Blue Edward, Blue Edward," until the reader is sufficiently impressed.

IV.

The writing of a detective story, without a doubt, gets

---

[1] *Irkutsk:* one of the largest cities in the Siberian region of Russia; *mujiks:* An archaic Russian word meaning peasant; *Epsom salts:* An inorganic salt that has a number of uses in the home, such as treating skin inflammations and to remove splinters; in agriculture to improve the soil; in the kitchen to make beer and tofu; and in industry. It is named for a spring in Epsom, Britain, where salts were originally prepared.

harder and harder towards the end. It is not merely the difficulty of finding a suitable criminal; there is added the difficulty of knowing what to do with him. It is a tradition of three centuries of novel writing that a story ought to end happily. But in this case, how to end up happily?

For example, here we have Blue Edward, caught at last, with handcuffs on his wrists — Blue Edward, the most dangerous criminal that ever interwove the underworld into a solid mesh; Blue Edward, who — well, in fact the whole aim of the writer only a little while before was to show what a heller Blue Edward was. True, we never heard of him until near the end of the book, but when he did get in we were told that his Gang had ramified all the way from Sicily to Oklahoma. Now, what are we to do?

If it is not Blue Edward, then we've got to hang the Tramp — the poor tattered creature who fried potatoes by the hedge. But we are called upon to notice that he now has "a singularly vacant eye." You can hardly hang a man with a vacant eye. It doesn't do.

What if we send him to prison for life? But that's pretty cold stuff, too — sitting looking at four stone walls with a vacant eye for forty years. In fact, the more we think of it, the less satisfied we are with hanging the Tramp. Personally I'd rather hang Meadows the Butler, as we first set out to do, or I'd hang the Nut or the Thoroughly Bad Woman, or any of them.

In the older fiction, they used to face this problem fairly and squarely. They hanged them — and apparently they liked it. But nowadays we can't do it. We have lost the old-fashioned solid satisfaction in it, so we have to look round for another solution. Here is one, a very favorite one with our sensitive generation. If I had to give it a name, I would call it —

The Criminal with the Hacking Cough

The method if it is very simple. Blue Edward, or whoever is to be "it," is duly caught. There's no doubt of his guilt. But at the moment when the Great Detective and the Ignorant Police are examining him, he develops a "hacking cough." Indeed, as he starts to make his confession, he can hardly talk for hacks.

"'Well,' says the criminal, looking round at the little group of police officers, 'the game is up — hack! hack! — and I may as well make a clean breast of it — hack, hack, hack.'"

Any trained reader when he hears these hacks knows exactly what they are to lead up to. The criminal, robust though he seemed only a chapter ago when he jumped through a three-story window after throttling Sub-Inspector Juggins half to death, is a dying man. He has got one of those terrible diseases known to fiction as a "mortal complaint." It wouldn't do to give it an exact name, or somebody might get busy and cure it. The symptoms are a hacking cough and a great mildness of manner, an absence of all profanity, and a tendency to call everybody "you gentlemen." Those things spell finis.

In fact, all that is needed now is for the Great Detective himself to say, *"Gentlemen"* (they are all gentlemen at this stage of the story), *"a higher conviction than any earthly law has, et cetera, et cetera."* With that, the curtain is dropped, and it is understood that the criminal made his exit the same night.

That's better, decidedly better. And yet, lacking in cheerfulness, somehow.

It is just about as difficult to deal with the Thoroughly Bad Woman. The general procedure is to make her raise a terrible scene. When she is at last rounded up and caught, she doesn't "go quietly" like the criminal with the hacking cough or the repentant tramp. Not at all. She raises — in fact, she is made to raise so much that the reader will be content to waive any prejudice about the disposition of criminals, to get her out of the story.

"The woman's face as Inspector Higginbottom snapped the handcuffs on her wrists was livid with fury.

"Gur-r-r-r-r!" she hissed."

(This is her favorite exclamation, and shows the high percentage of her foreign blood.)

"'Gur-r-r-r-r! I hate you all. Do what you like with me. I would kill him again a thousand times, the old fool.'

"She turned furiously towards my friend (the Great Detective).

"'As for you,' she said 'I hate you. Gur-r-r! See, I spit at you. Gur-r-r-r!'"

In that way, the Great Detective gets his, though of course, his impassive face never showed a sign. Spitting on him doesn't faze him. Then she turns on the Heroine and gives her what's coming to her.

"'And you! Gur-r-r! I despise you, with your baby face! Gur-r-r! And now you think you will marry him! I laugh at you! Ha! Ha! Hahula!'"

And after that she turns on the Nut and gives him some, and then some for Inspector Higginbottom, and thus with three "Gur-r-r's" for everybody and a "Ha! ha!" as a tiger,[1] off she goes.

But, take it which way you will, the ending is never satisfactory. Not even the glad news that the Heroine sank into the Poor Nut's arms, never to leave them again, can relieve the situation. Not even the knowledge that they erected a handsome memorial to Sir Charles, or that the Great Detective played the saxophone for a week can quite compensate us.

---

[1] A long growl. The whole phrase is usually "three cheers and a tiger" and is called for to honor a notable person. For example, in Mark Twain's "The Man That Corrupted Hadleyburg" can be found "...finishing up with cheers and a tiger for 'Hadleyburg purity and our eighteen immortal representatives of it.'"

The Six O'clock Mystery

Anonymous

Advertisers never let dignity get in the way of getting their message across. If you're advertising soap, then someone needs to be in the bathtub sans clothes, even Sherlock Holmes. This ad appeared in numerous magazines, including the March issue of Adventure *magazine.*

The six o'clock mystery...

Herlock Sholmes and his good friend Batson had noticed the man when he came in at precisely 6:03½ P. M.

"A dangerous looking fellow," murmured Sholmes. "Notice the twitching nerves around his eyes, and the smoldering impatience in every gesture. He'll bear watching..."

At 6:27 the man reappeared... a beam of loving kindness in his eye, a low jolly whistle on his lips.

"I say, Batson!" said Herlock, "the man must be a Dr. Jekyll and Mr. Hyde. I never saw such an astounding change in a personality! We must find the cause."

Picture Herlock and his faithful Batson in the man's apartment... measuring, digging through drawers, peering into corners. But pill or powder found they none!

Then Herlock threw open the bathroom door. A tropical warmth still lingered in the air, and the mirror was misted with steam. A splash of water on the floor... a heap of damp towel... and in the soap dish, a smooth, alabaster-white rectangle.

"Eureka!" he cried, "I have it!"

"Have what?" asked Batson, who never was very bright.

Herlock scorned to answer. He drew a tub... he threw off his clothes... he tossed the rectangle upon the water... and as he slid luxuriously into the steaming bath, he uttered these cryptic words—"It floats."

... kind to everything it touches · 99 44/100 % Pure · "It floats" © 1930, P. & G. Co.

Kindly mention Adventure in writing to advertisers or visiting your dealer.

Herlock Sholmes and his good friend Batson had noticed the man when he came in at precisely 6:03½ P.M.

"A dangerous looking fellow," murmured Sholmes. "Notice the twitching nerves around his eyes, and the smoldering impatience in every gesture. He'll bear watching..."

At 6:27 the man reappeared... a beam of loving kindness in his eye, a low jolly whistle on his lips.

"I say, Batson!" said Herlock, "the man must be a Dr. Jekyll and Mr. Hyde. I never saw such an astounding change in a personality! We must find the cause."

Picture Herlock and his faithful Batson in the man's apartment... measuring, digging through drawers, peering into corners. But pill or powder found they none!

Then Herlock threw open the bathroom door. A tropical warmth still lingered in the air, and the mirror was misted with steam. A splash of water on the floor... a heap of damp towel and in the soap dish, a smooth, alabaster-white rectangle.

"Eureka!" he cried, "I have it!" [1]

"Have what?" asked Batson, who never was very bright.

Herlock scorned to answer. He drew a tub.... he threw off his clothes... he tossed the rectangle upon the water... and as he slid luxuriously into the steaming bath, he uttered these cryptic words — "It floats."[2]

---

[1] An ancient Greek word meaning "I find," but more colloquially defined as "I found it." The phrase was popularized by the Roman architect and engineer Marcus Vitruvius Pollio (c. 80-70 B.C.- 15 B.C.). In one of his books, he told the story of Archimedes (c. 287-c. 212 B.C.), the mathematician who had figured out the solution to a problem involving a golden crown that the king had suspected had some of its pure gold removed and substituted with the same weight of silver. While submerging himself in his bath, Archimedes realized the volume of water displaced must equal the volume of the submerged part of the body. Because gold was twice as dense as silver, he reasoned that if the crown was weighed under water, the theft could be proved.

[2] Ivory Soap's slogan, introduced in 1891. It became so popular a catchphrase that in 1928, *The New Yorker* published a cartoon by Gluyas Williams (1888-1982) captioned, "Industrial Crisis: The day a cake of soap sank at Procter & Gamble's," showing executives attempting to rescue the soap in various ways from a swimming pool.

The Case of the Missing Patriarchs: Translated from the Thyroid

Logan Clendening

In his memoirs, Conan Doyle mentioned three apocryphal stories about himself and Sherlock Holmes that he had read in the press. He described two of them, then added, "There was a third about how Sherlock entered heaven, and by virtue of his power of observation at once greeted Adam, but the point is perhaps too anatomical for further discussion."

Fortunately, Dr. Logan Clendenning (1884-1945) not only decided to tell the story, but do so in an amusing fashion. Clendenning was a doctor who not only was a popular medical columnist, but an author whose The Human Body was a best-seller. He was also fascinated by the writings of Charles Dickens and Conan Doyle's Sherlock. This first appeared in 1934, in a limited printing of 30 copies by Edwin B. Hill, making it one of the rarest of Holmesian parodies. This also places it four years after the end of this series, and for that I have to beg your indulgence. You see, it appeared in Ellery Queen's Mini-Mysteries *(1969), which I encountered as a boy in the stacks of the Charlotte Public Library. It was my first encounter with Sherlock Holmes as a parody, so publishing it here makes a fitting capstone to the series.*

Sherlock Holmes is dead. At the age of eighty he passed away quietly in his sleep. And at once ascended to Heaven.

The arrival of few recent immigrants to the celestial streets has caused so much excitement. Only Napoleon's appearance in Hell is said to have equaled the great detective's reception. In spite of the heavy fog which rolled in from the Jordan,[1] Holmes was immediately bowled in a hansom to an

---

[1] Despite its appearance here, the Jordan does not flow through Heaven. The 156-mile-long river flows north to south through the Sea of Galilee and into the Dead Sea. This made it a natural boundary line as well as a primary water source. Moisture from the river, combined with the intense heat of the Rift Valley, also created a humid, fertile microclimate. The Israelites fleeing Egypt were said to have crossed the Jordan to reach the

audience with the Divine Presence. After the customary exchange of amenities, Jehovah[1] said:

"Mr. Holmes, we too have our problems. Adam and Eve are missing. Have been, as a matter of fact, for nearly two eons.[2] They used to be quite an attraction to visitors, and we would like to commission you to discover them."

Holmes looked thoughtful for a moment.

"We fear that their appearance when last seen would furnish no clue," continued Jehovah. "A man is bound to change in two aeons."

Holmes held up his long, thin hand. "Could you make a general announcement that a contest between an immovable body and an irresistible force[3] will be staged in that large field

---

Promised Land, and Jesus was baptized by John the Baptist in its waters.

[1] What you get when you change into Latin the Hebrew name for the God of Israel. In Jewish tradition, the name of God is too sacred to be pronounced. No less than seven substitute names for God were passed down, the most common one being the Tetragammaton (Greek for "[consisting of] four letters") that translates from the Hebrew into YHWH. A group of scholars called the Masoretes developed a guide to speaking the text in the Jewish Bible. They added notes to the Hebrew word that indicated it should be pronounced Adonai ("my Lord"). In the 12th century, the word was translated into English as "Iehouah" and "Jehovah." The latter form appeared in the Geneva Bible and the King James version, but has been dropped in favor of "Lord" in most modern translations.

[2] The word translates to "age," and while in astronomy it is defined as a billion years, the length is undefined in Biblical terms. Biblical commentators divide the whole of time into three eons: the time before man was created, the span of mankind's existence on Earth, and the end times when Christ will return. Note that the word is spelled two ways in the story, with "eon" the Americanized version of the English "aeon."

[3] While the pairing of incompatible premises that creates a paradox is of ancient vintage, this particular formulation is only from the mid-19th century. Its earliest appearance was in an 1862 issue of *Harper's New Monthly Magazine*, although it was described as "an old paradox of the schoolmen." The earliest known example comes from the *Han Feizi*, an ancient Chinese text dated from the 3rd century B.C. In it, Han Fei (c. 280-233 B.C.) tells the story of a man who sells a spear and a shield by claiming that the spear could pierce any shield, and the shield could defeat all spear attacks.

In another example, this time from the ancient Greek mythologies,

at the end of the street —Lord's, I presume it is?"

The announcement was made and soon the streets were filled with a slowly moving crowd. Holmes stood idly in the divine portico watching them.

Suddenly he darted into the crowd and seized a patriarch and his whimpering old mate; he brought them to the Divine Presence.

"It is," asserted the Deity. "Adam, you have been giving us a great deal of anxiety. But, Mr. Holmes, tell me how you found them."

"Elementary, my dear God," said Sherlock Holmes, "they have no navels."

Logan Clendening

---

the giant Teumessian fox was sent by the gods to eat the children of Thebes as punishment for a state crime. Amphitryon, the son of a Theban general, was tasked with killing the fox. He found the magical dog Laelaps, who could catch everything it chased, and sent him after the fox, who could never be caught. Zeus resolved the paradox by turning the two beasts into stone and becoming the constellations Canis Major and Canis Minor.

Appendix
The Adventure of the Fight Club

Bill Peschel

This story presents a mystery within the mystery. Previous stories in the series filled chronological gaps in Twain's life, such as when Twain met Mycroft Holmes in Tangier during a trip that inspired The Innocents Abroad, or when he visited London as recounted in "The Adventure of the Stomach Club." There are few hints in this story as to when it took place. Holmes' references to Twain's Hartford home places this story after "The Adventure of the Missing Mortician" and before the events recounted in "The Adventure of the Whyos." For those reasons, a provisional date of May 1887 was chosen.

This story is also unique in that it contains chronological errors, which the knowledgeable reader will recognize. It is also the only story in the papers that was narrated by Holmes' friend, Dr. Watson, who was known for fudging when some of Holmes' cases took place. But if Watson is the author, how did it get into the Twain papers? Handwriting analysis will not help, as the manuscript was typewritten. Could this be an account of a real story with the details disguised to protect the innocent, or a pastiche written as a joke? If it was the latter, was it Watson poking fun at Twain, or the other way around?

1. The Friend

During my long association with Sherlock Holmes, he never lost his capacity for surprises. I knew well his acting skill and ability with disguises. Yet he still confounded me with an unusual characterization. His deductive ability is unparalleled, yet he developed new ways of seeing deeper into the world what we skim over. His pronounced indifference to women was belied by his gentlemanly behavior towards them. His demeanour was as stern as a Glasgow preacher, yet ...

Imagine my surprise when I came downstairs in my dressing gown one unseasonably clement morning in early May and saw Holmes by the glowing coals of the fireplace. He was in his favorite attitude for listening, his head slightly forward, nodding as if asleep, his fingers steepled, but he was laughing! He emitted undignified snorts of merriment, like a train building a head of steam.

My surprise was redoubled when I saw in the chair opposite him a man I hadn't seen since we romped about San Francisco's Chinatown on the American Independence Day several decades before.

"Good morning, Watson," Holmes wiped a tear from his eye. "I assume you recognize our guest. Mr. Samuel Clemens was one of my clients early in my career when I was living in Montague Street."

"The honor of the introduction should be mine, Holmes, for I knew Sam out West before you did."

"Indeed? I wasn't aware of that." It was rare that I felt on the same level as Holmes and I resolved to enjoy it. "You must tell me about your adventure with him sometime."

It had been decades since I saw Clemens. Then, he was a young man whose spirits were as untamed as the West. He was older now, and his adventurous life and achievements had molded him. He was dressed in a proper suit, but it was rumpled. He slouched comfortably in the chair, smoking a cheroot that by the smell had been bought in a junk shop. He regarded me from underneath brows that could bristle with fire, then suddenly arch with good humor and warmth. Only a foot, bouncing on the floor like a piston, betrayed any anxiety.

"I'm pleased to shake the hand of friendship again after all these years, Watson," he drawled. "We've come up in the world since San Fran. How's your neck?" He went on to Holmes, "we've been swapping lies about our time on the stage, but your boy here has topped both of us. He played the most convincing imitation of a man being hanged it has ever been my pleasure to witness."

Holmes' surprise was startling. His confoundment by Irene Adler remained green in my memory, but that was minor compared to now.

"Your story intrigues me, Clemens. Watson will have to tell me about the measure he trod later. But we are awaiting a young lady, and it wouldn't do if two men were to receive her in dressing gowns."

"One is the room's limit," Clemens said grinning. "Or so I've read, John."

I took the hint, and rushed upstairs and changed. I returned to find my chair occupied by what I mistook for a girl in women's clothing. She barely occupied the seat, her feet barely touching the floor. She bore herself like a doll, but the tightness around her mouth and the twisting of her kerchief in her hands betrayed the state of her nerves.

Holmes said, "Dr. Watson, this is Lady Maud Tapp. Lady Maud, this is Dr. Watson, my companion on my cases. You may treat him as you would me. His discretion is on a par with my own."

She turned her attention to me, her gaze challenging. "And yet, you disclose your confidences to *The Strand*, do you not? And for money?"

"Only with the permission of the client," I said in my best bedside manner, as if I was talking to a fractious patient. I heard Clemens chuckling and felt my ears grow warm.

"She got you there, Johnny. Or do you go by Jack now?"

"Even so," Lady Maud said, "it would pain my father extremely if he knew that I told anyone about this. It would be terrible enough for him that I engaged your services, but if this appeared in The Strand, that would be—" she turned to Holmes as if he could divine her concerns.

Holmes's sympathy for her distress was palpable. "You need not fear. For every 'Speckled Band' or 'Hound' there are dozens that will never appear in the press."

"Simply to mention their existence would be indiscreet," I said.

She turned to me. "And yet, aren't your stories filled with mentions of other cases? We hear of the trained marmoset, the aluminum crutch, and Huret, the Boulevard assassin, do we not?"

"You're assuming, my dear, that those cases really exist," I said. "I mean, only a fool would believe in the existence of a giant rat in Sumatra, am I right, Holmes?"

Clemens choked on his cigar smoke. The mood was broken as he pounded his chest, and I leapt to his aid with a glass of water. Clearly, he had seen the look that had passed between Holmes and myself and found great merriment in it. Damn him!

When Clemens was settled, I moved to the breakfast table, pushed aside the remains of Mrs. Hudson's kippered herrings, unfolded my notebook, and with a warning glance at Clemens, set to work.

Maud Tapp was from the Tapp branch of the family that had resided in Liverpool since King James' reign. On the table next to me was one of Holmes' encyclopedic volumes, open to the T's, enabling me to learn that her father was Sir Henry Fawcett Tapp. It was a brief entry that made clear that this cadet branch played an insignificant role in the nation's affairs. I sighed and considered that it's the presence of these aristocratic families that make the achievements of our betters shine all the brighter.

"All his life," Lady Maud said, "Sir Henry preferred to spend his time tinkering in the basement of his castle near Rising Mildeau. We were a poor family for many generations, thanks to a duke with a taste for flashy women and paying blackmail, but we came into money recently."

"Married well?" Clemens said.

"Hardly," the lady spoke with a rasp. "My father had invented a new type of handle for the -- well, I can hardly say it out loud, it would not be proper -- but the porcelain throne that has lately come into fashion."

"The necessary box," Clemens said, the smoke from his stogie wreathing his head like a Satanic undertaker.

Lady Maud nodded. "It was a small fortune, but most welcome. News of his success brought inquiries for my hand in marriage, to invest in company bonds, to finance inventions that only a simpleton would fall for: difference engines, perpetual-motion devices, typesetting machines."

Clemens' face grew as red as his hair. He had been a long-time investor in the Paige machine and no doubt had been filling Holmes' ear with his calculations for the fortune he would make. He considered raising an objection, but chose to clench his cheroot in his teeth and puff furiously.

"My father was subjected to all of these traps. I had been mostly successful in keeping him away from them."

"Until the moment when you weren't," Holmes said, catching the qualifying adjective.

"He invested thousands of pounds into a scheme to extract silver from the tailings of a Roman-era mine on the estate. He had been told that the process was nearly finished and needed only a few thousand pounds to finish it."

"How did they get to your father?" Holmes asked.

"They were very clever," she said, a faint blush mantling her cheeks. "I was being courted by Lord St. Simon."

Holmes and I shared a look. We had encountered his lordship in a previous case.

"He won an audience with my father under the pretense of discussing a settlement should we be married. Instead, he introduced to him the man behind the scheme, an odious man named Charles Stuart Everhardt."

Holmes was reaching for the "E" volume when an explosion of horrid language erupted from Clemens. He thrust himself from his chair and paced the sitting room, waving his arms in rage and scattering ashes on the furniture.

"Clemens, behave!" Holmes said.

"Fetch me a rope and I'll show you manners! Could it be the same jackass who infested the territories back in the 1870s?" He pointed his cigar at Lady Maud. "This man, you eyeballed him?" She nodded. "Was he a balding gent with scrub pads over his ears, a belly like jelly, who affected to talk like a pouncey Englishman?"

"I'm unfamiliar with 'pouncey,' but he matched your description, yes," she said.

"And he favors snuff over honest tobacco?"

"But not the proper use of the kerchief in containing it."

"And did he call this process of his 'The Secret of Erasmus'?"

This sent her rocketing from her chair. She gripped his arms and would have shaken him like a terrier with a rabbit in its teeth. "Yes! Yes! That's the man."

Clemens held her hands. "Then you have been fleeced by one of the greatest swindlers to hail from the Pacific Slope. By God, tell he where he is, and I'll horsewhip him, gratis!"

"He's staying at the Alexander."

"Then I'll corner him there. Why that —"

Propriety forbids me from transcribing any more of his monologue, which he conducted on his feet and between cigar puffs. It was plain that he knew Everhardt and did not approve of his company. Clemens in the grip of an emotion was unstoppable. I shot a look at Lady Maud when some of his more fruiter phrases hit the air, but she showed no signs of distress. In fact, it appeared from the glow of her cheeks and heightened breathing that she enjoyed it.

At the first sign of a pause, while Clemens was searching for an appropriate word to describe Everhardt's ancestors, Holmes interjected, "Clemens, are you willing to work with us on a plan to recover Lady Maud's fortune?"

"If it means seeing Everhardt dangle from the end of the rope, then I'm your man!"

"Lady Maud, is that your desire as well?"

She looked apologetically at Clemens. "I understand Mr. Clemens' feelings. I really do. But it is more important to me that it not be known that my father led himself to be embarrassed in this fashion. I prefer to recover the money Everhardt stole. So long as my heart's desire is fulfilled, I have no objection to a hanging."

Holmes clapped his hands in appreciation. "We'll need to

discuss this matter in detail. First, I must reconnoiter." He got up and left the room. He returned wearing a rough coat, dusty pants, and a cloth cap. "I should return later tonight, but don't wait up, Watson. Clemens, let us meet here tomorrow and discuss the matter. Lady Maud, if you excuse me, I wish to begin work immediately."

2. The Plan

Holmes was as true as his word. He did not return that night. When I came down the next morning, he was taking his breakfast, looking trim and fresh as usual.

"I spent a most productive day yesterday with Mr. Everhardt, although he did not realize it," was all he said of the matter. He evaded my questions and said he preferred to wait until Clemens arrived. He spent the morning at the table digesting the pile of newspapers and clipping relevant stories for his scrapbooks. Sometimes, a piece of news would inspire commentary from him, and it was a delight to hear him outline how a scientific discovery in Germany could affect the future price of Newfoundland cod. Afterward, we went for a long walk, which allowed Holmes to gather fresh intelligence about the city, and we returned home well exercised.

When Clemens arrived that evening, Holmes suggested we dine out. "Simpson's serves an excellent roast, and with the help of a private table, we'll feed mind and body at the same time."

We engaged an upstairs room with a fireplace where we could talk in private. We laid our plans over platters of rare roast beef and Yorkshire pudding, that hearty English cooking that built and sustain our worldwide empire from John O'Groat, South Africa, India, Hong Kong, Vancouver, and Halifax. As the coal fire warmed us, Clemens described several schemes that he had encountered during his mining days out west.

"There were the stock schemes, where you form a company around a juicy land claim and sell shares in it. Reporters would be given shares in the mine, and in return pump up the noise about how much silver could be mined per foot. If need be, a visit to the test dig was arranged, and the mine 'salted' with silver so's the mark could discover the silver for himself. The stock would be bought and sold for ever-higher prices until the original investors had pulled out. Then it's revealed the claim contained dross and the company collapses."

"Would Everhardt know about that?" I asked.

"What he didn't know by experience he concocted himself. He's an old hand in that game. He took me for several hundred dollars, at a time when I didn't have them to spare."

"Does he know that?"

"Not as such. Shares get sold and resold. I was the one left holding the bag when the Conquistador mine folded. I've been itching for revenge ever since."

Holmes shook his head. "A stock scheme will take too long to get going."

Clemens suggested, "There's crooked games and bent sports like horse racing."

Holmes smiled, "England has a rich tradition of those kinds of fixes." He put his fingertips together and stared into the fire. "We need something big. There's the matter of several thousand pounds Lady Maud's father invested that needs to be recovered."

"A few fixed races won't cover that amount," Clemens agreed.

"Then you need a bigger scheme," I said.

"There is a possibility worth exploring. Last night, I shadowed Everhardt. In my guise as a common laborer, I waited outside the Alexander until he came out. He stopped at the Alhambra where Dan Leno has been such a success. He moved on to the Savage Club where he is a member. I was able to observe him from the window at the card table for awhile until the patrolman on his beat chased me off."

Clemens grumbled, "That's my club. Bad enough for their reputation that they let me in. Did you know he also loves boxing? He was a big one for staging bouts in the camps, just so's he could bet on them."

"Does he?" It appeared as if a light switched on inside Holmes. He gently tapped the arms of his chair. An idea was clearly forming. "There is a club in London called the Hellfire. Some of its members stage boxing matches with high-stakes wagers."

Clemens frowned, "Isn't that illegal here?"

"Yes. They organize their matches outside of the club, usually in isolated buildings south of the Thames. My observations revealed that Everhardt was a gambler who pushed a bet as far as it would go. We can take advantage of that." He outlined his plan, and the more Clemens heard, the more he was excited, to the point where he took to his feet and paced before the fire.

"That's a capital plan!" he said. "We'll need help to carry it off."

"I've already thought of someone who could help." Holmes suggested allies we could recruit from among the criminal class. Although we had roomed together for only a few years, we had experienced the events outlined in *A Study in Scarlet*, "The Speckled Band," and a few other stories. At that time, Holmes was a nonentity, known only by reputation to the Metropolitan Police and by word of mouth from grateful clients. It was at that moment that I understood how deep his knowledge of the criminal class ran. Had he chose to run an empire along the lines of Professor Moriarty, he would have at his fingertips a gang to run it.

Sated and feted, we were inclined to resume our labours to-morrow, but Holmes vetoed the motion. "You need to beard the lion in his den, or in this case, the Savage Club. Meet up with him, mention the fight club and the next match two days from now." He described further what he wanted Clemens to do, and suggested I go along with him.

"You'll play a member of the Hellfire Club, Watson, so you'll need a new name. Someone from the nobility. Americans do love a lordship. A minor noble, too obscure to be noticed by anyone and not easy to contradict." He searched his capacious memory. "I have it! You shall be Lord Dingwell. The title was recently revived in the Scottish highlands, so no one in London knows what he looks like."

Clemens objected. "If I'm to introduce him to that rapscallion as a friend, I won't be calling him Lord Dingwell. He'll need a plain name as well. Something easy to answer to. What's your middle name?"

"Hamish. After my grandfather."

"We'll call you Ham, how about that?"

I shuddered at the memory of the nicknames I was inflicted with at school. "How about Winston? It sounds similar to Watson. John Winston."

"Winston? For a last name?"

He was right. It is not a common name in Scotland. "How about Winston Moore?"

He puffed out the remains of his cheroot and tossed the stub into the fireplace. "It's your funeral. Anyway, once we're introduced, let me do the talking. Hang around if you must, but not with your ears flapping or your notebook open like you're a penny-a-word reporter." He pulled out another cheroot and sparked a wooden match alight with his thumbnail in the Western manner.

I should have taken umbrage at his insult, but I had grown accustomed to being treated this way by Holmes. "Tell me about it afterward," I said.

So instead of taking a hansom home, Clemens and I walked down The Strand and turned right on Savoy Street. The Savage Club was midway down the block, and beyond it the silent waters of the Thames shimmered in the moonlight. It was a cool night but our furious pace quickly warmed us. We rehearsed our scheme as Clemens' foul cigar scented the air.

The club's gaming room was jammed with bodies and the air damp with humidity. The uproar of shouted bets, cursing, and commentary on the table action was doubled and redoubled in the closed room. Coming in from the street, we welcomed the warmth at first, until we, too, were sweating and gasping for air like stranded trout like the rest of the members.

From underneath the thatch of his eyebrows, Clemens scanned the field like a native inhabitant of his country. Then he nudged me hard in the ribs and pointed.

"He's banking at the faro table with his back to the fireplace. Look for that ghastly olive-green checked coat."

Sitting stiffly in his chair, his arms spread and his palms caressing the green baize table, Charles Stuart Everhardt beamed at his fellow gamblers like a benevolent demon. His wool-pad sideburns were especially puffed, and most of his hair had fled to the nether regions of his scalp. He sat at the notch cut into the table, where the banker dealt the cards from a wooden box called the "shoe." The tabletop was marked with outlines of the 13 card suits where the bets were placed. Everhardt dealt the cards with one hand, while he rolled a thin flexible stick over the cloth with the other.

There was an outburst from the table. An elderly gentleman with a red beezer tossed his cards with a curse. He had been broken by Everhardt and was quitting the field. Clemens raced to snare the empty seat. He opened his folding leather case from his breast pocket and casually tossed a handful of bank notes on the table. He shouted:

"Pop in a fresh prayer book, banker, and prepare to be catawamptiously chawed up! Clemens is here from the Pacific rim, and I'm here to cavort until the cat wagon pulls up!"

Everhardt jerked like he had been electrified. His piggy eyes glittered in the candlelight, then he shouted, "Clemens! Cap the climax! I thought I recognized your clap-trap. When did you blow into England?"

"Long enough to hear you been raising hell like there's no heaven." Clemens tapped the pile of bank notes and said, "Are you gonna fish or cut bait?"

"Fish!" Everhardt shouted. "We'll blather later."

Play resumed, and it wasn't long before Everhardt found an opportunity to employ his stick. While the bets were being settled and many hands were placing and removing their chips, one of the players risked sliding his marker from a losing suit to a nearby winner. Quick as a rattler, Everhardt slapped the young man's wrist with his stick. The youth yelped and gripped his injured wrist.

The sudden violence silenced the table. Everhardt smiled like a serpent: "Now, I know you weren't planning to honey-fuggle the house, but I wasn't sure if your hand knew it. We do it according to Hoyle, here, or we'll be on the proddy." He shook his stick at him for emphasis. "You twig?"

It was an incident that could have led to a tragic outcome. The young man was a member of an old, noble house, and while he commanded no authority, he was backed by powerful family members who could cause trouble on his behalf. Some of them were even in the room.

Clemens barked a laugh "We're burning daylight here. Let's play!" The young man was either intimidated or he couldn't understand a word he said. Either way, he nodded, still clutching his injured wrist.

The gentlemen resumed play, if only to catch up with Clemens' play. He had placed several bets and was calling for cards. I breathed a sigh of relief, grateful that I wouldn't have to explain to Holmes how we started a riot at the Savage Club.

The hours passed. I grew bored watching the play. I found an empty chair and kept an eye on the men and made use of the opportunity to discreetly scribble a few notes. I heard a name similar to mine being called. Then twice more and louder. Then I was grabbed by the arm and hauled to my feet.

"Winston, you blatherskite," Clemens pressed his face close to mine. I weathered a blast of stale tobacco and fresh whiskey. "Didn't you hear me yelling for you? Are you drunk already? Come on, we're going to eat!"

There was a cackle of laugher from the members at my discomfort. I glared at him resentfully, but mindful of

Everhardt's presence, I stood on my dignity, removed his hand from my shirt and pulled it down. He turned on his heel, and walked away without a word, and we followed him.

We found ourselves at a table in the club's restaurant, and over toasted cheese on bread and more whiskey, Clemens and Everhardt reminisced about San Francisco and their days in the mining fields. If Everhardt knew of Clemens' stock misfortune, he didn't show it, and Clemens was good fellowship personified.

"One of my favorite games is Baccarat," Clemens said. "Have you seen it? The croupier uses this curved oar to gather in the money and chips."

"Are you good at it?" Everhardt said.

"Oh, I'd never play it," Clemens replied. "If I could have borrowed his oar I would have stayed. Otherwise, I didn't see the point."

As he told his stories, I watched the clock closely, and at the time we agreed, pulled my watch from my vest and opened it.

"It's getting on, Clemens," I said. I adopted a Scottish burr that I recalled a sergeant-major using from my soldiering days. "We need to get moving if want to get in a flutter before the first round."

"Is it? Ah, you are correct, Lord Dingwell."

"Round?" Everhardt said. "Where are you going?"

Clemens traced his lips with a finger. "I'm sorry, Everhardt. I can't let the cat out of the bag. His lordship invited me to a special event, but on the promise that I don't say a word about it."

"And yet you did, Clemens," Everhardt said maliciously. "You never could keep your yap shut. So you might as well spill to an old chum. Is it a sport? Ah ha! I see by your map that I twigged it. It's a boxing match, right? Why, I haven't seen a good mill since I left America. Where is it?"

Clemens shook his head, and I broke in to say, " 'Fraid we can't say. Strictly club business, you know. Enjoy your stay in London, Everhardt." I got up, and Clemens followed.

I walked out of the room without looking back, assuming the uncomfortable persona of a lordship. It was only when I reached the lobby that I realized Clemens had not followed me. I considered going back, then I remembered who I was, straightened my back, and stalked out.

I summoned a hansom and ordered the driver to wait. When Clemens appeared at the door, I waved to him, and he stepped up looking as pleased as the cat who lapped up the spilled cream.

"We hooked him, Johnny," he said as the carriage pulled away. "He stalled me to pinch out the location of the mill."

"What did you say?"

"Only that you knew and I didn't. But he's hungry for more. He wants to lunch with me tomorrow."

"Then we'll have to move quickly."

3. The Bait

The next day, while Clemens met Everhardt as arranged, Holmes and I traveled to St. Giles. The hansom slowly worked its way through the crowded streets until Holmes ordered the driver to pull up outside a large brick building. The building was shabby, but not quite as bad as those found several streets over. Several shops occupied the street level, while stairs led to the three floors of apartments above it.

Holmes opened the street door and led us upstairs to a landing with several doors. A knock on one was answered by a short man whose most prominent features were his jug ears and drooping moustache. Looking around his legs were two little girls. He caught sight of Holmes, paled, and attempted to close the door, but Holmes had already pushed his way in and grabbed his arm, the girls scattering in alarm. "Padraig Collins!" he said with good humor. "We come in peace this time."

Padraig eyed the taller man with suspicion. "So you say, Mr. Holmes? Then peace it shall be. Clara, Louisa, quit your grizzling! Mr. Holmes is a guest. But what would you be wanting with me otherwise?"

"We have need of your unique abilities. But, come, let's have a drink first, and then we'll talk."

Padraig brightened at the suggestion, but said there was none in the house. Holmes' offer to pay was accepted, and the girls were sent down to the pub for a bottle of gin.

At the table, his undrunk glass of gin in front of him, Holmes laid out the plan. Padraig drank his portion and set the glass carefully on the table, smacking his lips.

"This is a story for the ages, Mr. Holmes, I must say."

"Can you do it, Padraig? Can you help?"

"If I can't set this up then no one in the three kingdoms can. Let me see, you want to stage a fight, but in a place that'll attract the gents as well as people like us. I know of an abandoned warehouse across the river, Vauxhall way. We can do it up a treat, but cleaned up, like for the gentry on the slumnibuses. But you don't want the real moneyed gentlemen to be walking in, do you?"

"Correct. Only the men we hire will be in the room."

"So you'll need at least a hundred of them, some togged out as gentlemen and given roles to play. The rest will look like locals. They can outfit themselves. Then another dozen to run the fights, provide security. Some of them should be bruisers with fighting experience in case we need muscle." Padraig chuckled as he refilled his glass. "I've heard about plenty of cons, but don't this beat all! Setting up a scene to take in one gentleman. Will the payoff be worth it, you think?"

"If I know my man and his resources, enough to pay you all off and pay back the people he conned."

"You know," Padraig said thoughtfully. "If it works for one, it'll work for more. You could run several marks through the scene in a day. Spread the cost out with a chance for a greater return. Sure you won't consider—? Ah, it's something to tuck in the back pocket for a rainy day. How soon do you need them?"

"To-morrow night."

"Ohhhh," Padraig frowned and rubbed his chin in contemplation. "That'll take some doing."

Holmes pulled from his pocket a heavy bag and dropped it on the table. "Will this provide enough incentive?"

Padraig's eyes widened as he lifted the bag of coins and weighed it in his palm. "This'll do nicely. In fact, I'm thinking of some shortcuts that will help."

"Send a message when you're ready."

On the way back to Baker Street in the hansom, Holmes was uncharacteristically jubilant. "Padraig was one of the best stage managers in the business. He was a field marshal when it came to organizing a cadre of actors and actresses, stagehands, and directors, and leading them into mounting the production. It was only his intense fondness for drink that rendered him unfit, even for the theater. Perhaps this exercise in stage managing will help him return to his true calling." Holmes stared at the passing scene, lost in thought. "I hope you are taking notes, Watson. There are elements to this case that have the potential to make it truly unique. I've never experienced planning a criminal act from the criminal's point of view. This will bring a unique perspective to bear on my future work. There may even be a monograph in it."

4. The Hook

Across the city of London, wheels were set in motion. Everhardt lobbied Clemens to intervene with Lord Dingwell on his behalf to admit him to the next round of fights. Padraig organized his work crews and seamstresses into setting the stage at the warehouse. Holmes sat and played his violin in a thoughtful manner, reviewing the details of his plan, while I organized my notes and set this account down to paper. That afternoon, Padraig sent one of his daughters with a message to Holmes stating that the warehouse was ready. Clemens and myself met Everhardt at the Savage Club that evening, and we took a hansom down the Embankment to Vauxhall Bridge.

We turned south of the notorious pleasure gardens and into the side streets where residences ran cheek by jowl with manufacturers. I filled Everhardt's ears with stories of our activities in the Hellfire Club, and how some of the members, bored with the round of sinister rituals and drunken revelries, had banded together to create what we called the Fight Club.

"We go about this business with the utmost discretion," I said. "Prize fighting is deeply frowned upon, and has been for many a year. So we formed this club and recruit bonny-looking pugilists to battle for prize money. We even have a club champion, 'Mad Mike' O'Connor from County Cork, fourteen stone of hard muscle with a right hand that strikes like lightning."

"Is this bare-knuckle or Queensbury rules?" Everhardt said, the gleam in his eye betraying his eagerness.

"Queensbury," I shook my head as if regretting the decline in standards since the days of bare-knuckle boxing. "Although the gloves they wear don't merit the name. And if during a match they fly off, well, the referee knows not to object."

"And betting. Is that allowed as well?"

"Of course! It wouldn't be sporting if we didn't."

At my order, we were dropped off on the South Lambeth Road. I led Clemens and Everhardt down several streets and into a darkened alley. A gas lamp at the street cast a reddish light that lightened the gloom and reflected off the damp cobblestones. At the far end, we stopped at a wooden door wide enough to admit a wagon. Behind it could be heard the muffled shouts and cheers of many men. I knocked up the door in a particular pattern. The sound of a bolt being drawn back could be heard, and a man's face glared at us from under his cloth cap. The effect was so startling that I stammered out the password.

His eyes shifted to my companions. "Who're they, then?"

"Friends of mine," I said in my most fruity and noble voice. "Stand aside and admit us."

He sneered and pulled back the door, and we walked into a cacophony of cheers, hoots, and shouts. The room had once been a staging area where wagons were loaded and unloaded. It was wide and high and lit by gas jets. The floor above was open in the center, offering a balcony-like view of the action below. The remains of ropes dangled from above like the remains of giant spiders.

At the center, a makeshift ring had been set up, and a crowd of gentlemen and locals were gathered about a fight already in progress. The boxers were shielded by the press of men, but we could see their heads bobbing above the spectators, and the sound of their punches punctuated the noise. The air was hot and fetid, dust motes drifted in the lamplight, and the violence stimulated the senses. My breathing grew heavy and deep, as it did in Afghanistan when battle was imminent.

Mindful of my role, I led us over to the far side of the room. On a platform of crates, Padraig had set up a table. A timekeeper was studying a watch. He rang a bell with a hammer and to the general cheering the fighters parted and returned to their seconds. As they swigged water and their friends staunched their wounds, men crowded around the table demanding to place bets. We could see more bookies walking through the crowd, calling the new odds and arranging bets.

The timekeeper rang the bell and the men returned to battle. One of them, a pale ginger-haired fellow, was clearly getting the worst of the fight. His swings were wild and unfocused, desperate measures to avoid the inevitable. Everhardt' face was flushed with excitement, and he took in the battle with evident pleasure. Clemens grabbed Everhardt' shoulder and leaned over to shout something in his ear.

I glanced over at Padraig and caught his eye. He nodded at my unspoken signal and waved his arms like a semaphore. The ginger fighter seemed to take the message. He stepped in, swung and missed, took two punches to the head, and he collapsed to the floor. The fight was over. The referee raised the arm of the winner to a chorus of cheers, groans, and catcalls from the crowd. A few fistfights broke out, presumably by those who had bet on the loser. A couple of bruisers waded in with truncheons and quickly suppressed them.

Everhardt turned to us and said, "That was top-notch, Lord Dingwell."

"Wait for the next fight," I said. "He's a lad from Norfolk. Shows great promise. We've hopes of backing him against Mad Mike if he wins tonight."

"Are you?" he said. There was a thoughtful gleam in his eye. He pulled out a roll of bank notes and riffled through them. "Do you enjoy the sport, Clemens?"

"Oh, I enjoy making money off it more," he drawled. "Beats scribbling for thieving publishers for a living."

Two new men entered the ring. One was a fleshy older man, bull-faced, with a flattened Michelangelo nose. The other was younger, lighter, and considerably more energetic. He strutted around the ring, his arms up, as if he had already won, while his opponent contented himself with flexing and warming up.

"I recognize Warren the prizefighter," Everhardt said. "Who's the new buck?"

"Name's Ford. Sherrin Ford. The Norfolk man I was telling you about. He's the one I'm betting on."

"You're loony! Warren has got two stone on him. He nearly took down Nonpareil Dempsey in his prime."

"Stone and a half. If you're so sure, place a bet."

"That I will. Hi! You there!" Everhardt waved his bank notes at a nearby bookie. "What're the odds? All right. I'll lay ten pounds on Warren! No, twenty!"

"A hundred on the lad," Clemens said. Everhardt looked startled.

"You are flying high, Clemens." He shrugged at Everhardt's comment as if risking a hundred pounds were nothing.

Nearly an hour later, the fight was over. Warren still had a powerful right, but Ford was quicker and evaded most of the blows. He wore down the boxer until two sharp rights and a powerful left laid the bigger man down.

The audience was thrilled, even the losers, by the display of fighting prowess. From behind the table, Padraig stood up and waved his arms to get the crowd's attention.

"Thank you all for coming to see our exhibition of pugilistic skill and tenacity." Cheers and laughter greeted him. "Come back again three nights from now, when we'll see Ford take on Mad Mike!" The audience dispersed, the winners to buy the drinks and the rest to hope to be the recipients of their largess.

"That's it?" Everhardt said.

"We have to be wary of the peelers," I said. "So we only run two fights, maybe three at a time. Wouldn't do to get run in, you know."

Clemens collected a wad of bills from the bookie. He commiserated with him and promised that he'd be back later and give him his chance at revenge.

We stepped out into the street. Clemens flagged a hansom and directed him to head back to the Ritz.

"I still can't suss it," Everhardt said. "Warren should have pounded him into the ground."

"Told you that you should have bet on him."

"That you did, that you did," he said slowly. He looked out the window at the people walking along the streets. "Is all this on the up and up?"

"To the ones in charge of the carnival, yes," Clemens said. "They set the odds so that the house don't lose at all. But there's a gang, see, who know how to get to the fighters. They sniff the wind, find a long shot, and figure out a way to make it pay off."

"And you know these people."

"We've done business," Clemens said simply. "They do me a favor here, I do them a favor back home. Introduce them to people. Open doors."

"Yeah, I can see that," Everhardt said. "You're pretty tight with those Wall Street boys. Morgan. Diamond Jim. General Grant. Use your influence with 'em, eh?" He laughed with the knowledge he knew something dirty about his friend and pounded him on the back.

5. The Threat

"So, Holmes, what is next?" It was the next morning. A cheerful sun was shining through the bay windows, warming the brick fronts of Baker Street and polishing the streets of

London to a golden glow. Holmes had taken a few bites of breakfast, pushed aside his plate, and lit a cigarette, watching the curlicues of smoke rise to the ceiling. He looked like he was calculating the atmospheric effects on smoke and its use in detection, possibly for another in his interminable series of monographs that he insist I read as if part of my obligation lodging with him was to act as his unpaid editor.

"Humph?" he blinked and focused his attention on me. "Pardon me, Watson, I was wool-gathering."

I swallowed my blood pudding and spoke. "We were successful last night in hooking Everhardt. He's looking forward to the match with Mad Mike. I assume that's when we'll fleece him, right?"

"Yes, yes, you're correct," he said. "However, not entirely. I have another wheel that I need to set in motion."

"Have you?" I resolved to update my notebook at the first opportunity.

"Yes, in fact —" There was a knock on the door. The voice of Mrs. Hudson could be heard asking the visitor his business. In his loud American voice, Everhardt asked if he could see Sherlock Holmes.

"Watson, into the alcove! Stand behind the curtain."

I fled to the bay window where a curtain had been installed to create a private reading nook. I pulled out my notebook and hurriedly scratched a few sentences until I froze, my breath caught in my throat, at the sound of the door opening.

"I got your note this morning demanding an interview," Everhardt gave the impression that he was in a terrible mood. Given the amount of brandy and whiskey we consumed last night after the fight, his head must have felt like he'd gone several rounds with Mad Mike. "What do you want?"

"Sit down, Mr. Everhardt, I prefer my conversations at eye level. Thank you. I asked you here for a favor."

"Oh? And who are you to ask a favor of me?"

"I am a consulting detective. No, sit down! We can have this conversation either here or at Scotland Yard. It is your choice. Good. Know this: I am not an official representative of the police. Sometimes, our goals and desires coincide, but sometimes not. This is not one of those times unless you insist. I asked you here to talk about Samuel Clemens."

"What do you want to know about him?"

"What he is doing in England."

"I assume doing whatever authors do in England. Beg publishers to accept their works. Pawn their watch to buy food for their families. Gossip about writers they hate and critics they despise."

"Your humor is typically American, but I am deadly serious. Clemens displays the appearance of a genial writer of humor, but behind the mask is a criminal mastermind of the first water."

The silence that followed was so long I thought Everhardt had left. Then he burst out laughing. He carried on for several minutes, and when it bubbled down, he caught another aspect of that remarkable statement and launched into another round of wheezes.

"Criminal ... mastermind. That is good turn of phrase. You should go on the stage. In moustache, tall hat, and cape. That is very good! Oh, let me wipe my eyes a moment. There. Sam and I have known of each other for too many years for that to pass muster. Why, I'd make a better criminal than he!"

"That, my dear Everhardt, is what makes him so effective. Have you seen his house in Connecticut? I have. It is a palace. He entertains on a lavish scale. He invests in numerous business enterprises. He counts President Grant and the wealthiest members of Wall Street his friends. When he published Grant's memoirs, he turned over the majority of the profits to the president's widow. Is that the action of a rational publisher? Of course not! He lives on a scale far beyond that of other best-selling writers. The inference is obvious: Clemens heads a criminal enterprise far beyond anything in history. He is here in England for a reason, and you're going to help me."

"You threaten me?"

"I make a promise, Everhardt." Even from behind the curtain, I could sense Holmes' power. When angry, he can present himself as a terrible, even avenging figure.

"You have nothing on me."

"Do I? See that scrapbook on the table? That is one of many I keep." There was a pause as Holmes walked to it and the sound of the cover opening could be heard. "Let us see, there's Eadweard, the nefarious terror of Eton. Dr. Evans, the notorious clairvoyant physician from Liverpool, who I helped hang. Here you are. Charles Stuart Everhardt, born Ryszard Scymanski in Piotrków. Why, here's an article in which one Harrison accuses the owners of the Stafford and Lone Star Silver Mines of swindling investors! I quote from the Marysville Daily Appeal: 'Harrison denounces by name Major J.D. Wooley, Cheyenne; Colonel W. J. Jones, of San Francisco; and Colonel C.S. Everhardt, of Salt Lake, as projectors of the swindle.'" Holmes punctuated his revelation by slamming the scrapbook shut. "Shall I go on?"

"All right, you got me," Everhardt lost much of his steam under the force of Holmes' personality. "What do you want?"

"What Clemens is planning."

"Then you'll have to wait. We went to a boxing match last night. Some setup involving the Hellfire Club. There's going to be another bout a few nights from now."

"Then I need for you to keep your eye on him. Accompany him everywhere. Tell me who he meets and what he says."

There was another pause, then Everhardt said, "I'll need money. He flies pretty high for a criminal mastermind."

"Here's twenty pounds. You shouldn't need more."

"Thankee."

"I expect daily reports. Telegram or messenger will do."

When I heard the door closing, I peeped through the curtains to see Holmes shaking in quiet laughter.

"There you are, Watson. Did you hear everything? Everhardt must think me a dangerous fool, conning me out of twenty of the best and lying about the fight as well."

"But why should he shadow Clemens? You don't really suspect him of criminal acts?"

"Only of letting improper manuscripts fall into the hands of unscrupulous publishers. No, my intentions are the opposite of my orders. I don't want Everhardt to watch Clemens, I want Clemens to watch Everhardt. Left to himself, he might see the flaws in our plan, or ask uncomfortable questions. He needs to be kept busy until we're ready to fleece him. In fact, that's where you come in. Clemens insists on spending his mornings and afternoons at his writing. That means you'll have to befriend Everhardt during those times."

"What will I do?"

"Play Lord Dingwell. Show him London. Lunch with him. Drink with him. Gamble with him. Whatever, but keep him occupied. You'll meet Clemens for dinner and pass him off then. Will you do that?"

"Of course. You can count on me. I confess I was also impressed by the quality of your intelligence. How did you get California newspapers here?"

"That was a mere subterfuge. I wired the San Francisco police after Lady Maud's visit and received the particulars. It looks more impressive if he thought I had my eye on him all along."

The next two days passed quickly in my memory, but from the increasingly desperate tone in my notes that didn't appear to be the case at the time. In my guise as Lord Dingwell, I showed Everhardt cricket at Lord's, which bored him. We visited a Rugby League match between the Civil Service and Guy's, which he found more to his taste. We also visited the Savage Club and White's, where he left me to the reading room while he indulged his taste for cards. Every evening, we met Clemens at dinner where he read his day's writing to us before heading out for the evening.

This part of the plan was the hardest for Clemens to fulfill. Whatever injury Everhardt had done to him out West still hurt him deeply, for on the first evening, as we walked out of the restaurant, he grabbed my sleeve, leaned in, and hissed, "Even a damned soul as myself should be admitted to heaven for not stoving in his skull at the first opportunity."

Meanwhile, the clock continued its infinite turn, and day passed into night and back again. I saw little of Holmes, and when I did he refused to speak about the case, beyond rehearsing my part in what follows.

6. *The Visitors*

The day of the fight was more eventful than anyone expected. First, we received a visit from Padraig.

"I never expected to come here unless I was under arrest," he said. He settled into the basket chair by the fireplace and accepted a small glass of brandy. He downed the drink with evident enjoyment and set the empty glass on the small tray table.

"How go the preparations?"

"As you planned, Mr. Holmes. We installed a ring to give the proceedings some tone, and I've been recruiting a few more lads to fill the house. The seamstresses have been working late to finish dressing the toffs."

"And they understand the new script?"

"We rehearsed it until they could do it in their sleep. There is one question that I needed your advice on. I was approached by Lady Maud, see. She wanted to attend tonight's fight. In disguise, of course. But she wanted to see justice done, as she put it."

"Interesting. So long as she's well-costumed and unrecognizable."

Padraig nodded, "We'll have women in attendance, most of 'em serving drinks to the lads, like you'd see at any mill."

"We'll detail Watson to keep an eye on her. Anything else?" There wasn't, and he left to return to Vauxhall.

The next visitor was much more surprising.

Sherrin Ford was a tall, strapping lad whose wheat-colored hair poked from his bowler in unexpected places. For someone who faced violent men who outweighed him in the ring, his nervousness was unexpected and concerning.

"I appreciate this opportunity, Mr. Holmes, but something has come up that I think you should know about. Early this morning, I received a visitor at my home. I live with me mum in Spitalfields, you see, and this bald cove came with his bruiser to knock me up. He says he knew about the play and wanted in on it. I asked him what he was talking about, and he says, 'I know you're planning on throwing the fight. Don't worry, I want you to. I just want you to throw it when I say so.'"

Holmes said, "Everhardt."

"He didn't give me a name, sir. He says he'll make it worth my while, right now, and later. He wants me to come to America. Prizefighting's legal there, see, and he says he can manage me. If I do well enough, I could get a shot at a real championship." He looked down in shame.

"What did you say to that?"

"I didn't really know what to say. I know what you want me to do and why, so I said I'd have to think about it. That's when he said ... he said if I didn't do what he wanted, that I ..."

"That's all right, Sherrin. I think I know what he said."

"Mr. Holmes, what should I do?"

"I think you should agree. Did he say how he would tell you?"

"He said he would signal my second during the fight. I'd have to stay up during the first dozen rounds, then he'd decide when I should take the fall. He'll tell the second, who will tell me. Are you sure you want me to do this?"

"Yes, I think you should. You didn't go into this to risk your life, or your mother's. I'm sorry it came to this, but we'll have to adjust the plan in light of this information."

"Will he come after me? If it don't go right for him?"

Holmes smiled and laid a reassuring hand on the lad's shoulder. "He'll be too busy trying to save his own skin to worry about you." Holmes continued to console the young man as he escorted him down the stairs to the street door.

"There's an example, should you need one, of the degradation to a society caused by gambling such as this," he said upon his return. He picked up his violin and began tuning the strings. "Take the clean competition and exercise that sport lets us indulge in, add a way to make money off it, and moral decay must follow sure as night follows day. Give me a moment, Watson. I must clear my head," and he launched into a long, plaintive movement that better expressed his feelings than mere words.

That afternoon saw our third visitor, this time from Everhardt himself. As before, I hastily retreated behind the curtain by the window, notebook in hand.

"Mr. Holmes, you asked me what I thought Clemens was doing," Everhardt said, "and at the time I would have called you insane at the suggestion of any criminal doings. But I admit you're right. Clemens has been fixing fights!"

"Indeed, tell me more," Holmes said, and together we heard about the fight he had witnessed a few nights ago, and Clemens' 'confession' to him.

"Thank you, Mr. Everhardt. That is most satisfactory."

"Now that you know this, Sherlock, what are you going to do about it?"

"Uphold the law. Apply to the police for a warrant for his arrest. If we can catch him in the act, all the better."

"Excellent. You'll be able to catch him tomorrow."

"That's the next fight?"

"Yes, at the same place and time. And if he resists," he reached into his pocket to pull out a derringer, "we'll let Mr. Remington make the arrest."

"Impressive," Holmes said. "You don't see many of those these days." The men could be heard standing, and I received the impression Holmes was shaking his hand. "We'll see you to-morrow then."

"Holmes, I congratulate you," I said after Everhardt closed the street door behind him.

Holmes accepted my hand but more out of friendship than pride.

"Belief is a powerful human trait," he sat back in his chair and reached for his pipe. "The essence of a successful con is to convince the 'mark' of the veracity of the reality you construct. We created a nonexistent gentleman's club, faked a boxing match, and recruited a fake audience to watch and lay fake bets, all to fool one man that it was all real. On top of that, we had to ensure that Everhardt fooled me by lying about the date of the next fight. Running a criminal organization is much more work than I had anticipated. This has been a most educational exercise. I look forward to writing the monograph. But first, let's have dinner. Tonight's fight will tax our energies."

7. The Play

The fight had been going on for over two hours. True to his name, Mad Mike O'Connor came charging out of the corner early, forcing Sherrin Ford to backpedal repeatedly to avoid the Irishman's broad swings. This gave him the opportunity to step in and hammer the champion's midsection, then retreat to await the next onslaught.

I was seated on the large crate where Padraig Collins had set up his table. I had to play the cool, unflappable Lord Dingwell, but my heart was hammering and restraining myself from showing anxiety was draining. Although I had been watching Everhardt palling about with Clemens, there was no sign that he had placed a bet. Clemens kept a rein on his true feelings as well, but several times during the match he looked my way and his bushy eyebrows signaled that he was just as perplexed.

Only Lady Maud felt free to express her concern. Dressed in filthy clothes common to the women of the neighborhood, a large hat shading her features, she looked nothing like the trim, self-possessed woman who had sat in our rooms a few days before.

"What's keeping him?" she hissed in my ear. "Why doesn't he bet?"

"I do not know," I answered, tilting my head in her direction so she could hear me better. Although Everhardt had not recognized her, it seemed prudent to not give him the idea we knew each other at all.

As for Holmes, I know he was around even though I could not see him.

The timekeeper next to Padraig ran the bell, and round 39 had finished.

The slam of a Gladstone bag on the table drew my attention. It was Everhardt. "Ten thousand pounds," he said in a clear, strong voice. "Ten thousand pounds that the champion puts away the lad in the next round. What odds?"

Padraig reached over and, his hands shaking, unclasped the lock and pulled the handles apart. The bag was crammed full of bank notes of various denominations. I know that I have never seen so much money in one place at one time.

Padraig gazed thoughtfully off in the distance and pursed his lips. "Three to one," he said. Everhardt nodded.

"Right," Padraig said and snapped the bag closed. "We'll mark this a provisional bet. We'll be wanting to count this first before we pay."

I looked over at Clemens, who was deep in conversation with a laborer. They looked over briefly in my direction, and I thought I discerned the sharp features of Holmes under the cap! It took every particle of control not to wave back.

Then I heard my name. That is, I heard "Lord Dingwell! Your lordship!"

Padraig handed the case to me. "Mr. Everhardt does not feel comfortable with meself holding the stakes. Would you be so kind as to perform that function?"

I hadn't expected this. I knew most of what was to come, but I couldn't refuse. I clasped the bag and held it tight in my lap. The bell rang, and the fight was on. Everhardt leaped down and pushed his way to the ropes that formed the ring.

As before, Mad Mike stalked to the center. Two hours of hard fighting had taken its toll on him. His charges seemed to have no effect on the younger man, and he had taken enough blows to the head to make him cautious. A cut over one eye had opened, and a sheet of pale red painted his face. He had slowed down, jabbing to keep his opponent off-balance, and waiting for the right moment to unleash a still-powerful roundhouse.

There was a flurry of rapid blows between the two men. They parted, circled around each other energetically, then closed again. Then Sherrin went down on one knee! His gloves were down and he appeared to be clutching at his chest. The referee leaped in to protect him from Mad Mike, who backed away, a puzzled look spreading over his face.

Ford was breathing heavily, his face a mask of pain, and it was apparent to all he was suffering from a heart seizure. I leaped down. Padraig shouted "the bag," and I realized I was still holding the stake.

I thrust the bag into Maud Tapp's hands. "Keep an eye on her," I shouted to Padraig, and I pushed my way to the ring, and through the ropes.

Ford had fallen face-forward and was lying still. I kneeled beside him and rolled him over. He wasn't breathing. More men had entered the ring, and they were moving his limbs. Someone shouted, "Pick him up." I looked up and saw Holmes, disguised as the laborer. Next to him was Everhardt. Together we lifted Ford's body.

His sudden collapse had thrown the crowd into a frenzy of cheers and boos. There were cries of "Murder!" and "Fake!" I heard the referee declare Mad Mike as the winner.

Then I heard screams and a chorus of police-whistles. Holmes looked over my shoulder. I turned my head, just enough to see Clemens. He looked furious, and he held a gun in his hand.

"Ford, you fraud!" he shouted over the noise. "I know you're shamming. Get up or I'll put you down for good!"

There were cries of "No!" and added to that were new cries of "Peelers!" "Crushers!" and "Coppers!" I could sense that men outside the ring trying to get out of the building at the same time more men were coming in, and Clemens continued to threaten to shoot Ford.

Then there was a shot. Everhardt looked stunned, his mouth falling open. Next to him, Holmes stood stock-still, frozen in amber, grimly aiming Everhardt's revolver at Clemens. Then he handed it back to Everhardt.

I looked around again, and Clemens was on the mat, blood trickling from his mouth. He still held the gun in his hand.

He was lost to sight as the policemen entered the ring, the ropes collapsing against their assault. They were led by Inspector Lestrade, who knelt briefly by Clemens, then stood and pointed out Everhardt and shouted "Arrest that man!" Some of them took Ford from us. I was pinioned in the arms of two policemen. The last I saw of Everhardt, he was being tugged away by Holmes, who was shouting something about not being caught up in a murder. Everhardt struggled and said something about his bag, but he realized the dangerous situation he was in and they fled toward the back of the building and out of sight.

The room slowly quieted down. I was still being held in place by the men, but they were no longer moving. They seemed frozen, looking around as if awaiting a signal.

Then we heard the cry, "They're gone!"

A general cheer went up. I was released. There were handshakes and jokes and even a few of the police officers clapping.

Clemens stood up and spat out the packet he had concealed in his mouth. "My that was filling," he pulled out a handkerchief, "but I wouldn't recommend it for the menu."

Padraig stood up from behind his table and said, "Thank you all. Police officers, please approach the table with your coats and helmets and give your name to the clerk. The gentlemen who are still around, please come to the address you were given tomorrow to return your clothes and pick up the rest of your pay. Teardown crew, please begin dismantling the ring. We want this place cleared in ten minutes!"

I was sore, sweat-drenched, and cheerful. It appears we had done it. We had cheated Everhardt of ten thousand pounds, and it looked like we got away with it.

Then I paused and looked around. Lady Maud was no longer in the room, and neither the money.

8. The Hangover

It was a glum gathering late that evening in Baker Street. I was laying on the couch, a damp rag cooling my forehead. Holmes was curled in his mouse-colored robe in his favorite chair. Clemens was furiously scowling and smoking by the fireplace. Only Padraig, seated at the table and dining on one of Mrs. Hudson's sandwiches, seemed unconcerned by the mood of the room.

Downstairs the door bell rang. I trudged downstairs and opened the door. Inspector Lestrade in his usual mode was sallow, sharp-featured and grumbling. He was in a much more cheerful mood tonight, going so far as to shake my hand and taking the steps two at a time. I caught up with him just as he was asking why it appeared like he was at a funeral rather than a celebration.

"It appears, Lestrade, that we were the biter bit," Holmes said. "But let's not cause our mood to ruin our hospitality. The gasogene, tantalus and cigars are open for business."

"I'm not sad about this business at all," Lestrade poured himself a generous helping of whiskey. "Although I'll deny everything if this gets out. Where did you find those police officers for me to lead anyway?"

"The theater. They're from the production of *Penzance*. The costumes, too."

"Ah, I remember. They have a chorus of policemen singing that cheerful song. So what happened?"

"It turns out that we were played, Lestrade. On the way to Victoria Station, to put him on the train to Liverpool, a carriage passed us. A woman inside shouted, "Yoo hoo!" and waved a Gladstone bag at him. Everhardt was furious. He broke off from me and ran down the street after her and was lost from sight. It turns out that Lady Maud Tapp was not the daughter of his lordship, but Tilly Busby, an American actress with a talent for mimicking English ladies—"

"And the former partner of Charles Stuart Everhardt," Clemens said. "She was in on the scheme from the get-go. She let herself be courted by his lordship and introduced Everhardt to him. With her help, his lordship forked over thousands of pounds for his silver scam, then when they were back in London with the cash, Everhardt refused to pay her share."

Holmes took up the story, "She had heard about how Everhardt defrauded Clemens all those years ago and sought him out. When she discovered his connection to me, she decided to run a con of her own. Yes, laugh all you want Lestrade. I'm not ashamed to say I earned it. I assumed her story was correct. Why would she lie?"

"So all this was for nothing," Clemens said. "I don't even get a good story to tell out of it. That seems to happen every time I encounter you, Holmes, or one of your minions. No offense meant, Watson. And Holmes, my thanks to you for getting to his derringer and switching the bullets. It is an noble feeling to be shot at and missed, but I wouldn't want to make a habit of it. The odds are not worth the game."

Holmes nodded, then he chuckled thoughtfully. "The education of a consulting detective never ends. Fortunately, my earnings from my other cases have been generous, so Padraig and his band of merry schemers won't lose out by it. I will consider it tuition paid on a lesson well-learned: Crime does not pay."

"Well enough," Clemens said.

"Hand me my violin, Watson. I'm in the mood for a merry tune tonight!"

Bibliography

----------------, *American Spiritualist Magazine*, vol. 3, https://books.google.com/books?id=Ix7L6GSci3sC&pg=RA1-PA287&lpg=RA1-PA287&dq=magog+spiritualist, accessed Nov. 11, 2018.

----------------. "City of Berkeley Police Department History The Earliest Years 1905-1925 'First In Policing'," https://www.cityofberkeley.info/Police/Home/History_The_Earliest_Years_1905-1925.aspx, accessed Nov. 11, 2018.

----------------. *The Illustrated Annual of Microscopy*. London: Percy Lund, Humphries & Co., 1900. https://books.google.com/books?id=Q3ZGAQAAMAAJ&pg=PA122&dq=microscope+diameters, accessed Nov. 11, 2018.

----------------, "Night Life in Havana Just a Cocktail Trail," *The New York Herald*, 19 Feb. 1922, https://chroniclingamerica.loc.gov/lccn/sn83045774/1922-02-19/ed-1/seq-75/, accessed Feb. 6, 2019.

------------. "The Original, World-Famous, and Patented Six-Shooter Pipe," *High-Tech Presses, High-Tech Pipes*, https://hightechpipes.com/products/six-shooter-pipe, accessed April 21, 2019.

------------. *Rules of the Friendly Fountain Lodge of the Loyal Order of Ancient Shepherds*. London: Wisbech, 1862.

------------. "War Story; 'News' Secures Serial Right; "Her Privates We"; "It Is Not Nice — But It Is War!"", *Evening News*, March 25, 1930. https://trove.nla.gov.au/newspaper/article/125973401, accessed Feb. 18, 2019.

Anonymous, "Dawn," *Yale Daily News* (no. 82, January 17, 1929), http://digital.library.yale.edu/cdm/compoundobject/collection/yale-ydn/id/147474/rec/1, accessed Dec. 3, 2018.

Bechtel, Stefan, and Laurence Roy Stains. *Through a Glass, Darkly: Sir Arthur Conan Doyle and the Quest to Solve the Greatest Mystery of All*. New York: St. Martin's Press, 2017.

Bible references are from the King James Version at Biblegateway.com.

Decker, Kris de. "Fruit Walls: Urban Farming in the 1600s," *Low-Tech Magazine*, https://www.lowtechmagazine.com/2015/12/fruit-walls-urban-farming.html, accessed April, 22, 2019.

Ford, John Anson, "When Justice Hangs by a Hair," *Popular Mechanics* (April 1922),https://books.google.com/books?id=LtoDAAAAMBAJ&pg=PA571&lpg=PA571&dq=popular+mechanics+%22when+justice+hangs+by+a+hair%22

Longworth, Karina. *Seduction: Sex, Lies, and Stardom in Howard*

Hughes's Hollywood. New York: Custom House, 2018.

Marshall, Marguerite Mooers, "World Is Suffering From a "Hangover"; Kill-Joy Reform, Left on Safety Valve, Will Bring Explosion, Declares Novelist," *The Evening World*, 18 Feb. 1922, https://chroniclingamerica.loc.gov/lccn/sn83030193/1922-02-18/ed-1/seq-3/, accessed Feb. 6, 2019.

Michaelides, Lee, "Silly Goose," *Dartmouth Alumni Magazine*, https://dartmouthalumnimagazine.com/articles/silly-goose, accessed April 2, 2019.

Nevins, Jess, "The Nelson Lee Page," Oocities.org, http://www.oocities.org/jessnevins/lee.html, accessed Dec. 17, 2018.

Nix, Larry T., *Library History Buff Blog*, https://libraryhistorybuff.blogspot.com/2011/02/early-childrens-rooms-in-public.html, accessed Feb. 14, 2019.

Rood, Henry, "In Memory of the Cocktail," *New-York Tribune*, 4 June 1922, https://chroniclingamerica.loc.gov/lccn/sn83030214/1922-06-04/ed-1/seq-58/, accessed Feb. 6, 2019.

Schantz, Tom and Enid, "A Case of Identity," *The Adventure of The Lost Manuscripts*, Boulder, Colo.: The Aspen Press, 1974.

Seal, Graham. *Dog's Eye and Dead Horse: The Complete Guide to Australian Rhyming Slang*. Sydney: HarperCollins Australia, 2011.

Wikipedia

World Wide Words

About the Editor

Bill Peschel is a former journalist who shares a Pulitzer Prize with the staff of *The Patriot-News* in Harrisburg, Pa. He is also a mystery fan who runs the Wimsey Annotations at Planetpeschel.com.

The author of *Writers Gone Wild* (Penguin), he publishes through Peschel Press the 223B Casebook Series of Sherlockian parodies and pastiches and annotated editions of Dorothy L. Sayers' *Whose Body?* and Agatha Christie's *The Mysterious Affair at Styles* and *The Secret Adversary*. An interest in Victorian crime led to the republication of three books on the William Palmer poisoning case.

Peschel was born in Warren, Ohio, grew up in Charlotte, N.C., and graduated from the University of North Carolina in Chapel Hill. He lives with his family and animal menagerie in Hershey, where the air really does smell like chocolate.

Visit Bill at Peschel Press (www.peschelpress.com) or his personal website at Planet Peschel (planetpeschel.com). He can be reached at peschel@peschelpress.com or write to him at Peschel Press, P.O. Box 132, Hershey, PA 17033.

The Complete, Annotated Series

Classic novels by Agatha Christie & Dorothy L. Sayers with extensive footnotes showing the history behind the mystery

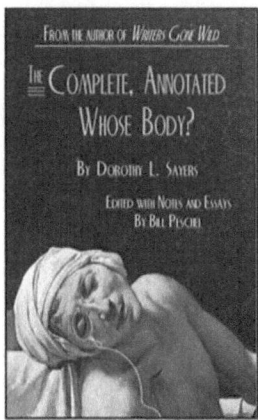  

The Complete, Annotated Whose Body?
Dorothy L. Sayers

Sayers' first novel introduces the witty Lord Peter Wimsey investigating the mystery of the body in the bath. Three maps and essays on notorious crimes, anti-Semitism, Sayers and Wimsey, plus two timelines. *282 pages.*

The Complete, Annotated Mysterious Affair at Styles
Agatha Christie

Mystery's most auspicious debut, Christie was only 25 when she introduced Hercule Poirot! With essays on Poirot, Christie, strychnine, women during the war, plus chronology and book lists. *352 pages.*

The Complete, Annotated Secret Adversary
Agatha Christie

Christie's conspiracy thriller in which Tommy and Tuppence —based on herself and her husband?—fight socialists plotting to ruin England! With art from the newspaper edition and essays on thrillers and her 11-day disappearance and more! *478 pages.*

Don't miss future Peschel Press books: Visit Peschelpress.com or PlanetPeschel.com and sign up for our newsletter.

The 223B Casebook Series

Classic and newly discovered fanfiction written during Arthur Conan Doyle's life, with original art plus extensive historical notes.

The Early Punch Parodies of Sherlock Holmes
Parodies, book reviews, & cartoons. Includes parodies by R.C. Lehmann and P.G. Wodehouse. *281 pages.*

Victorian Parodies & Pastiches: 1888-1899
With stories by Conan Doyle, Robert Barr, Jack Butler Yeats, and James M. Barrie. *279 pages.*

Edwardian Parodies & Pastiches I: 1900-1904
With stories by Mark Twain, Finley Peter Dunn, John Kendrick Bangs, and P.G. Wodehouse. *390 pages.*

Edwardian Parodies & Pastiches II: 1905-1909
With stories by 'Banjo' Paterson, Max Beerbohm, Carolyn Wells, and Lincoln Steffens. *401 pages.*

Great War Parodies and Pastiches I: 1910-1914
With stories by O. Henry, Maurice Baring, and Stephen Leacock. *362 pages.*

Great War Parodies and Pastiches II: 1915-1919
With stories by Ring Lardner, Carolyn Wells, and a young George Orwell. *390 pages.*

Jazz Age Parodies and Pastiches I: 1920-1924
With stories by Dashiell Hammett, James Thurber, and Arthur Conan Doyle. *353 pages.*

Jazz Age Parodies and Pastiches II: 1925-1930
With stories by August Derleth, Frederic Dorr Steele, and Edgar Wallace. *373 pages.*

ALSO: The Best of the 223B Casebook, featuring the best stories from 1888 to 1930.

The Rugeley Poisoner Series
Meet the murderer who inspired Christie and Sayers

The Illustrated Life and Career of William Palmer *(1856)*
- Gossip about Palmer, racing scams, and London's fleshpots.
- More than 50 restored woodcuts.
- Excerpts from Palmer's love letters.
225 pages.

The Times Report of the Trial of William Palmer *(1856)*
- The *Times'* trial transcript edited, corrected, & annotated.
- More than 50 original woodcuts restored to better-than-new condition.
426 pages.

The Life and Career of Dr. William Palmer of Rugeley *(1925)*
- Written by a doctor who interviewed witnesses and jurors.
- Rare photos and art.
- Essays on Palmer's impact on culture, strychnine, and Rugeley. *227 pages.*

The trial in London's Old Bailey, from "The Times Report of the Trial of William Palmer."

www.ingramcontent.com/pod-product-compliance
Lightning Source LLC
Chambersburg PA
CBHW030146100526
44592CB00009B/139